Fulke Greville, Lord Brooke

# Fulke Greville, Lord Brooke, 1554-1628

## A Critical Biography

*The years like great black oxen tread the world,*
*And God the herdsman goads them on behind.*
W. B. Yeats

Joan Rees

UNIVERSITY OF CALIFORNIA PRESS
Berkeley and Los Angeles   1971

UNIVERSITY OF CALIFORNIA PRESS
Berkeley and Los Angeles, California

ISBN: 0–520–01824–9
Library of Congress Catalog Card Number: 79–132064

Printed in Great Britain

# Contents

# Illustrations

# Preface

Charles Lamb once astonished his friends at an evening party by choosing Greville and Sir Thomas Browne as the two writers whom he would most have liked to meet face to face: 'The reason why I pitch upon these two authors', he said, 'is that their writings are riddles, and they themselves the most mysterious of personages. They resemble the soothsayers of old, who dealt in dark hints and doubtful oracles; and I should like to ask them the meaning of what no mortal but themselves, I should suppose, can fathom. . . . As to Fulke Greville,' he continued, 'he is . . . a truly formidable and inviting personage; his style is apocalyptical, cabalistical, a knot worthy of such an apparition to untie; and for the unravelling a passage or two, I would stand the brunt of an encounter with so portentous a commentator!' 'I am afraid', remarked a sceptic, 'that if the mystery were once cleared up, the merit might be lost.'[1]*

Sir Thomas Browne has long ago been rescued from the limbo of 'old crabbed authors', as Hazlitt calls them, but Greville has had to wait a long time for the sort of scholarly commentary and editing which has illuminated his obscurity and made it at last possible to read him, much, at any rate, of his 'mystery' having been cleared up. His 'merit' as a poet has not yet been tested in the light of the new knowledge. This is the endeavour of the present book, in which I have attempted to describe the nature of Greville's work and to suggest that once it is

* Hazlitt's essay 'Of Persons One Would Wish to have Seen'. In the margin of Lamb's copy of the 1633 *Certaine Learned and Elegant Workes* there is written out against *Caelica* LXXXIV Coleridge's sonnet 'Farewell to Love', which was partly modelled on Greville's poem.

understood it is revealed as being, in fact, highly accomplished and of very great interest.

Some explanation is required about the arrangement of the material. The principal difficulty confronting anyone who attempts to give a coherent account of Greville is that the chronology of his works is largely unknown. He published nothing himself in his lifetime though a few of his shorter poems and an early version of his play, *Mustapha*, did appear.

In 1633, five years after his death, a volume of his poems and dramas was published, entitled *Certaine Learned and Elegant Workes*. This contained the treatises *Of Humane Learning*, *Upon Fame and Honour*, and *Of Warres*; the plays *Alaham* and *Mustapha*; the sonnet sequence *Caelica*; and *A Letter to an Honourable Lady* and *A Letter of Travell*. In 1670 a volume of *Remains* appeared consisting of the treatises *Of Monarchy* and *Of Religion* which had not previously been published. The prose *Life of Sir Philip Sidney* appeared for the first time in 1652. There was until recently, when they were acquired by the British Museum, a collection of bound volumes of his works at Warwick Castle consisting of scribal copies with corrections in Greville's own hand. It appears that Greville kept his works by him and added to them and revised them over a period of years, perhaps right up to the time of his death, but we do not know when the Warwick transcripts were made nor at what dates Greville made his corrections. Every work, consequently, is composed of a number of strata and it is impossible now to recognize and date these. Professor Bullough, in his edition of *The Poems and Dramas of Fulke Greville*, based on *Certaine Learned and Elegant Workes* of 1633, has described the manuscripts and conjectured possible dating on the basis of the physical evidence which they offer, but there are few certainties in this region. More recently, Professor G. A. Wilkes has edited the *Remains* of 1670 and has taken a fresh look at the question of chronology in an article published in *Studies in Philology*, Volume lvi (1959), pages 489–503. He argues there, from some remarks in Greville's *Life of Sidney*, that much of Greville's writing was done in the later period of his life – post 1612 or 1614 – and that this later work bears testimony to a complete reorientation of Greville's outlook, away from worldly concerns of love and politics to an other-worldly religious rigour. I do not think that Professor Wilkes's chronology, or the account of Greville's poetic career and his thought which it posits, is acceptable, for reasons which will emerge in the course of this study.

I am myself inclined to think that the crucial point in the formation of Greville's mind was the death of Sidney and that the characteristic style of his writing with its interweaving of moral, political, and religious motifs is observable in all his works written after that: that is, in everything except the first seventy-six or so of the *Caelica* poems. This being so, I have not attempted to make any chronological arrangement of the works. It does not appear to me that, as we now have them, they present any line of development. It seems rather that they have in general been so worked over that each presents a fully integrated statement of its author's mature attitudes and beliefs. I have, consequently, so arranged my discussion of the various works as to enable me to bring out as well as I can the characteristic features of Greville's work. These features make a pattern, but hardly a progression.

This study begins with an account of Greville's life, a necessary introduction because he is not a very familiar figure and because knowledge of his background and his career is essential to an understanding of the poetry. There is a mass of material relating to Greville in state papers and elsewhere and the brief biography offered here does not pretend to be comprehensive. My main interest is in the poetry, and the biographical chapters are intended simply to serve as an introduction to the man and to facilitate an informed approach to what he wrote. A full biography by Mr R. A. Rebholz is in course of preparation for Oxford University Press.

Anyone who writes on Greville must be deeply indebted to the editorial work of Professors Bullough and Wilkes who have between them made all his poetry available in modern editions. For the *Life of Sidney* Nowell Smith's edition of 1907 is indispensable. Greville's *Letter to an Honourable Lady* and his letter on travel have not been reprinted since A. B. Grosart's edition of 1870.

The list of critical studies, apart from the introductory material in these editions, is small. Morris W. Croll's *The Works of Fulke Greville* (Philadelphia, 1903) was a pioneer study, and in recent years Peter Ure's article on 'Fulke Greville's Dramatic Characters' in *Review of English Studies*, New Series i–ii (1950–1), pages 308–23, has been notable for its recognition that Greville's dramas may be valued as something other than political tracts. Yvor Winters, in his articles on 'The 16th Century Lyric in England' just before the war (*Poetry : A Magazine of Verse*, Chicago, volumes liii and liv, February, March, and

April, 1939), claimed Greville as one of the most considerable lyric poets of the century. 'The great lyrics of the 16th century,' he wrote,

> are intellectually both profound and complex, are with few exceptions restrained and direct in style, and are sombre and disillusioned in tone. If we regard as the major tradition of the century the great poems of Gascoigne and Raleigh, and those most closely resembling them by Greville, Jonson, Donne, and Shakespeare, we shall obtain a very different view of the century from that which we shall obtain by regarding as primary Sidney, Spenser and the song-books; we shall bring much great poetry to light; and we shall find the transition to the next century far less obscure.

I did not read Professor Winters's articles till this book was completed, but I think he is right in his general view that a whole strain of sixteenth century poetry is insufficiently regarded, and I think he is right too in his high estimate of Greville. Whether the term 'plain style' which he and others use in relation to Greville offers a really useful description of so sophisticated a poet, however, is doubtful. As Winters recognized, he can employ 'the elaborate Petrarchan machinery' and he has a considerable range of rhetorical skills at his command. In some of the *Caelica* poems and in the play *Mustapha* a language which may appear monotoned reveals itself on closer reading to be a subtle combination of meanings and suggestions. Some of his verse is genuinely austere, but when it is so it is because Greville is choosing for clearly-conceived purposes a particular style out of the range of possibilities which he can master, and the choice and the motives of it are as ambitious in their way as a daring *jeu d'esprit*.

It might add enormously to our knowledge of Greville if a manuscript, once known apparently to Byron, could be traced. In Thomas Moore's *Letters and Journals of Lord Byron* there occurs the following passage from a letter to Murray dated 22 November 1812:

> I have in charge a curious and very long MS. poem, written by Lord Brooke (the friend of Sir Philip Sidney), which I wish to submit to the inspection of Mr. Gifford, with the following queries: first, whether it has ever been published, and secondly (if

not), whether it is worth publication? It is from Lord Oxford's library and must have escaped, or been overlooked, amongst the MSS of the Harleian Miscellany. The writing is Lord Brooke's except a different hand towards the close. It is very long and in the six-line stanza. It is not for me to hazard an opinion upon its merits; but I would, if not too troublesome, submit it to Mr. Gifford's judgment, which, from his excellent edition of Massinger, I should conceive to be as decisive on the writings of that age as on those of our own.

Later, in June 1813, Byron writes again to Murray: 'Have you got back Lord Brooke's MS.? and what does Heber say of it?' The British Museum has no information about this manuscript and, even assuming that Byron is wrong in ascribing the body of the text to Greville's own hand, none of the scribal copies at Warwick, as described by Geoffrey Bullough in his edition, appears to be written mainly in one hand with another 'towards the close'. I have so far not been able to discover anything about the manuscript which Byron describes, though a letter of mine to the *Times Literary Supplement* (8 May 1969) asking if anyone had any information brought a reply from W. Hilton Kelliher of the B.M. Department of Manuscripts adding some detail to Byron's references (29 May).

I have to acknowledge with gratitude the Earl of Warwick's permission to consult and make use of Warwick Castle documents. The present County Archivist, Mr M. W. Farr, in whose keeping the documents are, has been most helpful. The Marquess of Lothian allowed me to consult manuscripts in the Muniments Room at Melbourne Hall and has taken a kind interest in my use of them. I also acknowledge gratefully permission to use documents from the Marquis of Anglesey's collection in the Staffordshire Records Office and the kindness shown me by the County Archivist and William Salt Librarian, Mr F. B. Stitt, when I visited Stafford. The City Archivist of Coventry supplied me with copies of three Greville letters in his care. Dr Giles E. Dawson of the Folger Shakespeare Library, Washington, very helpfully answered my letter of enquiry about Greville papers and assisted me to get the ones I wanted. I have been allowed to consult and make use of a manuscript of part of *A Treatise of Monarchy* by courtesy of the Harvard College Library. Mr Philip Styles, Reader in History at the University of Birmingham, kindly brought to my notice the newly recovered manuscript entitled *The Genealogie, Life and Death of the Right Honourable Robert, Lord Brooke, Baron of Beauchamp Court in the Countie of Warwicke*. Professor Ellis Waterhouse of the Barber Institute of Fine Arts gave me valuable advice and information about the Greville and Sidney portraits. To these people and all the others who have helped me in innumerable ways, and especially to my colleagues in the University of Birmingham, I wish to offer my sincere thanks.

# 1   An introduction to the man and his mind

Greville lived a long life, from 1554 to 1628, and was known to his contemporaries as an important public figure, a courtier, a man of property, a holder of state office near the centres of political power. The poetry which he wrote throughout these years he kept back for posterity and not his own times to see, and into it he put the fruits of his observation and experience in all the roles which he played in his life. It grew beside him as a kind of *alter ego* recording the furthest reaches of his speculative thought about politics and morals and also his deep and powerful religious conviction of the inherent and ineradicable sinfulness of the world and the tense situation of men, who are called to be in the world but not of it and the acceptability or otherwise of whose lives will be known when God recognizes His elect.

Two stories told by Greville himself in his *Life of Sir Philip Sidney* will give some introduction to the kind of man he was. The first dates from Sidney's lifetime and it is Greville's account of how he and Sidney, both then in their early thirties, steal away from Court with the secret intention of joining Sir Francis Drake in one of his expeditions to the West Indies. Greville recounts the episode vividly and wittily. He tells how Sidney, by arrangement, joins the ships at Plymouth under the impression that all is ready for the voyage, but Greville himself, who is with him, scents that something is wrong. Sidney has made an excuse to get away from London; the Queen is unaware that he is planning to join Drake and would certainly forbid it if she knew; and Greville begins to suspect, though Drake welcomes them both heartily enough, that he has had second thoughts about risking the Queen's anger if he takes Sidney with him and that he is trying to back out of the agreement. Greville describes how on the first night of their arrival Drake feasts them

> with a great deal of outward Pomp and complement. Yet I
> that had the honor as of being bred with him [Sidney] from his
> youth; so now (by his own choice of all *England*) to be his loving,
> and beloved *Achates* in this journey, observing the countenance
> of this gallant mariner more exactly than Sir *Philip's* leisure served
> him to doe; after we were laid in bed, acquainted him with my
> observation of the discountenance, and depression which
> appeared in Sir *Francis*; as if our coming were both beyond his
> expectation, and desire. Nevertheless that ingenuous spirit of Sir
> *Philip's* though apt to give me credit, yet not apt to discredit
> others, made him suspend his own, and labor to change, or
> qualifie my judgement: Till within some few daies after, finding
> the shippes neither ready according to promise, nor possibly
> to be made ready in many daies; and withall observing some
> sparcks of false fire, breaking out unawares from his yoke-fellow
> daily; It pleased him (in the freedom of our friendship) to
> return me my own stock, with interest.

Then Drake sends word secretly to the Queen and a messenger comes from her with orders to Sidney to return, a message 'as welcome as Bulls of excommunication to the superstitious Romanist, when they enjoyn him either to forsake his right, or his holy Mother-Church', but Sidney has the messenger intercepted before he can deliver the orders and he ignores the message. But next there comes 'a more Imperiall Mandate, carefully conveyed, and delivered to himself by a Peer of this Realm; carrying with it in the one hand grace, the other thunder.'[1]* The grace was the offer of immediate employment under the command of his uncle, Leicester, in the Low Countries, and though reluctant to abandon the Drake project, Sidney felt he had no real alternative but to obey.

The story is splendidly told and would serve as a text for several commentaries. At the moment its prime interest is the glimpse it offers of Greville. In his account of this episode he accords, as he always did, the first place to Sidney and he is content to stand a little way back while the chief honours and attention are paid to his brilliant friend.

* Notes to chapters appear on pages 213–26.

1. Fulke Greville. The portrait of which this is a photograph is in the
possession of Lord Willoughby de Broke by whose permission it
is reproduced here. The painting now hangs in London at the St
Martin's Theatre. It was inherited by Greville's sister Margaret, Lady
Verney, and passed from her to her grandson who in 1695–6
successfully claimed the barony of Willoughby de Broke. There is a
copy of this portrait at Warwick which was made at the end of the
eighteenth century by William Patoun.

2. Philip Sidney. This portrait of Sidney was in Warwick Castle in 1734 and may have been there in Greville's time. The photograph is reproduced by permission of Lord Brooke and the Courtauld Institute.

While Sidney is engaged in business and courtesy, Greville keeps watch and he sees what Sidney in the hurry and excitement of the occasion misses. The 'outward pomp and complement' do not conceal from him the 'discountenance and depression' within. He reports it quietly and maintains his judgement though Sidney tries to dissuade him from it; and he proves to be right.

The enterprise that Sidney and Greville had ventured on was a bold one. To flout the Queen was to risk heavy penalties and their taking such a risk measures the extent of the frustration they felt at the restricted scope they were allowed at Court. It measures also their idealism, the extent of their desire and determination to take an active part in shaping their world and to put their gifts and their education at the service of their country. Sidney's high idealism has become a legend and Greville is not often thought of in these terms. Yet it is evident at least that he was so much in sympathy with Sidney as to be willing to take the chance of ruining himself with Elizabeth and for-feiting his hopes of future advancement in order to be a partner in this project. It is also plain that though he sympathized with Sidney's views and ambitions and had the daring to act upon them, yet he was not a man to be carried away in the enthusiasm of the moment from his normal habits of watchfulness and cool judgement. He seems to have been not altogether surprised to find that Drake was playing a double game, whereas Sidney, when he is convinced of it, is disgusted and expresses himself with some violence.

The picture of Greville at thirty offered to us by the story suggests a strong character but also, perhaps, an ambiguous one. He is capable of a wholehearted and unselfish devotion to a friend and of sacrificing with him for great causes; but the qualities which made him a good guardian in this episode hint also at darker strains in his character. The shrewdness which is so effective in penetrating beneath the surface may end by destroying enthusiasm and producing cynicism. What will become of Greville when the influence of Sidney is removed becomes, in the light of this story, an interesting question.

For some years, at any rate, intelligence, wit, and the ability to read men and situations were evidently among the qualities which helped Greville, after some early disappointments, to hold his own at Eliza-beth's Court. He made other attempts to leave England and see service abroad. Sometimes he was stopped before he could get away; some-times he was punished on his return. He served under Navarre against

Henry III of France and on his return was refused the Queen's presence for six months, a heavy punishment. After that he settled down to accommodate himself to what the Queen ordained, and he had his rewards. He had, so Robert Naunton reports, 'The longest lease and the smoothest time without rub, of any of her favourites.'[2]

The second story belongs to a later period. Both Sidney and the Queen are dead. James I is on the throne and the man in power is Robert Cecil. The date is probably early 1610 or 1611, when Greville would have been fifty-six or fifty-seven years old.[3] By this time he was deeply experienced in the world of policy and court intrigue. The spirit of the times and of the men who fashioned them was very different from what it had been in 1585 and Greville was suffering under Cecil for his friendship with Essex whom he counted second only to Sidney among his Elizabethan heroes. Deprived of office, he sought to write history and to memorialize the great reign of the recent past. But Cecil feared what an avowed Elizabethan would make of the opportunities of contrast and comparison which a work of such recent history would offer.

The story which Greville gives of his approach to Cecil[4] is an altogether remarkable one, partly because in his still active anger he writes more openly and straightforwardly than he commonly does; and again because of the vividness with which Cecil's self-seeking, devious and insincere methods (as they appear to Greville) are described; and also because of the light it sheds on Greville's attitudes. It is a masterly account, tracing the stages of Cecil's conduct step by step: first friendliness and acquiescence in Greville's request to have access to state papers for, as Greville savagely remarks— 'Where to bestow a Queen *Elizabeths* servant with lesse disadvantage to himselfe it seems readily appeared not.' Three weeks later, when Greville by appointment presents himself again, Cecil is even more friendly, and with gracious condescension asks Greville why he should 'dreame out his time in writing a story' when he was as likely a man to prosper in the new reign as any Cecil knew. From 1604 to 1614 Greville was excluded from public office, largely because of Cecil's distrust, and this remark of his appeared to Greville as a piece of malicious irony. Then Cecil asked, 'in a more serious, and friendly manner examining me, how I could cleerly deliver many things done in that time, which might perchance be construed to the prejudice of this.' It was a shrewd question. Greville was confident in his own discretion but Cecil thought the risk too great. Greville, seeing that he must give up the project or submit to close censorship, chose to abandon it. It is very obvious, none the less, that at the time of writing the account in the *Life* he feels the sting of this interview very sharply. He writes now what he vows will never be seen in his lifetime and he writes by the light of his own judgement of what is right and proper to be known, accepting no-one else's dictation: 'herein it may please the Reader to beleeve me the rather by these Pamphlets, which having slept out my own time, if they happen to be seene hereafter, shall at their own perill rise upon the stage, when I am not.' The time will allow no work but such as flatters it, but though he may be muzzled in his lifetime he will not be silenced for ever.

To compare this episode with the tone of the earlier one describing the Drake affair is to recognize at once some fundamental changes. Greville wants again to break away from a crippling present, not now to a new world but to a past time, and his comments on Cecil seethe with rancour and a sense of injustice. His protest at the position he is doomed to is no longer an open act of defiance but a resolution to take his revenge in secret, to make his memorial after all, but to suppress it till after his death and to make it more barbed than it would otherwise have been; and he will fix this biting character of Cecil in action into the fabric of it.

Greville's stance may not be a heroic one but it is easy to see how the older Greville as he reveals himself here might grow naturally out of the young one who absconded with Sidney to join Drake. He is not likely to have become rasher as he grew older and in the Drake affair, as has been seen, he was the one who stood back and calculated. But though Greville at fifty is not prepared to risk royal displeasure as he had at thirty, he is not prepared either to make a total sacrifice of intellectual independence. The full flavour of the Cecil episode can be appreciated if Greville's conduct is put alongside that of Bacon in similar circumstances. In 1610 Bacon was thinking of composing a history of the current reign and he was writing to James about the project: 'if your Majesty do dislike any thing, you would conceive I can amend it upon your least beck.'[5] Living history, of course, required to be handled with special prudence but it is to Greville's credit that he was not prepared to make an offer like Bacon's or to accept such conditions when they were proposed to him, whatever advantage might have been gained for the moment by compliance.

The combination of circumspection and respect for high standards in motive and conduct remains with Greville, then, through the middle years of his life. The pressures upon him are clearly more insidious in 1611 than in 1585 and the possibilities of resistance are less clear-cut. Nevertheless, he *does* resist, he does make his protest, though in his choice of means he exercises a politic and unheroic caution.

It is important to understand rightly the implication of this episode from the life of the mature Greville. 'I know the world and believe in God', he once wrote. The form of this sentence is conjunctive, not disjunctive. As Greville grew older his faith in daring gestures and dramatic enterprises failed. He believed that all human nature and activity are deeply tainted with sin and for him it followed that an intelligent man might fittingly exercise policy, calculation, and watchfulness and study to make these arts effective. Although this seems a long way from the daring optimism with which he and Sidney embarked on the Drake escapade, the progressive darkening of Greville's mood does not lead to cynicism. In Greville, contempt for the world bred a powerful religious energy and justified him in using worldly policy in order to gain, as far as he could, the ends that he thought were good. Because no man can hope to be exempt from the consequences of the Fall, temporizing in the affairs of the world becomes an inevitable necessity, but awareness of this serves only to intensify for the believer a sense of the ineffable righteousness of God. This is a point of view which is evident throughout his public career and throughout much of his writing.

In his biographical article, 'Fulke Greville, First Lord Brooke' (*Modern Language Review*, xxviii (1933), pages 1–20), Professor Bullough interprets 'I know the world and believe in God' as indicating a radical split in Greville's mind.[6] Professor Una Ellis-Fermor in an elegant essay prefacing her edition of *Caelica* (Gregynog Press, 1936) writes in the same vein of an 'unresolved dualism' in Greville's outlook. In her book *The Jacobean Drama* she describes Greville's as 'a mind typical of its generation, bitterly at war with itself and deeply divided'. But these are mistaken views. Greville's work does not at all reflect a conflict between two warring halves of experience. Far from being unable to reconcile his experience of the world with his belief in the ways of God, Greville has a firm view of the relation between them which nothing can disturb. He writes consequently from a position of great strength which allows him to survey and assess the various manifestations of human life, analysing with subtlety and precision the motivations at work and the likely consequences of courses of action, and at the same time keeping before the mind's eye the other scale of reference by which the most dextrous manipulation or gorgeous display of pomp are as nothing in the eyes of God. No doubt his world-view as he expresses it in his writings is loftier and more consistent than the actions of his life always appear to be. But his account of the episode concerning Cecil and the state papers shows, through one small but not unimportant crisis, how knowing the world and believing in God might actually work out in terms of conduct.

His point of view and the kind of expression he gives it in his poetry come out clearly when he writes on one of the greatest of the humanist themes, fame and honour.

Greville's *An Inquisition upon Fame and Honour* is, as the title suggests, a penetrating enquiry into the nature and worth of these much vener-ated names. In fact, he identifies the two, for the essential quality of both is that they depend upon reputation in the world. He goes at once to the heart of his theme without preamble:

> What are Mens lives, but *labyrinths of error,*
> *Shops of deceit,* and *Seas of misery?*

Yet the love of gain and honour and pleasure seduces men into esteem-ing life, and of these three, the desire for honour is the most effective bait. Desire of good fame is the spur which urges men to undergo toil and danger and assume burdens of responsibility, and states do well to encourage the pursuit of honour for by it they are strengthened and exalted. Having conceded so much use to fame and honour, Greville then proceeds drastically to qualify what he has said by explaining that they can only be described as good and useful relative to the utterly corrupt state of the world. The light of God's truth shines only dimly to the eyes of men and so they create for themselves codes of conduct and standards of judgement according to their own limited and im-perfect conceptions:

> Now in this *twilight* of Deliberation,
> Where Man is darke, because he will not see:
> Must he not trust to his selfe-constellation?
> Or else grow confident, he cannot be?

> Assuming this, hee makes himselfe his end,
> And what he understands, that takes to friend.    (Stanza 11.)

Fame and honour are, therefore, no more than the signs of man's fallen nature. But men who affect to despise them because they think, in the pride of their hearts, that they can live well without these ideas to restrain or excite them, fall even deeper into sin. These are the philosophers who teach 'Mans power to make himselfe good', who 'seat Felicities' within the heart of man, and open the way to moral anarchy; for even merely human light such as that provided by the desire to achieve fame and honour is better than no light at all in our 'humane darkeness'. Only when men know, believe, and obey God's truth, can the lesser lights be put out.

There is nothing in the least inconsistent or dual-minded in this. It is a perfectly coherent and integrated argument which in the rest of the poem Greville develops more fully. Aristotle, the father of pagan philosophy, made magnanimity his chief of virtues, but the true Christian knows that the greatest of man's virtues is humility:

> True knowledge of his wants, his height of merit;
> This pride of minde, this *Magnanimity*,
> His greatest vice, his first seducing spirit.    (Stanza 33.)

The way of mortal life is '*Vice*, gilt with hypocrisie' and fame and honour have their parentage of both these things. To him who has a perception of the nature of true virtue, such man-made ideals are in themselves worthless, for it is not they that are capable of

> New making Paradise, where we began,
> Not in a garden, but the heart of Man.

The line of thought presented in this poem runs throughout Greville's work and the hostility to Stoic teaching, which is also a feature of this poem and of others, is part of the same point of view. The Stoics centred virtue within but for Greville they lie, man being 'all foule within', to 'speake as God were there.'

In so far as Greville's position can be summed up in some such way as this, it is of slight interest and would scarcely warrant a close examination of his poetry. The same would be true of most poets. Where the interest of Greville's poetry lies is not in the position itself but in the ground which he covers in order to establish it. He is no unworldly recluse and his mind is far from narrow and uncultivated. He is knowledgeable about people and capable of attachments, a man deeply experienced in politics and the ways of the world. Though he disbelieves in human virtue and is sceptical about the human intellect, he is at the same time a scholar and steeped in humanist learning. His powerful intelligence plays upon his total experience and produces a commentary on life which is full of matter, sharply pointed, and deeply perceptive. To express it he evolves a kind of language which needs some study before it yields its full meaning but which, once understood, can be seen to have its own kind of effectiveness and at times a surprising beauty. These are the things which do not merely justify the attentive reading of Greville but make it a memorable experience and these are the qualities which the study that follows will attempt to demonstrate.

Greville's father, Sir Fulke senior, was a great man in Warwickshire, and Greville himself kept a firm grip on the soil of the county to the end of his life. Though the centres of power were his real stage and he was never content to be simply the great local man his father was, nevertheless Warwickshire looms large in Greville's life and the name of Greville is important in the county.

The foundations of the family fortune were laid by successful wool trade in the fourteenth century and one William Grevel, 'the flower of the wool merchants of the whole realm of England', purchased Milcote in Warwickshire.[1] He died in 1401 but his beautiful medieval house is still standing in Chipping Camden. Milcote House, in the parish of Weston-upon-Avon, was the seat of the older branch of the family till it died out in the reign of James I. The house itself survived till the Civil Wars when it was burnt by Parliamentary troops sent, ironically enough, from Warwick Castle, then also belonging to the Greville family, to prevent it being turned into a Royalist garrison.

The first descendant of immediate interest is Sir Edward Greville who died in 1528 and is buried in the church of Weston-upon-Avon. He had the wardship of Elizabeth Willoughby, heir to her grandfather, Robert Willoughby, Lord Brooke, and her grandmother, daughter and co-heir of Richard, Lord Beauchamp of Powick. She was one of the richest heiresses of her time and Sir Edward intended her for his elder son, but she said she liked the younger one, Fulke, better. Edmondson, in his *Account of the Noble Family of Greville* (1766), quotes this story from a manuscript life of Robert Greville, second Lord Brooke, which was written in 1644 and until very recently was lost (it has now reappeared and been acquired by the Bodleian Library): Sir Edward, the story goes,

> made a motion to his ward to be married to John, his eldest son; but she refused, saying that she did like better of Foulke, his second son. He told her that he had no estate of land to maintain her, and that he was in the king's service of warre beyond the seas, and therefore his return was very doubtful. She replied and said that she had an estate sufficient both for him and for herself; and that she would pray for his safety, and wait for his coming. Upon his return home, for the worthy services he had performed, he was by King Henry honoured with knighthood; and then he married Elizabeth, the daughter of the Lord Brooke's son.

Through this marriage the foundations of later Greville wealth were established. By legacies falling to Elizabeth Willoughby extensive holdings of land and property in some eight counties came to the Grevilles[2] and important connections were formed with powerful families. Robert Willoughby's great estates in Wiltshire, Dorset, Devonshire, and Cornwall were settled on the two daughters of his second marriage but a reciprocal entail provided that the heirs of neither marriage could alienate their property without the permission of the other parties and new legislation would also be required. As a result of this the Fulke Greville of the end of the century had a lien on the property of Charles Blount, Lord Mountjoy, and on that of the Marquis of Winchester, both of whom were the heirs of the second Willoughby marriage.[3] A fourteenth century ancestor in the Beauchamp family gave this Fulke Greville his 'cousinship' with Robert Devereux, Earl of Essex.[4]

The manor of Alcester, seven and a half miles from Stratford-upon-Avon, was among the properties which came to Elizabeth Willoughby's husband, and here he and his wife settled themselves at Beauchamp's Court, about half a mile north of Alcester on the Arrow Road, and they purchased land in the neighbourhood. In Alcester Church where they are buried there is a handsome monument in alabaster to them both.

The eldest son of Elizabeth and Fulke Greville was another Fulke, who married Ann Neville, daughter of Ralph, Earl of Westmorland,

and became the father of the poet with whom this study is concerned. Sir Fulke senior was reputed to be 'a gentleman full of affability and courtesy, and much given to hospitality, which got the love of the whole country. For in his time no man did bear greater sway in the county of Warwick than himself.'[5] He was born probably in 1526 and he was knighted at Kenilworth by the Earl of Leicester in August 1565. He was twice sheriff of Warwickshire, in 1572–3 and 1584–5, and also a Justice of the Peace from about 1570 onwards. He was Recorder of Warwick and also of Stratford-upon-Avon from 1591 to his death in 1606. He was a man of boldness and decision: 'Upon the news of the death of Queen Elizabeth, he being at Warwicke at the great assize, came down from the bench, and with some of his friends, proclaimed King James, which the judges of the circuit refused to doe.'[6] At the time of the Gunpowder Plot he responded to the challenge of the hour with alacrity and high spirits. As Deputy Lieutenant of the County of Warwick, 'when he heard the alarm of taking the horses from Warwick with the vulgar opinion that it was only a robbery, apprehended disorder of higher nature, from the nature of the place, the insolent manner, and that the kind of horses were heavier, and not breathed or ridden for that trade', and so he roused the towns and warned the countryside.[7] Afterwards he wrote exultantly to Lord Salisbury that he hoped to be able to send him a traitor's horse taken in his town.[8]

He was a convivial and hearty man, perhaps not a prudent one. His will indicates that he had run into debt[9] and his son's letters confirm both this and his good qualities:

> God has taken from me a most worthy and kind father and, if I
> be not much deceived, the poor country [county] has in him
> lost a father too. The world, his debts, his will and executors shall
> bear witness with me that the ruins of his estate, which he has
> left behind him, will for divers reasons sink me lower than I was
> before, so that I assure myself my own end will come upon me
> before I shall see any end of these misfortunes which have
> constantly followed me since the death of my blessed mistress.[10]

So Greville wrote to Cecil on his father's death in 1606. He may have been darkening the picture for Cecil's eyes for at this period he lost few opportunities of referring to the change in his fortunes since Elizabeth died and Cecil became James's right-hand man, but an earlier letter too hints at some irresponsibility in old Sir Fulke: 'Commend me I pray you', Greville writes to John Coke, 'to all the little ones. I joy in them and by my own defects know how happy their youths may be to them that are set young in a right way.' His own father, he goes on, is a good man but 'pleasure is the commonest end of men and the greater tide hath carried him that way.' He must be referring to indiscretions of his father's youth for he acknowledges that 'ever since I knew him he hath been wise with the wise and provident among good husbands' but he was not always 'trained up in the best company.'[11]

Sir Fulke's weaknesses, whatever they may have been, did not prevent him being a man of standing who performed honourable public service and could claim the favour of great men in the realm. The senior branch of the family at Milcote was less reputable. Ludowick, old Sir Fulke's nephew, seems to have suffered from a sixteenth century *folie de grandeur* and decided to embattle a new house at Milcote and call it Mountgrevell. The ruins of this were still standing in 1730 but it had never been completed, probably because Ludowick ran short of money. To raise funds he resorted to a piece of picturesque, if macabre, villainy. He caused two of his servants to murder one Richard Webb, a wealthy tenant of his Oxfordshire manor of Drayton. Then he gave out that the man was very sick on a visit to him and put one of his henchmen in bed to personate the unfortunate Webb. In the presence of witnesses the impersonator made a will in Webb's name, leaving his property to Greville. Afterwards the real body was put in the bed and it was announced that Webb had died of his sickness and Greville inherited. But murder would out even in 1589 and retribution caught up with Ludowick. At his trial he refused to plead, and was pressed to death, but by 'standing mute' he saved his estates from forfeiture and his son Edward inherited at Milcote and lived to be a nuisance in the county and earn a reputation as 'the rapacious son of the crazy Ludowick.'[12]

The Grevilles at Alcester were meanwhile strengthening their position and in 1601 Sir Fulke senior made a bid to enhance it further by acquiring possession of Warwick Castle, which was then in a ruinous state. His letter requesting the grant is addressed to Robert Cecil and combines wiliness and charm in a blend which is probably characteristic: 'I have a house much older than I,' he begins, referring to the family house, Beauchamp's Court,

and so kind as, lest I should think it had any purpose to last after
me, it threateneth every day to fall upon me. Now, Sir, the
Queen hath the ruins of a house in the country, which hath been a
common gaol these ten or twelve years; the walls down in many
places hard to the ground; the roof open to all weathers; the
little stone building there was, mightily in decay; the timber
lodgings built thirty years agone for herself [when the Queen
visited Warwick in 1572], all ruinous; the garden let out for
forty four years, the barns fallen and stolen away, the court made
a common passage, wherein the people prescribe already;
so as in a very short time there will be nothing left but a name of
Warwick. This, Sir, I beg not, but desire to buy for as much as
it is worth; because the stone is ready cut and the love of my
country will give me carriage.

He refers to a survey of the castle made on behalf of the Queen during
the preceding twelve months and which entirely corroborated his
account of its condition.[13] But Elizabeth still hesitated and it was James
in 1604 who finally acceded to a renewed appeal from the younger
Fulke. There is a copy of Greville's letter to James among the castle
archives in which he asks permission to buy the property and adds that
he would like also the 'Garden thereunto belonging, called the Vine-
yard' and the two watermills which adjoin the castle walls and a 'little
narrow plott of ground' called the castle-meadow. Underneath in
another hand is an instruction to the Treasurer: 'His Majesty is pleased
that your lordship and the rest of the lords in commission of sale do
take order to pass to my cousin Greville this sute.' It is signed 'Suffolke'
and dated 14 May 1604.[14]

There are a number of documents at the castle dating from this time
and relating to the conditions of sale and the value of the property.
The 1601 survey that old Sir Fulke had referred to confirmed that the
rain came in in most places and that windows and walls had fallen
down.[15] The surveyors had estimated how much the stone, timber,
glass, tiles, iron, etc., would fetch if taken down and sold, but though
they contemplated dismantling they did not estimate how much it
would cost to repair it all. According to Dugdale, it cost Greville
(junior) £20,000 for he not only repaired the castle but beautified it
'with most pleasant gardens and walks' and adorned it 'with rich furni-
ture.'[16] There is an interesting inventory in the castle archives [17] drawn

up by Greville's executors for the benefit of his heir which lists all the goods and chattels in his various houses, including Warwick, at the time of his death. The castle was certainly well-equipped and judging by the stores of bed linen, well-inhabited. Bishop Corbet went there sometime after 1614 and found both the place and the host delightful:

> Please you walke out and see the castle? Come,
> The owner saith, it is a scholler's home;
> A place of strength and health: in the same fort,
> You would conceive a castle and a court.
> The orchards, gardens, rivers, and the aire,
> Doe with the trenches, rampires, walls, compare:
> It seems nor art nor force can intercept it,
> As if a lover built, a souldier kept it.
> Up to the tower though it be steepe and high,
> We doe not climbe but walke; and though the eye
> Seeme to be weary, yet our feet are still
> In the same posture cozen'd up the hill:
> And thus the workman's art deceaves our sence,
> Making those rounds of pleasure or defence.
> As we descend, the lord of all this frame,
> The honourable chancellour, towards me came.
> Above the hill there blew a gentle breath,
> Yet now we see a gentler gale beneath.
> The phrase and wellcome of this Knight did make
> The seat more elegant; every word he spake
> Was wine and musick, which he did expose
> To us, if all our art could censure those.[18]

Dugdale's prose is more controlled than the Bishop's verse but his praise is equally warm: 'now it is the most princely Seat that is within these Midland parts of the Realm.' James himself paid a visit in 1617 and was treated to an oration which recalled the castle's recent past. The castle is represented as overcome with modesty:

> After she became the jaylor's lodge, enterchangeinge the golden
> chaines of her noble erles with the iron fetters of wretched
> prisoners, given over to be inhabited by battes and owles, shee is
> ashamed to speake before you. Hee whom your never decayinge

bountie hath made Master of his House, this Towne his patron, and his humanitie mee his servant, hath with noe small care of thoughte and charge made it knowen that this signe of your Majesty's favour is pretious to him; and to the end the memorie of this guifte might remaine to all ages in the House, he hath restored unto her some luster of her former flourishing youth.[19]

Though Greville spent time, money and pains on Warwick castle, he retained still the family house at Alcester where he had been born. In 1614–15 he was writing to John Coke about 'the breaking up of the house at Beauchamp's Court' and finding a tenant,[20] but in 1621 or later he was still addressing letters from the Alcester house.[21] He remembered too to be a local benefactor. In 1613 his offer to build at his own expense at Alcester 'a good stone Bridge lykelie to enduier to Posteritye' was accepted (but the bridge now standing is not Greville's) and in 1618 he gave the town £300 to build a market hall.

Greville sought his first parliamentary seats outside Warwickshire. In 1580 he stood and was elected at a by-election for Southampton which was later declared invalid. In 1584 he sat for Heydon in Yorkshire, but in 1586 he established his claim to represent Warwickshire. In that year he was junior knight but in 1588, 1593, 1597, 1601, and 1621 he was returned to the senior seat. This, as J. E. Neale points out, was not a matter of course since he was no more than eldest son and heir to a commoner till his father's death in 1606 and not even a knight till 1603. 'Quality, not its trappings, mattered in this instance.'[22] When in 1601 the Sheriff (Sir Thomas Lucy) illegally postponed the election in an attempt, apparently, to break Greville's hold on the seat, the Privy Council severely rebuked Lucy for his misconduct in endeavouring to frustrate the election of one 'who both in respect of his bloud and quality, his sufficiency to do service to the State and estymacion in her Majesty's gratious opynion, deserveth to be preferred before others.'[23]

Greville inherited the Recordership of Stratford-upon-Avon at his father's death and held it until his own, but his principal impact upon the life of the county was as a land-owner. If to wish to have as much as possible of the land in one's own possession is a sign of affection – as Shakespeare's Henry V claimed to be a great lover of France because he would not willingly part with a village of it – then Greville was a devoted lover of Warwickshire. He acquired or inherited numerous land rights throughout the county as well as extensive holdings in and around Warwick itself. In the course of time he acquired property through the length and breadth of England and at his death had holdings in thirteen counties to dispose of.[24] In 1608 John Coke, his agent, calculated his net revenue for the year at £4,062. 5s. 5d.[25] A document at Warwick Castle drawn up at the time of his death lists his properties and other revenues which produced a total income of £7,088. 10s. 4d. made up of £3,635. 5s. 5d. from lands, £3,184. from fees and pensions, and £269. 4s. 11d. from leases.[26]

All this property inevitably produced litigation as well as money. In 1596 he was granted the rangership of Wedgnock Park in Warwickshire but in 1603 his right was challenged by Sir Robert Dudley who sought to establish that he was the legitimate heir to the Earl of Leicester and therefore entitled to Wedgnock. Greville was experiencing a number of reverses at this time and the affair gave him some anxiety. Coke had a word with the Attorney-General about it and received a promise that Greville's interests would be safeguarded.[27] Two letters at Coventry show the Grevilles, father and son, careful to have an arrangement concerning a house there put in writing, rather to the puzzlement of the mayor and magistrates who protested that it was not necessary.[28]

A particularly well-documented piece of property dealing concerns the granting to Greville of a twenty-one year lease of the iron works and woods at Cannock in Staffordshire. The property, formerly in the possession of Lord Paget, became forfeit to the crown when Paget was suspected of complicity in the Babington Plot and fled the country in 1583. The Queen granted the lease to Greville in July 1587 and the record of his subsequent transactions provides a good but not attractive example of Elizabethan interest-making and exploitation. Trouble began very quickly and Staffordshire County Record Office has an agitated letter of June 1588 from Gilbert Wakering to Thomas Poyntz, who acted on Paget's behalf after his flight: 'Mr. Grevill maketh much ado here', Wakering writes, 'he thinkes to have all the timber and hollies in canoke woode . . . it is to the utter undoing of the countrie.'[29] He is asking Poyntz, as one of the members of a commission sent to survey the timber, to intervene and put a stop to the despoliation if he can. Meanwhile Greville was exerting himself to secure favourable terms of tenancy of the Paget properties and in the same month that Wakering's letter was written, Poyntz received another, from Essex, addressed to him and his fellow-commissioner, Ainsworth: 'I do understand that you two are commissioners in a cause which doth concerne my Cosin Foulke Grevill. I do hold him very deare unto me, and I do especially labour in this cause to get him a good bargaine.'[30] In the same June, Thomas Cecil wrote to Richard Bagott— 'whereas there is a Commission nowe downe to enquire of the woodes and furnyses that nowe be in Her Majesties handes late the Lords Paggettes, which the Queenes Majestie is very willinge to graunt in Lease to a deare ffreinde of myne Mr. Foulke Grevill,' he knows that there are some who will try to arrange the terms to Greville's disadvantage to do good to themselves, and he asks Bagott not to increase the rates for Greville above what they have formerly been. He cannot ask his father to intercede for Greville 'by reason of his extreme sorrowe for the present deathe of my Ladie of Oxforde' but he finishes by exhorting Bagott to 'shew favour with expedytie'.[31] In the same month Cecil writes again:

> I am once more to putt you in mynde of my Cossen Fowlke
> Grevill. You are nowe putt upon two commissions with certaine
> bothe his creditt, and proffitt. Lett him finde favour for my
> sake, and I assure you yt shall not be forgotten. I knowe it is her
> Majesties pleasur to do Mr. Grevill good in this, and I dare assure
> you of my Lords my fathers good meaninge towards hym.

Cecil adds in his own hand: 'I pray yow show your favor herein to my cosyn Grevyll as to one whome my L. my father and I doe greatly favor.'[32] Paulet also wrote to Bagott at Greville's request asking him as principal commissioner to favour Greville and so did Sir Thomas Walsingham, begging his favour to a kinsman whom he loved.[33]

One commission after another sat to arbitrate on complaints that Greville was despoiling the land of timber. In 1591 and 1592 the complaints took a different turn and Bagott sent in an official report. The tenants of Bromley Hurst are complaining that great damage is being done to their cattle and corn because water in a water course that feeds the iron mill now being 'farmed' by Greville, is being kept at so high a level that the adjacent land is flooded. They have taken retaliatory action and stopped the supply of water to the mill. Bagott says the complaint is unjustified since the watercourse has run in the same channel for some twenty years without previous complaint and there has been no change in the situation since Greville took over the mill. He acknowledges incidentally that the tenants have suffered some losses, since he says that Greville's officers have offered reasonable recompense, but the tenants have refused it. The tenants themselves present the story differently:

> aboute January in the 33 yeere of her majesties raigne divers of us
> to our greate trouble, travell and charges (urged therunto by
> the violente dealings of Mr. Grevill his ministers and servants)
> did exhibite to the hands of the right honourable L. Treasurer
> of England our humble petition, shewing therein the injuries
> wronges and oppressions offered to us dayly by the officers of the
> saide Mr. Grevill.

An enquiry was instituted into the facts which they claim found in favour of their case. They maintain that the present dispute turns on the same points and should receive a similar verdict.[34]

In 1596 it was the felling of trees in Cannock Forest that was causing trouble again.[35] It was reported that trees marked for the Queen were daily being felled and taken away to the damage of the property and to the harm of the Queen's tenants, and the Government took action to prohibit the felling of any more marked trees. Three years later it was being suggested that some new plantations might be made 'where Mr. Greville's falls of woods weare whereby heareafter some woode myght come Againe for the releife of the countrie' but the idea found no favour with Greville who feared that he might be called upon to pay.[36] Relations with the tenants in Bromley Hurst and Cannock being so bad, it is not surprising, though equally not heartening, that in a letter of 1600 to John Coke, his agent, Greville should be specific about the rents— 'let care be had of the rents at Cannock for nothing must there be left to courtesy.'[37] Things seem to have settled down later and in December 1604, when the fourth Lord Paget was trying to get restitution of his father's confiscated property, Thomas Egerton, Lord Ellesmere, then Lord Chancellor, forwarded to Paget a petition from Fulke Greville and expressed it as his opinion that Greville should 'quietly enjoy' what Queen Elizabeth had granted him.[38] This was evidently a friendly gesture at a period when losses were threatening Greville from all sides, though 'quiet enjoyment' hardly seems an appropriate term for this turbulent and unedifying tenure.

There is not much to be said to exonerate Greville from the charge
of being a grasping landlord. What he says for himself is contained in a
letter to Burghley of 29 January 1596:

> Notwithstanding he [Greville] hath duly paid the rent and
> employed the woods according to the purport of the grant for her
> Majesty's benefit and contentment of the country, by the malice
> of some persons there, envying both her Majesty's title and
> the small benefit he raiseth thereby, he has been often vexed by
> frivolous complaints before his lordship, supposing he had
> exceeded his grant, and to his excessive charge and trouble [they]
> have proceeded to examine the matters in fact by several
> commissions.[39]

The high cost of royal service has also to be remembered. To be a
faithful servant of the Queen and conscientiously administer her affairs
might cost a man his private substance, as Sir Henry Sidney found, and
none of Elizabeth's courtiers could afford to be above the scramble for
whatever fees, perquisites, rents, or monopolies might be going.
Greville conducted his part in this jungle warfare as efficiently as he
could but it does not appear, in fact, that he was successful in his running
of the ironworks.

Despite continued references to his ill-health from quite early manhood, Greville nevertheless lived to the age of seventy-four, a very
great age in his day, and death in the end came by violence. He was
stabbed and fatally wounded by one of his servants, Ralph Haywood, on
1 September 1628 during a brief visit to London. The circumstances of
his death are described in a letter of 2 September from Edward Reed
to Sir John Coke, who was in Portsmouth at the time:

> My Lord Brooke being upon Saturday come to town and resolving
> to go down this day for Warwickshire was arrested here by
> his servant Ralph Haywood, who trussing his points stabbed
> him into two places in the left side, the upper blow is between the
> lower ribs and next the back (perhaps mortal): the second and
> lower blow is but a flesh wound and the cure not doubted.
> When Haywood had wounded him, being alone with him in his
> chamber, he ran from him, left him bleeding and locked him in
> with a double lock, and ran himself into his own chamber which
> he locked also, opened his doublet and with the same knife

gave himself four wounds into his breast, upon which he presently
died. My Lord Brooke calling loud, Mr. Wilson came unto him
and with his double key opened the door, found him bleeding
but not any whit amazed, neither did desire that if Haywood
were escaped out of the house that he should be prosecuted,
desiring not that any man should lose his life for him. After
I heard of his hurt I went to see him, and found him to speak
heartily, and not any whit to be troubled with the danger but
much with the pain. This morning my Lord's wounds are to be
opened again, upon which the surgeons think to give some
guess of the state of him. My Lord had given Haywood 20 *l.* a
year for his life now at his coming from Warwick.[40]

Hostile gossip at the time and later made the motive of Haywood's
attack Greville's allegedly inadequate provision for him in his will.[41]
Greville was renowned as a patron but he may nevertheless have been a
mean master: his dealings with the Paget property suggest that he
counted some situations as legitimately exploitable. The story of his
niggardly treatment of Haywood, however, is not very convincing.
Greville made generous provision for all his servants in his original will,
which Haywood signed. Haywood's name was omitted from specific
bequests made in a codicil which Greville added as he lay dying, but
as Haywood himself was by this time dead, no injury to him could be
in question. Greville's request, reported by Reed, that Haywood should
not be pursued and prosecuted, 'desiring not any man should lose his
life for him', bespeaks at any rate generosity of mind.

More might have been generally known about this act of violence if
another and more sensational one, the murder of Buckingham, had
not taken place soon after and absorbed public curiosity. The postscript
of a letter from Lord Brudenell to the Earl of Westmorland links the
two victims with unsympathetic impartiality: 'My Lord Brooke dyed
of corrupted fatt thrust into the wound of his belly, in place of his kell,
which putrifying, ended him, that fewer sorrows than the [Duke],
though not so many rejoyces.'[42] Martin Peerson's *Mottects or Grave
Chamber Musique* of 1630 contains a more gracious obituary. The
volume was dedicated to Robert Greville, Fulke Greville's heir:

Where shall a sorrow great enough be sought
For this sad ruine which the Fates have wrought:

Unlesse the Fates themselves should weepe and wish
Their curblesse powers had been control'd in this?
For thy losse, worthiest Lord, no mourning eye
Has flood enough: no Muse, nor elegie
Enough expression to thy worth can lend;
No, though thy Sidney had surviv'd his friend.

Dead, noble Brooke shall bee to us a name
Of griefe and honour still: whose deathlesse fame
Such vertue purchased as makes us to bee
Unjust to Nature in lamenting thee;
Wayling an olde mans fate, as if in pride
And heate of youth hee had untimely dy'd.

Greville lingered on for a whole month, then his body was wrapped
in lead and taken to Warwick where he was buried in a vault beneath
the tomb which had been erected during his lifetime.[43] The tomb is in
itself a document and it has a history. In a letter of 4 September 1615 to

*Opposite*  An extract from Greville's holograph letter of 1615 to John Coke,
discussion his plans for erecting a tomb for Sir Philip Sidney in St Paul's. The
letter is at Melbourne Hall in Derbyshire and this extract is reproduced by
permission of the Marquess of Lothian. It reads as follows:
I send you herewith the Inscriptions fyer hotte, for philips long promysed
tombe. The Latyn verses be his (i.e. they were composed by the candidate
whom Greville was at this time thinking of appointing to a History lectureship
at Cambridge) yet contracted from many to thes 4 by my direction. The rest
are my own. Touching the form and matter of the sepulchre it is shortly thus.
Two daynty large stones of touch delicately forbished, borne up, one above an
other, by 4 pillars of brass 3 foot and a half high and double guylt; the uppermost worthily his, the other myne. Now because I would not mar the delicacy
of the stones, or embase their lustre, with adding any thing to cover it, I have
devised a pillar of the same touch, raysed above and yet disjoyned from the
tombe, and placed at the upper end of sir philips which shall carry skutchions
for his arms, and Inscriptions, to be graven uppon it in guilded letters, and in
lyke maner at the lower end, saving only half the tombe high, a more humble
one to carry myne. The place is pawls church wher he lyes open, and because
there is or can be no severed Isle ther, my purpose is to encompasse the
sepulchre round and inclose with a high grate of Iron.

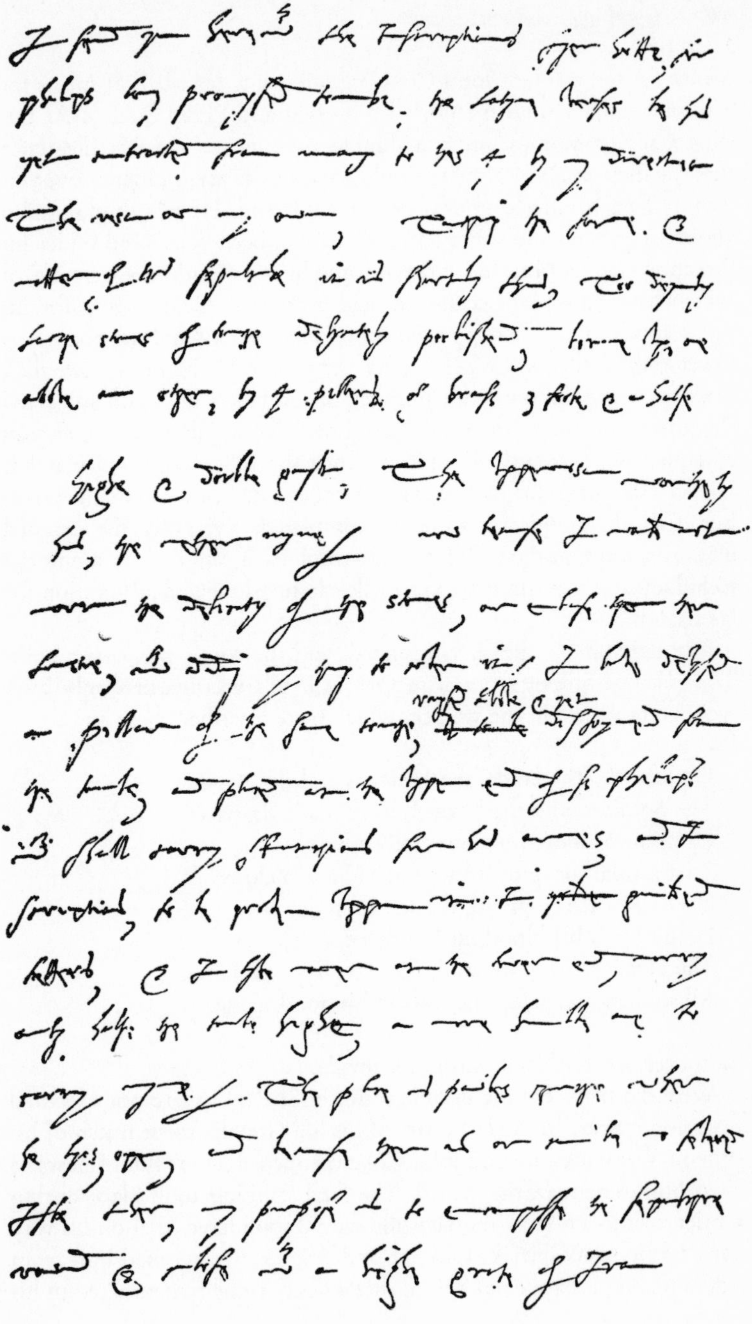

his friend and assistant John Coke, Greville had described his plans for
a tomb which should memorialize himself and Philip Sidney. At this
time Greville was planning a double monument and his insistence
that the memorials of Sidney should have a clear pre-eminence over his
own reflects his life-long devotion to his friend. He was thinking also
about an epitaph and some Latin verses had been composed under his
direction. He had himself written some lines in English, specimens of
which have survived because he sent a copy to Coke asking for his
opinion of them. The copy itself is no longer extant and the poem was
never published but Coke wrote a very careful critique of Greville's
draft in which he quoted a number of Greville's lines and subjected
them to rigorous comment.[44] Possibly *Caelica* number LXXXII, also an
epitaph and apparently unfinished since the following page was left
blank in the manuscript,[45] may represent an attempt to revise the poem
but if so the revision was never completed. Evidently the original
intention was that the poem, like the tomb itself, should be a memorial
to Sidney and a testimony to Greville's lasting love and admiration for
his friend.

The epitaph was never completed, and the tomb was never built.
Tha place of Sidney's burial in Old St Paul's was marked only by a
wooden tablet set in the wall on which were inscribed these lines:

England, Netherlands, the Heavens and the Arts,
The Soldiers, and the World, have made six parts
Of noble Sidney; for none will suppose
That a small heap of stones can Sidney enclose.
His body hath England, for she it bred,
Netherlands his blood, in her defence shed,
The Heavens have his soul, the Arts have his fame,
All soldiers the grief, the World his good name.[46]

Whoever wrote this, it was not Greville.

Why the plans for the double tomb in St Paul's were not executed
does not appear. In the last years of his life Greville spent much of his
time in Warwickshire and John Coke composed letters full of news to
keep him abreast of the world. The fatal stabbing took place during
a brief visit to London and Greville would soon have been on his way
back home to Warwick. Old age and sickness had weaned him from
London and perhaps even before that a desire to be remembered in his

native county prevailed on him to reserve his own body for Warwick. The tomb he built there is very large, much too big, in fact, for the chapter house of St Mary's Church where it is.[47] There are no verses and the only inscription reads: 'Fulke Greville, Servant to Queene Elizabeth, Concellor to King James, and Frend to Sir Philip Sidney. Trophaeum Peccati.' Brief as this is, it is in a high degree eloquent. After the titles of state but equal with them as a source of pride comes the claim to friendship with Sidney. This friendship is treasured to the end as one of the real prizes of a long and eventful life, and he places it in the brief list of things he wishes to be remembered of him as long as his memory lasts. He is proud that he can claim this friendship and there is great humility in such pride. So that after all there is a double monument to Greville and Sidney, as Greville originally planned, and the tribute that he pays to Sidney on the tomb at Warwick is not easily surpassed. His complete works, deeply influenced as they are by his acquaintance with and feeling for Sidney, make another kind of monument, as he recognized when, probably between 1610 and 1614, Greville collected all that he had up to that time written and dedicated them to his dead friend in the prose work now known as *The Life of Sir Philip Sidney*.

# 3   Public figure

Greville always had his eyes on wide horizons, sharing in Sidney's plans for a settlement in the West Indies in his youth, and concerning himself with the affairs of the East India Company in his age.[1] It may have been he who, remembering Sidney's plans, roused the interest of his cousin's young son, Robert Greville, in the possibility of creating a new society in the New World. Robert Greville, who became Fulke's heir, was a politically active man deeply hostile to Charles I.[2] He planned to found a settlement in North America and a town actually rose up, known as Saybrook (a compound of Brooke's title and that of his partner, Viscount Saye and Sele: the town exists today as Old Saybrook in Connecticut), but the Civil War intervened and Brooke was killed at Lichfield, leading Parliamentary troops.

Fulke Greville also had some experience as a soldier. He was stopped by the Queen on the point of embarkation when he volunteered for service in the Netherlands in 1578 and again in 1585, but he did serve briefly under Navarre in 1587,[3] and in 1588 he was encamped at Tilbury in command of a company of lances raised in expectation of a Spanish invasion.[4] He had more experience as a sailor, and countless images of the sea in his works bear witness to the deep impression it made on him. In 1580 he had command of a ship in a small fleet guarding the Irish coast so as to prevent the landing of Spanish aid to the rebels. He hurt his leg badly among the rocks in O'Sullivan-Beare's country but he had plenty to occupy his time while he rested. His cabin, it was reported, was stored with books and sea charts.[5] In the 1590s he was much concerned in naval affairs, including preparations for the Islands Voyage, and he spent some time on the ships themselves.[6]

In 1598 he was appointed Treasurer of the Navy[7] and in 1599 he was made Rear-Admiral and given command of the *Triumph*, the largest vessel of the fleet, at a time when a Spanish attack was expected.[8]

In point of fact he never came under fire in his ships at all, but preparing for the Spaniards was only part of his problems. His appointment as Treasurer of the Navy in September 1598 was not accomplished without delays and heart-burning. 'It is now almost two years since I have languished in the suit of this place,' he wrote earlier that year, in a letter in which indignation is only just contained by respect for the Queen and her officers,

> and I protest, without other glory or ambition in it than first to think I should be of her [the Queen's] own choice, and then that in her service I should have *pour un champ d'honneur un siècle corrompu* . . . she in her princely nature knoweth that I have commanded mine own genius, and left all courses in the world that advance other men, only for her sake.[9]

To obtain a footing and keep it was a perpetual struggle, even for a Greville, even in 1598. And when the post had been won, money was always scarce even for necessities and begging letters had to be framed very carefully. Greville, along with Lord Thomas Howard and Sir Walter Raleigh, is among the signatories of a letter written aboard the *Elizabeth Jonas* in the Downs on 31 August 1599, and addressed to the Lord High Admiral of England. It contains the following pathetic passage:

> We do further beseech you to believe us in this true complaint, that both our drink, fish and beef is so corrupt as it will destroy all the men we have, and if they feed on it but a few days, in very truth we should not be able to keep the seas, what necessity soever did require the same, unless some new provision be made, for as the companies in general refuse to feed on it, so we cannot in reason or conscience constrain them.[10]

In his naval activities and in other ways too during these years Greville was closely associated with Essex. They were linked by slight but effective ties of relationship and Essex's intervention on Greville's behalf in 1588 in the negotiations over the Paget property was only one instance of his willingness to protect the interests of his 'cousin'. In November 1590 they took part together in a tilt at Court[11] but their real association was much more than a formality. Public records of the eighties and nineties contain plenty of evidence of friendship, but the strongest evidence comes when things begin to go wrong for Essex. Greville was at his right hand during the preparations for the unlucky Islands Voyage and the disaster seems only to have drawn them closer. A letter Essex wrote to Greville at this time is in terms of close confidence and intimacy[12] and in 1600 the relationship was still unimpaired: 'my lord of Essex deals clearly and kindly with me,' Greville wrote to his friend and agent, John Coke, 'which makes whatsoever comes else the lighter, for my eyes have ever been upon the goodwill and not the power of my friends and I have both strength and kindness to suffer with them that can love.'[13] Suffering with Essex was all that his friends could now do. In March 1600 Greville, together with Bacon and others, was ordered by the Queen to leave the apartments he had occupied for some time in Essex House[14] but he had to return in 1601 to take part in the siege of this great mansion after the rebellion. He was present in the Star Chamber when Essex was charged[15] but what he felt about all these proceedings he left, characteristically, for his posthumous testament, the *Life of Sidney*. There he speaks very plainly. Essex, he declares, had been 'worthily beloved' of Queen and people but Greville himself had

> in the Earles precipitate fortune, curiously observed: First, how
> long this Noblemans birth, worth and favour had been
> flattered, tempted, and stung by a swarm of Sect-animals, whose
> property was to wound, and fly away: and so, by a continuall
> affliction, probably enforce great hearts to turne, and tosse for
> ease; and in those passive postures, perchance to tumble some-
> times upon their Soveraignes Circles.

We remember Greville 'curiously observing' Drake's behaviour to Sidney, and the knowledge of how shrewd an observer he was adds conviction to his account here. Essex, he goes on, fell into their trap and 'his enemies took audacity to cast Libels abroad in his name against the State, made by themselves; set papers upon posts, to bring his innocent friends in question.' Greville may have been one of them.

'His power, by the Jesuiticall craft of rumor, they made infinite; and his ambition more then equall to it. His Letters to private men were read openly, by the piercing eyes of an Atturnies Office, which warranteth the construction of every line in the worst sense against the writer.' Seeing clearly what means were being used to destroy him, Greville did what he could, but was defeated.

> My selfe, his Kinsman, and while I remained about the *Queen*, a
> kinde of *Remora*, staying the violent course of that fatall ship,
> and these winde-watching Passengers (at least, as his enemies
> imagined) abruptly sent away to guard a figurative Fleet, in
> danger of nothing, but these *Prosopopeia's* of invisible rancor; and
> kept (as in a free Prison) at Rochester, till his head was off.
>                                          (*Life of Sidney*, pages 157–8.)

Before he went on this 'sudden journey', as he calls it, his assessment of the situation at Court left him in no doubt that the Queen was so surrounded by Essex's enemies that 'it was impossible for her to see any light, that might lead to grace, or mercy.' What the real effect of his own presence at Court had been he leaves in some doubt, half suggesting that Essex's enemies thought it greater than it actually was: in any case he seems to have thought that there was no more now that he could do. In the *Life of Sidney* he defends Essex: he was a favourite who exposed himself to protect his Queen, he served in all the sea and land actions of his time, he never sought to usurp the sovereign's prerogatives and he used the weapons only of 'greatnesse of worth and incomparable industry' to combat envy and enmity: 'that active heart of his freely chose to hazard himselfe upon their censures, without any other provisionall rampier against the envious, and suppressing crafts of that party [those who were against him], then his owne hope, and resolution to deserve well.' (*Life of Sidney*, page 161.) As well as giving evidence of his personal faith in Essex, Greville is concerned also to note his history as a political exemplum: 'So that let his heart bee (as in my conscience it was) free from this unnaturall crime [i.e. treason], yet these *unreturning* steps seemed well worth the observing. Especially in the case of such a Favorite, as never put his Soveraigne to stand between her People and his errors; but here, and abroad placed his body in the forefront, against all that either threatened, or assaulted Her.' (*Life of Sidney*, page 159.)

The story of Essex fed Greville's knowledge of life and of high politics and exemplified also his view of the corruption of worldly affairs. It also had practical consequences in his own life. Because of Essex's fall he destroyed a play he had written on the theme of Antony and Cleopatra, 'many members in that creature (by the opinion of those few eyes, which saw it) having some childish wantonnesse in them, apt enough to be construed, or strained to a personating of vices in the present Governors, and government.' (*Life of Sidney*, page 156.) Greville does not say or even imply that his play really did make a commentary on the factions and vices of the contemporary Court and courtiers: only that he thought it might be interpreted in that way, Essex's fall providing a demonstration of how hostile interpretation might wrench innocence quite from its true nature. Among those who saw the Antony and Cleopatra play before it was consigned to the fire, the poet and playwright Samuel Daniel may have been one, for he was in close touch with Greville at this time. If this were so, the situation would have its ironies, for Daniel was himself engaged on a political play in 1600, a study of Philotas, the favourite of Alexander the Great, who had enemies and who fell and was executed. When Daniel's *Philotas* was performed in 1605, he was promptly called before the Privy Council and charged with seditious comment on the trial and execution of Essex.[16] He extricated himself from the charges with some difficulty but he was bold enough, in the 'Apology' which he wrote for the published version of the play, to acknowledge his debts to and his sympathy for Essex: 'for mine owne part having been perticularly beholding to his bounty, I would to God his errors and disobedience to his Sovereigne, might be so deepe buried underneath the earth, and in so low a tombe from his other parts, that hee might never be remembered among the examples of disloyalty in this King-dome or paraleld with Forreine Conspirators.'

Daniel was not a public man, as Greville was, and could perhaps more easily afford to say what he thought at the time. He could have come within the range of Essex's bounty through the good offices of either Charles Blount, Lord Mountjoy, or Greville, both of whom had befriended him in 1594-5. Mountjoy was a close friend of Essex, but evidence implicating him was suppressed at the Essex trial because his services as Lord Deputy in Ireland had by that time made him too valuable a man to lose. No evidence apparently could be found against Greville, but it is not unlikely that the charge brought against Daniel in 1605 was seen by some as a means of discomforting both Greville and Mountjoy who were known to support Daniel but who were themselves too powerful to touch.

The leader of the rival faction, the arch 'enemy' of all those whom Greville writes about in his account of the fall of Essex, was Robert Cecil, and it is an accumulation of dislike with a long history behind it which envenoms the story of Cecil's discouragement of Greville's application to use the state papers. Cecil and Greville had inherited a tradition of mutual friendship from their fathers and for some years after Burghley's death and Robert Cecil's appointment as Principal Secretary all continued to go well.[17] But as Essex's career developed, the rift between him and Cecil widened and Greville found himself caught between two powerful factions. He appears to have tried to be a faithful friend to Essex and also a loyal servant of the Queen and her appointed ministers: so he sought to repair Essex's reputation with the Queen but when the die was cast he took his place in the siege of Essex House. His attitude, perhaps not surprisingly, was too ambiguous for Cecil and though Greville's fall was not so spectacular or conclusive as Essex's he nevertheless did fall, kept out of office from 1604 till 1614. So long as Elizabeth lived Greville hung on, but James came to England as a stranger, already primed by Cecil about persons and events at Court and relying on the Secretary's knowledge and experience to guide him in his new responsibilities. Cecil wrote wearily to a correspondent of all the jockeying for favour which surrounded him. All the activity of place-hunting and eye-catching that was a normal feature of Court life was stirred into a fever by the advent of a new sovereign. If Greville took part in the 'hurrying, feigning, suing, and such-like matters',[18] as it is very likely he did, not all his intelligence and shrewdness served him. He was made a Knight of the Bath at the coronation, not a distinguished honour under James, and he received the grant of the office of Secretary in the Principality of Wales for life,[19] but these were small alleviations compared with the dark clouds that were threatening. In 1603 Sir Robert Dudley, illegitimate son of the Earl of Leicester, was disputing Greville's tenure of Wedgnock Park in Warwickshire which Elizabeth had granted to him in the last year of her life, and Sir Robert Mansell was attempting to gain a reversion in the Navy Office over his head.[20] Greville was unwell and short of money. He was obliged to pawn his plate to Michael Hicks for the sum of £500.[21] In 1604 he surrendered the treasurership of the

Navy to Mansell[22] and he had to borrow again from Hicks to secure the Welsh office.[23] In respect of his services at the Navy Office he was released of £1,000 worth of debts and a warrant was issued to pay to him £5,782. 8s. 0d.,[24] but however the financial situation was repaired, there was no doubt that power was slipping from him. He put a good face on it and kept up a friendly correspondence with Cecil in spite of occasional chilliness, apparently still with hope that his position would improve. The grant of Warwick Castle in 1604 gratified father and son: 'Your favour to my old father I will serve you for and I hope God will reward,' Greville wrote to Cecil, now Earl of Salisbury, in 1605,[25] and he even risked a playful allusion apparently to their estrangement over Essex: 'I am in part now gallantly revenged of your noble and kind reprehension of my negligence in the Queen's time and the world shall bear me witness that I have no worse thought in my heart against you.'[26] In 1605 he invited Salisbury to visit him in Warwickshire and Salisbury came.[27] Greville reported the visit to Hicks, with evidently some confidence of Salisbury's favour: 'when he shall please to command my service, he and the world shall see, that I am a more natural subject to love than power.'[28] But in 1606 things looked black again. Greville's father died and left Greville with new problems in clearing up his estate: 'the ruins of his estate, which he has left behind him, will for divers reasons sink me lower than I was before, so that I assure myself my own end will come upon me before I shall see any end of the misfortunes which have constantly followed me since the death of my blessed mistress.'[29] This was written to Salisbury and in 1607 he was writing to him again in another crisis:

> That I have not obeyed your commandment in speaking with the King before his departure, nor the message I received from you (while I was present with you in the same room) to go after him to Royston, will be found no error of mine; wherein I make this short apology because I see (be it spoken as far from unthankfulness to my other friends as my heart is) that whatsoever I shall receive either in justice or compassion comes merely from your ingenuous care and native industry, so as it were an ungrateful indiscretion for me to neglect any part of your directions, which I beseech you to accept for my true excuse.[30]

The trouble this time is connected with Greville's offices in the Council
in the Marches of Wales. Greville had been given his first foothold in
these lucrative offices by Sir Henry Sidney and in 1577 had secured the
reversion of the Signet and of the clerkship of the Council. He shared
the clerkship from 1581 to 1590 but from 1590 onwards he held the
offices of Clerk of the Council, Clerk of the Signet, and Secretary.
John Powell, whom Greville had appointed as his deputy in these
affairs, estimated that in the first year of Greville's holding both clerk-
ships he derived an income of £1,000 from them. When Edward,
Lord Zouche was appointed President of the Council in 1602 he took
exception to the amount of the fees which Greville was pocketing,
especially since he did little of the work in his own person. Zouche
was unpopular at Ludlow, where the Council headquarters were, but
he was an appointee of Robert Cecil and Cecil's support kept him in
office.[31] Greville, appealing to Cecil for what he sees as fair play, is
bitter about the whole business. Changes introduced by Zouche have
turned a profitable office into a liability: 'This office,' Greville reminds
Salisbury,

> was the main harvest of my youth, spent as you know; then by
> this change of instructions I have lost in the same office 1200*l.*
> yearly, wherein the records will not lie. Lastly, that I lose still
> while my loss is in repairing and find length of expectation and
> endless course of life heavy, among other alterations which I
> have found lately in declined years. All this I had rather write
> than speak, and if you forgive me this presumption you give me
> ease of heart besides. The rest I leave to God and the sense you
> were wont to have of your distressed friends. In which matters
> if any service of mine may be worthy to keep me, I should be
> proud, for I fear it is not chance that keeps you thus as you are
> in both these times, and whatsoever else it be men do in nature
> owe honour and reverence to it.

Salisbury appears to have taken action to relieve Greville's immediate
distresses, for a few months later Greville received a grant of fourpence
on every affidavit taken before the Council of the Marches of Wales[32]
but later again in the year there is a new complaint and a new appeal to
Salisbury for his assistance in some trouble that has arisen over a grant
to Greville of revenue derived from the impost on Rhenish wines.[33]

No wonder that he writes to Salisbury that he 'keeps watch upon his going and coming, as the poor mariner upon the star which he finds most propitious to him',[34] and yet in spite of the constant expressions of devotion and of gratitude and the repeated pleas for Salisbury's help in one matter after another, Greville must in these years have been seething with the bitterness which comes out in the *Life of Sidney*. So long as Salisbury lived he had to keep on the right side of him or go under altogether, but it seems likely that Greville held Salisbury largely to blame for the precarious state of his affairs at this time and his vulnerability to blows from every quarter.

There is not enough evidence to say whether he was right or wrong in this. Modern historians are inclined to take a much more sympathetic view of Salisbury than the contemporaries who called him Robertus Diabolus and thought of him as devious, tricky, cold-hearted and scheming, ever ready to betray a friend or ally. This seems to have been Greville's view of him and he was an experienced and penetrating observer, but his judgement may have been soured by his own discomforts during the years from 1603 to Salisbury's death in 1612. Salisbury only abandoned his friends when his allegiance to the crown demanded it, the apologists argue, and certainly the correspondence which survives shows him doing what he can to help Greville meet incidental difficulties as they arise while at the same time apparently keeping him firmly out of office.

'He was conceived to be a vessel of wrath.' So wrote Sir John Holles to the Duke of Lennox in October 1614, in a letter which expresses his surprise at Greville's appointment to the chancellorship of the Exchequer after his long years in the wilderness. 'I confess,' he goes on, 'he hath great parts and, if the King had sooner taken to him sooner had his service been found useful, but then he was conceived to be a vessel of wrath. Some had told tales of the Lady in the Tower and of councils held at Rufford and other places.'[35] The Lady in the Tower is Arbella Stuart and Rufford was one of the mansions of Gilbert, Earl of Shrewsbury, that unfortunate woman's uncle, whose wife was an accomplice in her secret marriage and flight. Holles seems to be suggesting that Greville was considered to be implicated in schemes to promote Arbella's slight claim to the throne of England and that for this reason the King never trusted him. But by 1614 Arbella was in prison and mad and James no longer feared her and could afford at last to make use of Greville.

There is no sound reason for taking this story very seriously. All kinds of rumours circulated at various times about Greville as they always do about any figure in a public position. The grain of truth in this one appears to be that Greville was friendly with the Shrewsburys and remained so through the troublesome years with Arbella. But P. M. Handover in his recent study[36] concludes that 'it is improbable to a degree that he [Fulke Greville] was concerned with Arbella's affairs' and it certainly seems highly unlikely, on the face of it, that a man of Greville's cautious temperament would mix with schemes so dangerous and so unpromising as those which centred on Arbella. Some seed of suspicion may nevertheless have lodged in James's mind or have been planted there by a rival but even so it seems unlikely that this would have accounted altogether for Greville's exclusion from public affairs for eleven years. Distrust on Salisbury's part seems much the more likely explanation, whether this was produced by some episode in Greville's career or whether it was fear of a clever and potentially powerful political rival whose subtle mind might conceivably constitute him a threat to Salisbury's own position.

Another letter of Holles, written two years earlier, in 1612, immediately on the death of Salisbury, supplies more political gossip. 'Sir Fulk Grevil begins to appear upon the stage for a Secretary,' he writes, and goes on to describe an alliance between Greville, Robert Carr, Lord Rochester, the reigning favourite, and Henry Howard, Earl of Northampton, which is evidently designed to bring Greville back now that Cecil is gone.[37] In January of the following year Naunton reported that 'Sir F. Greville has been lately sought violently by the King to be one of the Commissioners for the reformation of the Navy'[38] and in 1614 he became Chancellor and Under-Treasurer of the Exchequer.[39]

At this point his second political career begins. In 1614 Greville was sixty years old. He lived another fourteen years and for all that time he had a finger in affairs of many kinds. He took part in the early enquiries into the Overbury murder in 1615[40] – it need not much have disturbed him that he had sought Rochester's (now Somerset's) support in 1612 or that he had attended his wedding to Lady Frances Howard, for the whole Court, either in innocence or cynicism, had accepted this later so notorious marriage and the divorce which preceded it. He was a member of the Commission appointed in 1616 to enquire into Coke's conduct in the praemunire case.[41] In the 1620s he was among those appointed to examine trading disputes with the Dutch over the East India Company[42] and in 1624 and 1625 he sat on councils for war, foreign affairs, and trade.[43] In 1625 he was one of the commissioners appointed to form a noble household for Charles I, and in the same year the Venetian Ambassador described him to the Doge and Senate as 'one of the most privileged of the councillors.'[44]

No record suggests that he was a decisive or dominant figure in public affairs though he appears to have been an able administrator. He was perhaps too intellectual in his approach to be an effective executive. An account of his speech at a Privy Council meeting in 1615, called to advise James on whether or not to summon a Parliament and if so on what conditions, shows him opening up questions and propounding a general observation, whereas the contributions of his compeers are firmer and more specific. To those who are not under the obligation of coming to an immediate decision, however, Greville's words may be highly interesting:

> He said he would rather move some questions than deliver his advice; one question was whether their Lps would hold it fit that everything that was vulgarly complained of were of necessity to be amended. All impositions were not unlawful; nor all monopolies: in all ages and in all states some of both kinds have been done and held warrantable. Another question was whether their Lps would not think that many of those things which were moved for preparation were meet to be referred to Parliament and handled there. It was a pleasing thing and popular to ask a multitude's advice; besides, it argued trust, and trust begat trust; and such a mutual confidence might perhaps dispose their minds to a greater freedom towards the King.[45]

Bacon in his *Apophthegms* (no. 202) quotes from a speech by Greville in the House: 'Why should you stand so much upon precedents?' he asked them; 'the times hereafter will be good or bad; if good, precedents will do no harm; if bad, power will make a way where it finds none.' The characteristic standing back to enquire into the philosophy of an attitude is apparent in both these samples of his contribution to political discussion. The men whose minds were focused on the immediate moment may have found his perspective baffling or irritating.

Ill-health had always troubled him and in late years he was forced to

remit personal attendance at meetings connected with some of his
duties. Personal attendance in execution of his duties in the Welsh
offices was excused in 1625[46] but he did not relinquish his sense of
responsibility. In November of that year he wrote to John Coke to
protest against the rumoured appointment of Baronet Harris as Chief
Justice in Wales: 'He is very distasteful to that principality and as like
to help to ruin that court as any man I know. Beseech my Lord Keeper
to think of some other man for that eminent place of justice.'[47] In 1621
he was raised to the peerage as Lord Brooke, but his energy was de-
creasing and in 1622 he retired from the Exchequer. 'Age and sickness
(the gentlemen ushers of death)',[48] as he wrote, forced him to live more
quietly and he spent more time in Warwickshire and relied greatly on
his old friend and assistant, John Coke, to keep him abreast of the news
in London. But he was as deeply concerned as ever with affairs of
state and in October 1625 wrote characteristically to Coke, who had
just been appointed one of the Principal Secretaries of State:

> I ask you how this change of wounding our own church with our
> own weapons stole in since the first instructions which so provi-
> dently restrained that French desired liberty. Again why this fleet
> hath been so long suspended in this first undertaking of ours
> when good success against stirring adversaries commonly follows
> the preventing of expectation.

The reference to 'wounding our own church' is to the tergiversations
of Charles and Buckingham over the question of tolerance for Catholics. At the time of his marriage-treaty Charles had entered into
secret undertakings with the French to protect English Catholics but
he was under continual pressure from Parliament to apply the penal
laws. He vacillated between one policy and the other. The 'first undertaking' Greville writes about was an attack on the coast of Spain,
actually carried out with the greatest inefficiency in the last months of
the year. Buckingham had at one time intended to command the
expedition in person but instead he had gone to the Hague to attempt
to strengthen by diplomacy an alliance against Spain and the Emperor.
The enterprise still had something of the character of a Protestant
crusade against Catholic power such as had stirred Greville's and
Sidney's enthusiasm in their youth and, seeing it in this light, Greville
could exclaim with a good conscience: 'God bless the work and my

Lord Duke's journeys both into France and the Low Countries because the world will discover in it how bravely he takes upon him the hazard of being a public author of this revolution.'[49]

Greville's attachment to Buckingham is not one of the most edifying relationships of his life but it is easily explicable. His view of the world taught him that it is folly to expect much of humanity and equal folly to waste time in futile regrets at the un-ideal nature of man. Since James and after him Charles loved Buckingham so deeply it was entirely consistent with Greville's considered views that he should take this as a political fact to be accepted and worked with. If he himself could maintain good relations with Buckingham there was at least a chance that the young man might be receptive of his good advice and serve as a channel to conduct his thought to the King. In the letter quoted above, Greville adds to his congratulations to Coke on his secretaryship: 'Counsel I cannot give you other than not to change the many years acquaintance with yourself for any sudden or tempting liberties of a brave undertaking court,' and it is unlikely that he himself, shrewd, experienced and old as he was, would be swept off his feet by the 'brave undertaking' show of Buckingham or that he would act in any other way than that his many years acquaintance with himself and the world at large had marked out as the best path by which to tread through the dark wood of this world.

Two letters from Greville to Buckingham survive from 1623. The first has to do with Prince Charles's and Buckingham's journey to Spain to bring back a Spanish bride. It begins with some rather heavy-footed frivolity and we are apparently to understand a well-established joke in which Buckingham, then aged thirty-one, is addressed as 'grandfather' by Greville. But a more characteristic style soon establishes itself.

> More than Complement, what can you expect from him, to whom you command nothing; a man old, without office [Greville had resigned from the Exchequer in the previous year], imployment, or particular intelligence in anything. Nevertheless (worthy Lord) if the proverbe be true that lookers on maie see sometymes as much as players can doe, then believe, that I will carefully attend my Soveraigne's provident eye over all that concerns you and if I finde any draught play'd amisse in yor game, as confidently presume to acquaint him: Hee can doe what hee will, and in my conscience will doe what hee can.

After these various reassuring preambles, Greville comes at length to the matter in hand and here, if Buckingham were at all capable of reading between the lines, he might find a number of warnings:

> Touching this noble worke you are in hand with, I will say noe more but *Blessed be the woeing that is not long in doeing*; especially after soe many yeares spent in deliberate treaties about it: The God of love and honor forbidd, that anie advantageous wisdome whatsoever should eclipse, qualify, yea or mingle it selfe, with these hazardous travells of our brave Prince's affections to bring home his equall. I will therefore hope, that it is among Kinges and Princes as with private men, where wee see suspition to begett suspition, caution to bring forth caution; and contrari-wise, a gallantnesse of proceeding, to have as gallant a manner of retorne: Their part is yet behind for the consummation of all. In the carriage of which, your Lordshipp shall have just cause to observe, that howsoever (in petty thinges) the spreading Scepter of Spayne maie seeme to bend under the Myter of Rome, yet in regalities and things of high nature, I presume you shall see, it reserves a more suplatyve [superlative?] greatness, then other petty Soveraignes of the same faith doe, or dare imagine.

The deepest suspicion of Spanish intentions and of the wisdom of the whole enterprise is implicit in these lines and it is hard to believe, even if Buckingham had inspired more confidence in his powers to handle this situation than events would show was justified, that Greville would have been happy at the prospect of England being tied to the old enemy, Spain.[50] 'I seriously wish,' he concludes, 'this hasty errand ended, and your selves at home.' Buckingham of course took no notice of his 'old grandchild', but it is good to have this evidence of how Greville sought to use association with him as an opportunity to teach him some restraint and wisdom.

Later in the same year Greville wrote again to Buckingham in Spain. The matter is more urgent and Greville no longer gives his warnings obliquely. He begins, for form's sake, by expressing the hope that all is well with the marriage negotiations. But he comes quickly to the point of his letter: 'Wee heare of a new treaty sprunge upp, between the Palsgrave's oldest sonne, and the Emperor's younger daughter: A labarinth, into which what hope so ever leade us, I feare, no one threed will be able to guide us well out.' He goes on to trace the

dangers he foresees in this project and then advances the suspicion that
the mooting of this scheme may be a contrivance of the Spanish to
provide 'colourable and un-avoydeable delayes' in the concluding of
the marriage negotiations that Buckingham has in hand. Greville
separates one by one the various strands of interest and motivation as
he sees them in the situation implied by the rumour of the Palsgrave
marriage and does not mince words in his account of the roles played
by the King of Spain and the Pope. He concludes that: 'Except the
restitution of the Palatinate be instantly pressed (and like a worke of
fairies either finished or broken of at once), wee may easily be over-
shott in our owne bowes' and England may find itself 'compeld to
play an after-Game, among'st discouraged friends, and combination
of powerfull enmyes, Such, as under Caracters of Allyance will thinke
they have woone one great stepp, towards their inveterate ambition of
a westerne Monarchy.'[51] He signs himself 'loving grandchild and
humble servant' and apologizes for wearying Buckingham with such a
letter. It is an acutely perceptive diagnosis of the political situation as
well as a remarkably vigorous piece of writing, showing a highly
figurative use of language in the service of a mind long used to shrewd
observation of European politics and skilful at untwisting the ravel.
His lack of enthusiasm for the Spanish marriage project itself is very
obvious but he has not been able to dissuade James from his attachment
to it. It is curious and rather shocking to see so old and experienced
and able a man as Greville having to work so patiently on Buckingham
in order that he might exercise some guidance, however indirectly, on
the conduct of affairs. His efforts were, in fact, fruitless, for James
agreed to support negotiations for the Palatinate marriage.

It is consistent with Greville's lifelong interest in politics and his
profound reflections on the methods of state-craft that he planned to
endow a lectureship in History at Cambridge, his own university. As
early as 1615 he had called over from the continent a scholar who he
thought might be suitable for this post.[52] Nothing came of this and in
1624 he invited Vossius to take up the position.[53] This invitation again
came to nothing but in 1627 Isaac Dorislaus was invited and accepted.
He had a short and unhappy tenure and ran into trouble at once.
Dr Matthew Wren reported to Laud about him:

His first lecture passed unexcepted at, but the writer [Wren]
warned the Heads in private that the lecturer placed the right of

monarchy in the people's voluntary submission. The second
lecture contained such dangerous passages, and so appliable to the
exasperations of these villainous times, that the writer could not
abstain before the Heads from taking offence. The Vice-Chancellor
sent for his lectures, out of which the writer privately gathered
the principal passages, which he incloses.

Wren declined to incorporate the lecturer as a Doctor of Cambridge
but went on to describe him to Laud as 'of good learning, very ingenuous, and ready to give satisfaction in any kind.'[54] He was at first
forbidden to give any more lectures but later the decision by the
authorities was rescinded. Greville, however, was not prepared to
accept the anxiety and perhaps the odium of supporting a protégé who
seemed to have so little of that prudence which Greville had himself
adopted as his rule of conduct. He advised Dorislaus to return to
Holland though he continued to pay the stipend.[55] He attempted to
preserve the lectureship by a codicil to his will, which again nominates
Dorislaus, but this was contested and the foundation lapsed.[56] Dorislaus
lived to give even more overt expression to his democratic views and
was finally murdered in Holland in 1649 by a party of Royalists
because of the part he had played in the trial and condemnation of
Charles I. Greville's heir, Robert, who refused to refound the lectureship, shared nevertheless Dorislaus's political ideas and was a prominent
Parliamentary leader till his death in action in 1643. So Greville who
walked so circumspectly in his day not only preserved his real thoughts
to be released into the ferment of ideas later in the century, but he also
nourished two acknowledged revolutionaries, Dorislaus, whom
he chose as his lecturer, and his heir, whose upbringing he super-
vised from a child. The pliant courtier who was willing to indulge
in foolish jokes with Buckingham carried dynamite about him:
perhaps Cecil, who was a clever man too, had some awareness of
this to account for his keeping Greville down for eight important
years.

Although it is probably right to set the Dorislaus affair in its political
context it has another aspect, as one example of Greville's patronage of
learning and literature which earned him gratitude and respect and a
long-lasting reputation as a benefactor of distinguished men. Among
them was William Camden who was appointed Clarenceux King of
Arms in 1597 on Greville's 'incessant supplication' and who left him a

piece of plate in his will.[57] A more significant testimony is the tribute
he pays in his *Britannia*:

> Sir Foulque Grevill [this refers to the father] a right worshipfull
> person both for his knights degree, and for kind courtesie:
> whose only sonne, carrying likewise the same name, hath conse-
> crated himself so to true Vertue and Nobility, that in nobility
> of minde he farre surmounteth his parentage and unto whom
> for his exceeding great deserts towards me, although my heart is
> not able either to expresse or render condigne thankfulnesse,
> yet in speech will I ever render thankes, and in silence acknowl-
> edge my selfe most deeply endebted.[58]

John Speed likewise recorded his obligation to Greville: 'whose merits
to me-ward, I do acknowledge in setting this hand free from the daily
employments of a manual trade, and giving it full liberty thus to
express my mind, himself being the procurer of my present estate.'[59]
In 1601 Greville recommended Lancelot Andrewes for appointment
as Dean of Westminster[60] and in the same year he secured the deanship
of St Pauls for John Overall.[61] He came to the assistance of Samuel
Daniel in 1594 and used his influence with Robert Cecil on his behalf
in 1595.[62] David Lloyd has this to say:[63] 'One great argument for his
[Fulke Greville's] worth, was his respect of the worth of others, desiring
to be known to posterity under no other notions than of Shakespeare's
and Ben Johnson's Master, Chancellor Egerton's patron, Bishop
Overal's Lord, and Sir Philip Sidney's friend.' The references to
Shakespeare and Jonson whet the curiosity but unfortunately, as E. K.
Chambers remarks, there is no evidence to support them. Conceivably,
Chambers suggests, Greville might have found employment for
Shakespeare in the Marches when he left Stratford.[64] It is also possible
that Lloyd may have heard some story spread by Davenant who as a
young man was a member of Greville's household and who liked to
claim kinship with Shakespeare.[65] There may or may not have been
some basis of truth for it.

There is plenty of evidence of Greville's efforts to assist Francis
Bacon. Several letters survive between them from 1594[66] during
Bacon's long-drawn-out and at that time unsuccessful suit for the post
of Solicitor-General. Greville interceded with the Queen for him and
was confident of success but Essex was involved in the affair too and

probably his ill-judged solicitations were a cause why Bacon was disappointed. Bacon and Greville retained their respect for each other during these and other vicissitudes. In 1615 we find Bacon in a letter to James praising a speech made by Greville in Parliament[67] and in his *Apophthegms* (1625) he twice quotes Greville. Greville read Bacon's *History of the Reign of Henry VII* before publication and recommended it.[68]

Merely to list the names of the men with whom Greville was associated is enough to establish the importance and quality of his participation in the intellectual life of his time: but his contact with Giordano Bruno deserves a few more words. When Bruno came to London Sidney and Greville were anxious to meet him and to hear from his own mouth an explanation of his views about the movement of the earth and the infinity of the universe. Greville invited him to a supper party of professional scholars and intelligentsia and Bruno gives an account of it in *La Cena de le Ceneri*. John Florio and Matthew Gwynne came to escort him from the house of Mauvissière, the French Ambassador, where he was staying, to Greville's lodging at the Court at Whitehall. They had a very trying and dirty journey but at last they arrived and the supper took place. This was on 14 February 1584. Bruno dedicated his *Spaccio de la Bestia Trionfante* (1584) to Sidney and in his dedication he refers to 'that generous and humane spirit, Sir Fulke Greville,' and goes on: 'Even as you were born and raised together in bonds of genuine friendship, so he resembles you [i.e. Greville resembles Sidney], both in corporal and spiritual attainments. It was he who, after you, offered me his good offices.' Bruno hints that someone made trouble between him and Greville and so interrupted their association but the episode did not, apparently, diminish his respect for Sidney's friend. Greville himself makes no comment on Bruno but he may have been remembering him when, in *A Treatie of Humane Learning*, he illustrates his scepticism about the power of the human intellect to penetrate to any fundamental truth by pointing to the inability of astronomy to decide:

> Whether the heavens doe stand still or move,
> Were fram'd by Chance, Antipathie, or Love?

But the supper party and Bruno's compliments to him are evidence of his lively interest in intellectual activity of all kinds and his willingness to give encouragement to learned men.

Greville's associate in his connection with Bruno was Sidney, as he was in so many other enterprises. From childhood into manhood the centre of Greville's intellectual and personal life was his close friend and this chapter, like the previous one, must conclude on that point. Sidney was as important in Greville's literary career as he was in other areas of his life. It was through Sidney's example that Greville took to writing in the first place and his influence did not end with his death. Greville's editing of his dead friend's *Arcadia* and his so-called *Life of Sidney* provide a transition from his public career to his work as a writer and provide an opportunity also for studying some aspects of this celebrated friendship.

# 4  Friend to Sir Philip Sidney

The story of Greville's friendship with Sir Philip Sidney, like other major aspects of his life, does not lend itself to straightforward chronological and factual description. What Greville experienced acutely he took deep into his nature and there it acquired colour and shape from the tones and contours of his own mind. He probably brooded long before he wrote and he certainly held his works in mind long after he had first committed them to paper and constantly returned to them, thickening the web of meaning and reference as further thought and feeling accumulated round the subjects of his writing. His friendship with Sidney becomes the centre of some of the most powerful of this accretive activity, and what has its origin in a sequence of biographical facts acquires, especially after Sidney's death, an area of associations and significances which reaches far into Greville's political and also his religious experience. The sonnet sequence *Caelica* and the verse-play *Mustapha* are both deeply influenced by Greville's friendship with Sidney and what he made of it, but for the moment the two pieces of work which are most obviously connected with Sidney can usefully be detached for separate consideration.

Greville's edition in 1590 of Sidney's *Arcadia* presents one of the simplest situations in his literary career; the so-called *Life of Sidney* one of the most complex. We not only have a date for the edition of *Arcadia*, we also have external information relevant to it; and since Greville was dealing with another man's work he was not free to build multiple layers of meaning onto it as it was his usual tendency to do. His attitude to *Arcadia* is nevertheless very characteristic of his habits of mind and his interests and since it is so it gives a helpful introduction to the more complicated treatment in the *Life* of the material which came to cluster in Greville's mind about Sidney.

The facts of Greville's friendship with Sir Philip Sidney are recorded in all biographies of Sidney. They were born in the same year, 1554, they entered the same school, Shrewsbury, on the same day in 1564, and though they went to different universities, Sidney to Oxford and Greville to Cambridge, their companionship was scarcely interrupted and they began Court life together in 1575. 'foulke grivell is a good boy' Sidney scrawled one day in his school book[1] and there is plenty of testimony that it was a close friendship based on common interests and congeniality of temperament. Their natures were probably complementary rather than similar but they had the same fundamental seriousness of outlook and they shared the same aspirations toward public service and high endeavour to which they were born and trained. Greville writes of having been brought up with Sidney and he was evidently on close terms with the family as a whole. It was probably Sir Henry Sidney who sponsored Greville's first appearance at Court, and he who by his recommendation made the first opening for him in the Welsh Council. In 1577 the two young men were sent on a minor diplomatic mission to the continent when they took the occasion to make themselves known to prominent leaders of European Protestantism and when both of them, but especially Sidney, caught the attention of the elderly and experienced Huguenot, Hubert Languet, peripatetic scholar and statesman of European courts. In the next few years Greville and Sidney were feeling round for ways of establishing their careers and both suffered the dampening of their first enthusiasms by Elizabeth, but whatever else she frustrated, she did not weaken their attachment to each other. Sidney's death was a blow the impact of which was felt throughout Greville's life.

Sidney died in October 1586 and in November Greville wrote the following letter to his friend's father-in-law, Sir Francis Walsingham:

Sir this day one ponsonby a booke bynder in poles church yard,
came to me, and told me that ther was one in hand to print,
Sir philip sydneys old arcadia asking me yf it were done, with
yor honors consent or any other of his frends, I told him to
my knowledge no, then he advised me to give warning of it,
ether to the archebishope or doctor Cosen, who have as he says
a copy of it to peruse to that end. Sir I am lothe to reneu

his memori unto you, but yeat in this I might presume, for I have
sent my lady yor daughter at her request, a correction of that
old one don 4 or 5 years since which he left in trust with me
whereof ther is no more copies, & fitter to be printed then that
first which is so common, notwithstanding even that to be
amended by a direction sett down undre his own hand how &
why, so as in many respects espetially ye care of printing it is to
be don with more deliberation, besydes he hathe most
excellently translated among divers other notable workes monsieur
du plessis book against Atheisme, which is since don by an other,
so as bothe in respect of the love between plessis & him, besydes
other affinities in ther courses but espetially Sir philips
uncomparable Judgment, I think fit ther be made a stei of that
mercenary book to [so] that Sir philip might have all those
religious honors which ar worthelj dew to his life and death,
many other works as bartas his semayne, 40 of the psalm[s]
translated into myter &c which requyre the care of his frends, not
to amend for I think it fales within the reache of no man living
but only to see to the paper and other common errors of
mercenary printing Gayn ther wilbe no doubt to be disposed
by you, let it helpe the poorest of his servants, I desyre only care
to be had of his honor who I fear hathe caried the honor of thes
latter ages with him. . . . Sir I had wayted on you my selfe for
aunswer because I am Jelous of tyme in it, but in trothe I am
nothing well Good Sir think of it   ffoulk Grevill.[2]

This is an eloquent letter in spite of the ambiguity of some of its
references to Sidney's corrections of and 'directions' concerning *Arcadia*.
Greville rouses himself from distress of mind and body to defend his
friend's memory against the threat of a pirated edition of the old
*Arcadia*, and his concern for Sidney's reputation, not only that it
should not be besmirched by falling into the hands of a purely 'mercenary' publisher, but also that it should be established from the start
on what Greville considers the right grounds, is particularly notable.
The right grounds do not include the old *Arcadia* but they do include the
revised *Arcadia*, and Sidney's translations of the work of the French
Protestant, du Plessis Mornay, and of the religious verse of Du Bartas
and of the Psalms. The letter would evidently be a very valuable aid
in working out the textual history of *Arcadia* if only one could be sure

of interpreting it right,[3] but the more interesting topic in relation to the present study is the light which it throws on Greville's attitude towards Sidney's work.

Which of the versions of *Arcadia* is to be preferred, the old or the revised, has been a debating ground ever since the original version was recovered at the beginning of this century. Between the time of writing the original version during pleasant days at Wilton when the sheets were handed as they were written to Sidney's sister, the Countess of Pembroke, and her ladies, for whose especial pleasure and entertainment the book was written, and the time a few years later when Sidney conceived the idea of rewriting his romance on a much larger scale, Sidney's approach to his material radically changed. The entertainingly light touch of the old *Arcadia* became a sober handling of moral issues, the material being now organized not simply to amuse but to provide a series of *exempla* discriminating, principally but not exclusively, the different responses of a carefully-chosen gallery of rulers to the privileges and responsibilities of rule, and of an equally carefully chosen collection of lovers to love. The change has been regretted by some and Mario Praz has called it 'an instance of perversion which can find a parallel only in Tasso's travesty of his masterpiece into a lifeless Counter-Reformation epic.'[4] It is easy to understand that the twentieth century may rejoice in the insouciance of the early version and equally easy to see that a man of Sidney's own generation, sharing his serious preoccupation with statecraft and morals, would estimate more highly the epic qualities of the revised *Arcadia*. But it needs only a modicum of historical imagination and sympathy to find, even today, abundant riches in the revised *Arcadia*. The following passage, for instance, is a brilliant piece of subtle description in a mode which is foreign to us but which is not on any account to be underestimated:

But Amphialus (taking of his mother Philocleas knives, which he
kept as a relique, since she had worne them) gat up, and
calling for his richest apparell, nothing seemed sumptuous inough
for his mistresses eyes; and that which was costly, he feared were
not daintie: and though the invention were delicat, he
misdoubted the making. As carefull he was too of the colour; lest
if gay, he might seeme to glorie in his injury, and her wrong; if
mourning, it might strike some evill presage unto her of her
fortune. At length he took a garment more rich than glaring, the

ground being black velvet, richly embroidered with great pearle,
& precious stones, but they set so among certaine tuffes of
cypres, that the cypres was like blacke clowds, through which the
starrs might yeeld a darke luster. About his necke he ware a brode
and gorgeous coller; whereof the pieces enterchangeably
answering; the one was of Diamonds and pearle, set with a white
enamell, so as by the cunning of the workman it seemed like a
shining ice, and the other piece being of Rubies and Opalles, had
a fierie glistring, which he thought pictured the two passions of
Feare and Desire, wherein he was enchayned. His hurt (not yet
fully well) made him a little halt, but he strave to give the
best grace he could unto his halting.

That is a splendid paragraph presenting a sensitively observed and
even moving description of a particular man's behaviour, his senti-
mental care of what has belonged to the lady, his nervousness and
anxiety to please, and finally, the realistic touch of his limp. The limp
is a particularly fine detail in the characteristically rich texture of this
passage because it reflects not only Amphialus's physical disability, but
also a moral halting; for with all his worth Amphialus is fatally flawed
by allowing his mother to lead him astray and try as he may to give
'the best grace' he can to his behaviour the defect must be cured,
cannot be concealed.

The moral judgement is clear but Sidney has also a great deal of
sympathy for Amphialus and throughout the revised *Arcadia* there is a
delicacy – even a tenderness – in the treatment of individuals which, set
as it is in a world compounded of medieval chivalry, Greek romance,
a Renaissance preoccupation with statecraft, and a devout man's study
of the way to the good life, opens some unexpected prospects and
throws a revealing light on the characteristics of Sidney's own nature.
There are limitations to this sympathy, of course. The common people
when they leave the duties of their station in life are not included in it
and though Gynecia is, the infidel Cecropia is not; but the exceptions
do not invalidate the general point. There is humour also in the revised
*Arcadia*, ranging from the half-smile with which, in the passage just
quoted, Sidney describes Amphialus's preparations for his interview
with Philoclea, to the broad comedy of the combat between Dametas
and Clinias. Mopsa's story of the knight and the girl and the aunts and
the nuts is delightful in itself with its long sequential chain of 'And so

. . .'s and its medley of semi-literary extravagances and homely details – the comment that Sidney is here contrasting a crude medieval narrative style with its sophisticated setting, though no doubt just, seems faintly pedantic.

The letter to Walsingham makes plain that Greville preferred the revised *Arcadia* to the old and the *Life of Sidney* explains how he regarded it. Sidney's 'intent and scope', he writes (pages 15–16),

> was to turn the barren Philosophy precepts into pregnant Images of life; and in them, first on the Monarch's part, lively to represent the growth, state, and declination of Princes, change of Government, and lawes: vicissitudes of sedition, faction, succession, confederacies, plantations, with all other errors, or alterations in publique affaires. Then again in the subjects case; the state of favor, disfavor, prosperitie, adversity, emulation, quarrell, undertaking, retiring, hospitality, travail, and all other moodes of private fortunes, or misfortunes. In which traverses (I know) his purpose was to limn out such exact pictures, of every posture in the minde, that any man being forced, in the straines of this life, to pass through any straights, or latitudes of good, or ill fortune, might (as in a glasse) see how to set a good countenance upon all the discountenances of adversitie, and a stay upon the exorbitant smilings of chance.

Greville is obviously taking *Arcadia* very seriously indeed and he ignores in this account of it any possible interest attaching to the characters and their situations in themselves and gives no hint of any lighter moods or of literary, as distinct from moral or political, values in *Arcadia*. Nevertheless, his phrase 'turning the barren Philosophy precepts into pregnant Images of life' is no bad description of Sidney's work in the revised *Arcadia*. Greville does not expand the phrase 'pregnant Images of life', evidently thinking that the aspects of *Arcadia* which are implied in it will not be missed by readers of the romance. He is concerned, for his part, to point out what lies beneath the surface of this 'various and dainty work' (a description which he applies to *Arcadia* on page 14), for he was in Sidney's confidence, he seems to suggest, about the importance that Sidney attached to the deeper current of ideas running through the work and this is the aspect of *Arcadia* which he feels he needs to stress.[5]

There are indications in the *Life of Sidney* that Greville was very conscious of the apparent disproportion between his admiration for his friend and what Sidney can actually be seen to have achieved in a short life in which he held no office of importance. He is at pains to point out that in the limited field of action which was all that Sidney was allowed he gave evidence of powers of mind and qualities of character which would have made him, had he lived, one of the dominating figures of Europe. In establishing this point the revised *Arcadia* is obviously useful evidence, for it shows Sidney fulfilling in imagination the role of a governor, studying men and how best to make use of them in the service of the community (see Amphialus 'distributing each office as neere as he could, to the disposition of the person that should exercise it – knowing no love, danger, nor discipline can sodainly alter an habite in nature'), putting down a rebellion with full consideration of the processes by which the people have been incited to revolt and the means to be used to restore them to loyalty (more fully developed in the new *Arcadia* than the old), envisaging, in fact, every situation and combination of circumstances which might arise in the internal and external affairs of a state and weighing the courses of action to be taken at each juncture. A recent method of selection of candidates for higher administrative posts in the Civil Service and for commands in the armed forces has been – perhaps still is – to propose an imaginary situation such as they might encounter in their post and set the candidate to work out the best means of dealing with it. *Arcadia*, from one point of view, is an exercise of this kind on a grand scale, and this is the aspect which concerns Greville in these comments of his. The *Life of Sidney* does not touch on literary criticism: in Greville's eyes his friend was a candidate, the most brilliant that England had ever produced, for the highest political honours, and by the side of this his achievement in literature is a consideration not worth dwelling on.

Since then we have changed the priorities. General Wolfe who would rather have written Gray's *Elegy* than have taken Quebec, would have puzzled and perhaps disgusted not only Greville but Sidney too. It is true that there were stirrings in Sidney of a different spirit, a more modern consciousness of the claims of art and also of the claims of the individual identity apart from the social function: the coexistence of these two attitudes in him is part of what makes Sidney so deeply interesting a writer, and it may also have been partly responsible for the depression he appears to have been subject to. For Greville art was always second to action. It had its place when action was for some reason impossible but it should be directed to redound on life. In the *Life of Sidney* he does not mention *Astrophil and Stella* or any of Sidney's poetry – of all Sidney's writing it is only *Arcadia*, in fact, that he does mention. 'The truth is,' as Greville sums up his comments on *Arcadia*, 'his end was not writing, even while he wrote; nor his knowledge moulded for tables, or schooles; but both his wit and understanding bent upon his heart, to make himself and others, not in words or opinion but in life, and action, good and great.' (*Life of Sidney*, page 18.) Or, as he writes later:

And though my Noble Friend had that dexterity, even with the dashes of his pen to make the *Arcadian* Antiques beautifie the Margents of his works; yet the honour which (I beare him record) he never affected, I leave unto him, with this addition, that his end in them was not vanishing pleasure alone, but morall Images, and Examples, (as directing threds) to guide every man through the confused *Labyrinth* of his own desires, and life.'[6]

The consequence of Greville's letter to Walsingham was that the projected pirate edition was stopped, and in 1590 an edition of *Arcadia* appeared under the care of Greville himself and Dr Matthew Gwynne.[7] The 1590 edition was printed from the manuscript which the Walsingham letter says Sidney deposited in Greville's care (presumably at the end of 1585, when he left for the Netherlands) and the editors worked conscientiously to produce an edition corresponding to Sidney's intentions as far as they knew them. They were forced to exercise their own judgement in the selection and arrangement of the eclogues and they also divided the work into chapters, adding chapter headings, which listed briefly the matters included in each chapter. They were scrupulous in pointing out that these features of the work were without Sidney's authority. A note to the 1590 edition runs:

The division and summing of the Chapters was not of Sir Philip Sidneis dooing, but adventured by the over-seer of the print for the more ease of the Readers. He therefore submits himselfe to their judgement, and if his labour answere not the worthines of the booke, desireth pardon for it. As also if any defect be found

in the Ecologues, which although they were of Sir Philip Sidneis
writing, yet were they not perused by him, but left till the worke
had bene finished, that then choise should have bene made,
which should have bene taken, and in what manner brought in.
At this time they have bene chosen and disposed as the over-seer
thought best.[8]

No doubt in the collaboration the executant hand was Gwynne's and
the directing mind was Greville's. He probably thought of the chapter
headings as serving as an index for the use of those 'sounder judgements' who, he says in the *Life* (page 14), will 'exercise their Spirits'
in consideration of the depth and scope of Sidney's work. Gwynne's
digests are in fact very competent indexes of the matter but they have a
more than functional value, for they show that he also enjoyed the
story. His little summaries show his relish in the turn of phrase by which
he makes the most of a piquant situation – Philoclea, for example,
when Zelmane reveals herself as Pyrocles, 'feares much, but loves more',
and he takes the opportunity for a little fine writing on his own
account, the occasional pun, frequent alliteration – 'A Ladies kinde
comforts to Pyrocles comfortlesse unkindnesse' combines both –
and a vocabulary stored with inkhorn terms. The summaries are
miniature compositions by themselves: 'The two Princes policie to
reconcile two warring brothers. The unbrotherly brave combat of
Tydeus and Telenor. Plexirtus his viperine unkindness to the kindest
Leonatus. His conquest by the two brothers, and his dogtrick to
destroy them by themselves. The regreete of the dying brothers.' It is
lucky that Greville found in Gwynne a man who was able to give a
testimony to his own enjoyment of *Arcadia* in quaint and picturesque
terms.

The selection and arrangement of the eclogues was a more difficult
matter. Some changes from the order of the old *Arcadia* were inevitable
because Sidney had worked poems from the original eclogues into the
test of the revised version. Some omissions were also inevitable because
Greville and Gwynne were working with the revised manuscript which
goes only as far as a point towards the end of Book 3 so that not all
the poems included in the original third and fourth eclogues could
appropriately be used. They evidently made an effort, however, to
include in the 1590 edition as many as possible of the poems and when
choice was necessary, either Greville or Gwynne, probably Greville,

assessed relative merits. Thus the two poems of Strephon and Klaius, originally in the fourth eclogue, are included, one in each of the first two eclogues; the poem which tells Languet's beast fable is taken from the original third eclogue and put into the first,[9] and so is the discussion of marriage between Geron and Histor; and to make room for the additions in the first eclogue two poems in classical scansion contained in the original version are omitted and three classical poems are left out of the second eclogue. Greville, who was himself not much interested in experimenting with classical prosody, probably thought that these were the poems Sidney himself was most likely to have eliminated since they belonged to a vein of experiment which he later gave up as unsuccessful. He does, however, retain two classical poems, one in each of the first two eclogues, to represent the rest which have been cut out.[10]

A particularly interesting aspect of the changes which the 1590 editors made in the eclogues from their original state is their exclusion of Philisides from them. Sidney himself in the revised manuscript had redistributed among other characters the songs occurring in the text which had originally belonged to Philisides and Greville and Gwynne removed him also from the eclogues. It must have appeared to them that the changes Sidney had made in the handling of the Philisides story in the revised manuscript indicated his intention to cut him out of the eclogues, or perhaps when Sidney discussed his plans for the revised *Arcadia* with Greville he told him that he meant to reduce Philisides's part. Philisides appears once in the revised *Arcadia* but as this was now a work of a much more public nature than the old *Arcadia* had been, it perhaps appeared inappropriate to introduce the author-figure in any more conspicuous place.[11] It is surprising that the Countess of Pembroke in the 1593 edition ignored the plain hints that Sidney intended to change his account of Philisides and restored the poems to him, necessarily retelling also his original story. Her treatment of the eclogues is altogether less satisfactory than Greville's, and where an intelligent principle of arrangement and selection can be discerned in the 1590 edition, the task appears to have been carried out in 1593 in an arbitrary and inconsistent way.

Hugh Sanford, the Earl of Pembroke's secretary and for some time tutor to the Countess's elder son, William Herbert, assisted Lady Pembroke with her edition and signed the foreword, 'To the Reader'. This foreword begins with a reference to the 1590 edition:

The disfigured face, gentle Reader, wherewith this worke not
long since appeared to the common view, moved that noble
Lady, to whose Honour it was consecrated, to whose protection
it was committed, to take in hand the wiping away those spottes
wherewith the beauties therof were unworthely blemished. But as
often in repairing a ruinous house, the mending of some olde
part occasioneth the making of some new, so here her
honourable labour begonne in correcting the faults, ended in
supplying the defects; by the view of what was ill done guided
to the consideration of what was not done.[12]

This sounds harsh criticism of Greville and Gwynne whose edition,
though it contains some errors, is by no means a bad one. Lady
Pembroke's own major contribution was in supplying the end of the
story as it had been written for the old *Arcadia*, plus the rewritten
passages concerning Evarchus's journey and Pyrocles's visit to Philo-
clea's chamber. Greville had not printed these chapters, perhaps as a
matter of principle because he believed that, even amended by Sidney's
'direction', the older version of the work was far from representing
Sidney's later intentions and that Sidney would not wish it to stand.[13]
If this was indeed the reason for Greville's insistence on printing no
more than the revised manuscript authorized, actually breaking off in
the middle of a sentence, this might account for the acerbity of the
1593 preface. The Countess of Pembroke might have thought that
Greville took too much on himself. *Arcadia* was, after all 'done . . . for
her' and it was to *her* protection (i.e. not Greville's) that Sidney committed it, as the preface claims. Lady Pembroke does not seem to have
shared the view that there were two distinct books, one the light-
hearted private *Arcadia* which Sidney wrote for his sister and her
friends, the other the much more serious and ambitious work containing an exhaustive study of public and private ethics. Viewing *Arcadia*
as he did, Greville would hardly be likely to accept as a satisfactory memorial of his friend the mixed version which the Countess
offered. She, on the other hand, was anxious that nothing of her
brother's should be lost and was perhaps angered by what may have
seemed like Greville's contempt for the version that was so especially
hers.

Part of Sanford's foreword to the 1593 edition seems to be concerned with some private grudges of Sanford's own and it is a pity

that they should have been allowed a place here. The Countess of Pembroke's own irritation is easily forgiven, for though she under-estimated Greville's work, everyone would agree that the old *Arcadia* should not have been suppressed and many readers have pre-ferred what Sidney wrote out of 'a young head, not so well stayed as I would it were'[14] to the later rehandling of it. And it is under-standable that the devotion of sister and friend might easily lead to jealousy.

Florio picks up Sanford's quarrelsome tone in his dedication of Book II of his translation of Montaigne to Sidney's daughter and Lady Rich. Writing of the 1593 composite version he compares the old ending unfavourably with the revised text to which it is tacked on: 'this end we see of it, though at first above all, now is not answerable to the precedents', and he adds: 'though it were much easier to mend out of an originall and well corrected copie, than to make-up so much out of a most corrupt, yet see we more marring that was well, than mending what was amisse.' This, like the Walsingham letter, is ambiguous in detail and whether, in criticizing Lady Pembroke's edition, Florio had in mind the new verbal errors introduced in 1593, the rearrangement of the eclogues, the printing of the last books from the old *Arcadia* to add to the revised version, or what-ever else, speculation will not determine. It only seems a pity that any bad feeling should have been engendered in the history of these publications.

Greville's personal conduct in the affair seems to have been irre-proachable. His original action in taking steps to stop the pirate edition had been honourable and self-effacing, and he does not, in the *Life of Sidney*, make any comment on Lady Pembroke's edition, which perhaps shows a certain restraint on his part for Sidney's sake and for the sake of his affection for his sister. But he has a final word on his views at the end of the *Life* immediately following the passage already quoted about 'the Arcadian Antiques' beautifying the margin of his works. He has restated his belief that Sidney's intention was to provide 'morall Images, and Examples (as directing threds) to guide every man through the confused Labyrinth of his own desires, and life', and he goes on: 'So that howsoever I liked them too well (even in that un-perfected shape they were) to condescend that such delicate (though inferior) Pictures of himselfe should be suppressed; Yet I do wish that work may be the last in this kind, presuming no man that followes can ever reach, much lesse go beyond that excellent intended patterne of his.' (*Life*, pages 223-4.)

2

The 1590 *Arcadia* belongs to Greville biography for it comes directly out of his love for Sidney and their long and close friendship. It belongs also to the history of Greville's thought for, as this study has shown, Greville's attitude towards his friend's work reflects strongly his own political interests and his assessment of the moral value of literature. 'His end was not writing, even while he wrote' is the keynote of his commentary on *Arcadia*: Sidney bent all his endeavours 'to make himself and others, not in words or opinion, but in life, and action, good and great.' Greville's decision to confine his edition of *Arcadia* to the revised manuscript alone may very well stem from these attitudes. His explicit comments on the book occur in his *Life of Sidney*. There they are but one element in a compendious gathering of Grevillean topics and themes, and in turning to the *Life* next it will be as well to start, as before, by identifying the relatively simple biographical nucleus round which all the rest gathers.

The prose work known as the *Life of Sir Philip Sidney* was not published in Greville's lifetime but appeared first in 1652 under the care of an unknown P. B. who dedicated it to the former Lady Dorothea Sidney, Algernon Sidney's sister and Waller's Sacharissa, who was at that date Countess of Cumberland. As usual, we have no certain evidence about when it was composed but since Greville took no active part in public affairs during the years 1604-14 it is on the face of it very likely that this was the period when he composed the *Life*, with its nostalgia for the past and its soreness at the changed and degenerate temper of the present. There is a reference to Henry IV of France as 'the late renowned *Henry of France*' on page 31 which suggests a date of composition not long after Henry's death in 1610, but it is possible that Greville worked on and added to the *Life* over a number of years. If so, the original core of it was probably a shorter and simpler dedication of his works to Sidney, and various other material was added to it later.

Though the work is always known by the title its first editor gave it, it is not a biography in any ordinary sense and Greville himself did not claim that it was. By 1652 he had been dead for twenty-four years and

the title, *The Life of the Renowned Sir Philip Sidney*, was given by P. B.
and not by Greville himself. In the Cambridge manuscript the work is
entitled simply *A Dedication*[15] and the first paragraph of the printed
text confirms that this was what Greville intended it to be: a dedication
of the 'exercises of his youth' – a collection of his literary works, that
is – to 'that worthy *Sir Philip Sidney*, so long since departed.' A dedication of this kind might naturally contain a tribute to the friend long
dead and some account of the author's own writings and Greville
prepares us to find also a contrast made between the times of his youth
and the present in which he writes. He strikes this note of contrast at
the very beginning and draws deliberate attention to his choice of a
patron from among the dead rather than the living. The 1652 editor
recognized that to call what emerged from this combination of in-
gredients simply a life of Sidney was inadequate, if not misleading, and
he strove for greater accuracy in extensive subtitling. Even then some
aspects of Greville's work escaped him. The full title-page reads—

> The Life of the Renowned Sir Philip Sidney. With the true
> Interest of England as it then stood in relation to all Forrain
> Princes: And particularly for suppressing the power of Spain
> stated by Him. His principall Actions, Counsels, Designes and
> Death. Together with a short Account of the Maximes and
> Policies used by Queen Elizabeth in her Government. Written by
> Sir Fulke Grevil, Knight, Lord Brook, a Servant to Queen
> Elizabeth, and His Companion and Friend.

The suggestion of the title-page that the biographical material is set
in a political rather than a domestic context is fully justified. Indeed it
is tempting to describe Greville's *Life of Sidney* as political hagiography,
devoted to describing Sidney's preparation and fitness for the role of
European statesman and extolling the wisdom of his reading of men
and events and the policies he favoured. But though statecraft looms
large in Greville's mind, it is not everything:

> For my own part, I observed, honoured, and loved him so much;
> as with what caution soever I have passed through my days
> hitherto among the living, yet in him I challenge a kind of
> freedome even among the dead. So that although with *Socrates*, I
> professe to know nothing for the present; yet with *Nestor* I am

delighted in repeating old newes of the ages past; and will therefore stir up my drooping memory touching this man's worth, powers, wayes and designes: to the end that in the tribute I owe him, our nation may see a Sea-mark, rais'd upon their native coast, above the levell of any private Pharos abroad: and so by a right Meridian line of their own, learn to sail through the straits of true virtue, into a calm, and spacious Ocean of humane honour.   (*Life*, page 3.)

The eulogy here has its roots in personal emotion, a devoted friendship justified and exalted, Greville believes, by the surpassing worth of the young man dead years ago. Greville passed his life in the company of the great and had a busy hand in the affairs of his country but he looked back over his experience to account it perhaps his greatest honour that he was brought up with Sidney, and when he speaks of him it is with deep affection for his nature as well as admiration for his parts.

It was an intimate friendship dating from childhood and Greville was on terms of familiarity not only with Sidney himself but with his family and friends. He consequently writes with the special authority of close knowledge. Yet, of course, as a life of Sidney this work of Greville's disappoints many of our modern expectations. Greville has no interest in providing the homely detail which enlightens a personality or in revealing the lineaments of the private man behind the public figure. Like the Elizabethan portraitists in their formal pictures, Greville is less concerned with identifying an individual personality than with delineating his status in the society in which he lived and giving a representation of his contribution to it. It is useless to look to him for pleasant trivialities concerning Sidney's childhood, for example. We shall find more of Philip as a boy in Marshall's account book[16] than we shall in Greville. He takes for granted the childish features, having neither the psychologist's nor the sentimentalist's interest in them, and describes only what marked Sidney off from others:

Of whose Youth I will report no other wonder, but this;
That though I lived with him, and knew him from a child, yet I never knew him other than a man; with such staiednesse of mind, lovely, and familiar gravity, as carried grace, and reverence above greater years. His talk ever of knowledge, and his very play tending to enrich his mind: So as even his teachers found something

in him to observe and learn, above that which they usually read, or taught.   (*Life*, page 6.)

Eschewing much of the personality and detail which has been one of the most valued qualities of biographers from Dr Johnson onwards, Greville also neglects to give a full chronological account of Sidney's career. The most notable omissions to a modern way of thinking are any reference to his sister or to Penelope Devereux or even to his wife and his child.

From what point of view then does Greville make his selection of material and what manner of man does he intend to persuade us Sidney was?

He sets out to praise him, to show him as an example which all men were glad to follow: 'this one man's example, and personall respect, did not only encourage Learning, and Honour in the Schooles, but brought the affection, and true use thereof both into the Court and the Camp. Nay more, even many Gentlemen excellently learned amongst us, will not deny, but that they affected to row, and steer their course in his wake.' (*Life*, pages 34–5.) He was learned and accomplished and he had an unshakeable moral probity: 'Above all, he made the Religion he professed, the firm Basis of his life' (page 35) and he 'found no wisdome where he found no courage, nor courage without wisdome, nor either without honesty and truth' (page 36); 'his heart and tongue went both one way, and so with every one that went with the Truth; as knowing no other kindred, partie, or end' (page 35). All his great gifts of character and intelligence he was eager to put, as Greville's ideal man should, at the service of the State, and Greville is concerned to show how great his potentialities as a statesman were. The scope for action actually allowed him was minimal, as Greville acknowledges, but he accumulates the tributes of great men of the day attesting their sense of his superlative capacity. Among them was Languet whom Greville describes as 'wise by the conjunction of practice in the world, with that well-grounded Theory of Books' (page 7) and who gladly 'became a Nurse of knowledge to this hopefull young gentleman' (page 8). In spite of the great difference in their years and experience the true friendship of Sidney and Languet testified that 'wisdome and love, in good spirits have great affinity together' (page 9). Leicester and Walsingham, Henry of Navarre, Don John of Austria, and the Spaniard Mendoza are all called upon by Greville as witnesses to the extraordinary impression this young Englishman made upon some of the most experienced and exacting men of their day. William of Orange, he reports, went so far as to send a message to Queen Elizabeth via Greville, affirming with all his experience of European politics behind him 'that if he could judge, her Majesty had one of the ripest, and greatest Counsellors of Estate in *Sir Philip Sidney*, that at this day lived in *Europe*: to the triall of which hee was pleased to leave his own credit engaged, untill her Majesty might please to employ this Gentleman, either amongst her friends or enemies' (page 27).

The unqualified eulogy which Greville offers to the memory of Sidney might very well be tedious and at best a panegyric to an abstract virtue. It is not so because, although the enlivening personal detail is usually absent, yet the whole is firmly rooted in Greville's memory of particulars, of times, places, and individuals. His account of Sidney's boyhood, already quoted, ends with a recollection of an occasion when Greville, a boy himself, heard Sir Henry Sidney refer to his son as '*Lumen familiae suae*'. Greville evidently recalls this episode of his own childhood with particular vividness for he remembers that Sir Henry did not know that he was present to overhear. So that the description of the precocious, grave child, the light of the Sidneys, a little daunting, perhaps, in our eyes, is at least brushed over by a real touch from the past. The story of William of Orange's compliment is an extended example of this kind of authentication, for Greville has already given a circumstantial account of his own meeting with the Prince and their conversations so that there can be no suspicion that he is merely relating a legend or inventing a pious fiction.

What follows has also the ring of genuineness. Greville was to pass on Orange's comments to Elizabeth:

> At my return into *England*, I performed all his other
> commandments; this that concerned Sir *Philip* (thinking to make
> the fine-spun threads of friendship more firm between them) I
> acquainted Sir *Philip* with: not as questioning, but fully resolved
> to doe it. Unto which he at the first sight opposing, discharged
> my faith impawn'd to the Prince of *Orange*, for the delivery of it;
> as an act only intending his good, and so to be perform'd, or
> dispens'd with at his pleasure; yet for my satisfaction freely added
> these words: first, that the Queen had the life it self daily
> attending her: and if she either did not, or would not value it so

highly, the commendation of that worthy Prince could be no
more (at the best) than a lively picture of that life, and so of far
lesse credit, and estimation with her. His next reason was,
because Princes love not that foreign powers should have
extraordinary interest in their Subjects; much lesse to be taught
by them how they should place their own: as arguments either
upbraiding ignorance, or lack of large rewarding goodness in
them.   (*Life*, pages 27–8.)

This episode might have been used to show that Sidney was by nature
modest but it is typical of Greville's method that it is on Sidney's per-
spicacity and maturity of judgement that he wishes to focus attention.

There are, of course, more famous episodes in the *Life* where Greville
writes with a vivid sense of the people and occasions he is describing:
the tennis-court episode, for example. At the time when the court was
in a state of great tension over Elizabeth's projected match with the
Duke of Alençon and feelings were high between the supporters and
opponents of the marriage, Sidney was at tennis one day when 'a Peer
of this Realm [the Earl of Oxford], born great, greater by alliance, and
superlative in the Princes favour abruptly came into the Tennis-Court.'
Oxford ordered Sidney and his friends off the court and Sidney responded sharply to his insulting language and behaviour: 'In which
progress of heat, as the tempest grew more and more vehement within,
so did their hearts breath out their perturbations in a more loud and
shrill accent. The *French* Commissioners unfortunately had that day
audience, in those private Galleries, whose windows looked into the
Tennis-Court . . .' (page 65).

The little dramatic scene of the two young men, each challenging the
pride of the other, and the unwelcome observers at the windows is full
of character and political significance and Greville sketches it in well.
The account of Sidney's attempt to join with Sir Francis Drake in an
expedition to the West Indies has already been discussed and it is one
of the best pieces of sheer narrative writing in the *Life*. The story of
Sidney's death as Greville tells it is also skilfully managed in a different
style.

Greville was not with Sidney during these last months in the Low
Countries but he evidently collected as full accounts as he could of the
fatal skirmish on that misty day at Zutphen and the events that followed.
There is, in fact, more detail in Greville's account of the weeks when

Sidney lay dying than there is for any other period of Sidney's life and the details are far from indiscriminate. Greville sought deliberately to demonstrate how the inner quality of the man, which he had been attempting to describe throughout the work, was redefined by his behaviour in the last few days of his life. Sidney's and Greville's contemporaries attached much significance to the way a man died. As Greville's younger friend, Samuel Daniel, wrote of the Earl of Devonshire:

> But let it now sufficient be, that I
> The last scene of his act of life bewray,
> Which gives th'applause to all, doth glorify
> The work; for 'tis the ev'ning crowns the day.
> This action of our death especially
> Shows all a man. Here only is he found,
> With what munition he did fortify
> His heart; how good his furniture hath been.

These lines were written in 1606. They sum up very well the motivation behind Greville's choice of detail in his story of Sidney's last days. He maintains, of course, the tone of love and admiration which has been constant throughout but in addition to this, individual details recall earlier episodes and traits of character suggested at other points so that the narrative of his wounding and his dying shows in little the pattern of his life. The episode of Sidney's handing the bottle of water to the poor soldier on the battlefield in spite of his own thirst is an example of that quick sensitivity to the needs and feelings of others which appears to have been a rare quality among Elizabethans and which seems to have struck Greville particularly. Greville has laid stress on it earlier in his account of Sidney's actions after the frustration of his own plans for the West Indian project. Sidney's personal disappointment was very great but he at once took thought for the others involved, protected Drake, and encouraged the men by presenting the Queen's actions in the light most favourable to them and honourable to her. Again, the story of how Count 'Hollocks' (von Hohenlo) sent his own doctor to attend on Sidney when he was wounded, although he himself was in need of attention, and his anger at the man's bad report on Sidney's condition is in line with all the other instances of the admiration and love which Sidney inspired. The account of Sidney's own discovery of his worsened condition and his refusal subsequently to allow himself to be deluded into false hope of recovery illustrates in different circumstances the same strongmindedness and resolution which he had shown in composing his letter to the Queen concerning the Alençon marriage and in his conduct in the Oxford affair, and recalls also a remark, which Greville makes earlier in the book when he is commenting on Sidney's refusal to allow him to pass on to Elizabeth William of Orange's complimentary remarks about himself: 'after mature deliberation being once resolved, he never brought any question of change to afflict himself with, or perplex the business; but left the success to His will, that governs the blinde prosperities, and unprosperities of Chance; and so works out His own ends by the erring frailities of humane reason and affection.' (*Life*, page 28.)

Greville gives full weight, naturally, to the religious exercises by which Sidney prepared for his death, but he does not linger over them, and the end itself is described briefly and with great restraint: 'Here this noble Gentleman ended the too short Scene of his life; in which path, whoever is not confident that he walked the next way to eternal rest, will be found to judge uncharitably.' (*Life*, page 140.) Finally Greville concludes his account with some reflections of Sidney's on the character and probable future of the Dutch, thus by a final reference to his statesmanlike reflections rounding off his account of the last stages of Sidney's career.

So much for biographical narrative as such. It will be clear, even so far, that Greville is giving the material a highly individual treatment.

Indeed Greville, when he came to write the life of Sidney, might have said of his friend what Keats said of Shakespeare: 'he lived a life of allegory'. It is because he felt about him in this way that he did not concern himself with personal detail for its own sake (Sidney's wife was present at his deathbed, for example, but Greville does not mention her). The details which are included and the actions which are recounted are there not because they illuminate the figure of one individual but, on the contrary, because they have meaning far beyond the immediate circumstances and the individual life which gave birth to them. Sidney's life, as Greville looks back on it, has to his mind the quality of an emblem, or speaking picture, a 'pregnant image', in his own phrase: it manifests a perfectly proportioned nature, accomplished in all branches:

Indeed he was a true modell of Worth: A man fit for Conquest, Plantation, Reformation, or what Action soever is greatest, and hardest amongst men: Withall, such a lover of Mankind, and Goodnesse, that whosoever had any reall parts, in him found comfort, participation, and protection to the uttermost of his power . . . his heart, and capacity were so large, that there was not a cunning Painter, a skilful Engineer, an excellent Musician, or any other Artificer of extraordinary fame, that made not himself known to this famous Spirit, and found him his true friend without hire: and the common Rende-vous of Worth in his time. (*Life*, pages 33–4.)

Yet it was a nature truly modest, fit for great responsibility yet always preserving respect of place, a product of good stock developed by high culture, whose highest aspiration was service. In his death he combined the stoic virtues of strong-minded endurance and disregard of physical pain with Christian piety and humility: in his life he was unmindful of himself but sensitive to the needs of others. This is the good life as Greville saw it, and it is a powerful allegory of diverse applications. A sombre sense of the vanity of human wishes is part of it, for death came early and Sidney was never given any opportunity to try his trained strength in a major task. His life was one largely of frustration and renunciation and it makes a sharp contrast between worldly values and the triumphs of the spirit. Greville's Sidney is reminiscent of the figure of Mustapha in the revised version of his play and Mustapha himself is set in a vast drama of conflict between the world and the spirit. Sidney's life is part of the same drama. He is willing to serve the world on his own high terms but he is never a servant to it, always free within himself and able to renounce it.

This is the moral allegory of the *Life of Sidney*, the more absolute and the nobler kind; but like Spenser's *Faerie Queene*, *The Life of Sidney* is two-faced and contains also a political allegory. It is obvious from the title page of 1652 that Greville is much concerned in this book with political affairs.[17] The moral implications of the *Life* cut very deep, and Greville's convictions about the world and the spirit have a profound effect upon his selection of scenes and episodes: but on another level he is deeply engaged with affairs of the world, in particular with political affairs, and he treats Sidney's career in the central sections of the book in terms of his participation in these affairs. Thus he describes

Sidney's embassy to Germany when, charged with a purely formal mission of condoling the death of the Emperor Rudolf, he enlarges his scope and takes the opportunity of strengthening the Protestant League; he goes in detail into the episode of the letter which Sidney wrote to the Queen setting out arguments against her proposed marriage with the Duke of Alençon (the tennis-court incident which modern readers seize on as a piece of vivid colouring in the *Life* comes in the text as incidental to the discussion of the whole political situation at Court at this time, with rival factions on different sides on the marriage issue: Greville sees the quarrel with Oxford not only as a contrast between two kinds of courtier, one noble by nature, the other noble by blood but base by nature, but also as a reflection of a political crisis: the presence of the French ambassadors is a stinging reminder of the threat to the national honour); and he describes Sidney's plans for colonization beyond the seas and the preparations he made to forward them. The accounts of his gravity and love of learning in childhood and the insistence on the lessons in statecraft contained in *Arcadia* lead naturally into this account of Sidney as a public man and are linked by the desire to present Sidney as potentially a great figure on the European stage.

This is one strand of political interest in the book: Sidney as a political example as well as a moral emblem. But there are others. After the story of Sidney's life has ended on his deathbed, Greville turns to those works of his own which the memoir of his friend is to preface, but his attention is soon diverted in a remarkable manner. He tells how the last-written of his plays was about Antony and Cleopatra but he confesses that he burnt it. The play showed them acting 'according to their irregular passions, in forsaking Empire to follow sensuality' (page 155) and prudence urged that it should be destroyed: 'Many members in that creature (by the opinion of those few eyes, which saw it) having some childish wantonness in them, apt enough to be construed, or strained to a personating of vices in the present governors, and government.' (*Life*, page 156.) He calls to mind how, in inhospitable times, people and things are readily misconstrued against their true nature and he sees how that very thing had just happened in the slandering of Essex by his enemies and his death as a traitor. So, in or about 1601, he burnt his play. This little piece of personal history then leads by an astonishingly swift transition into an account and defence of the Earl of Essex, which interrupts Greville's commentary on his own works and which brings in its train reminiscences of the Queen. These occupy three lengthy chapters. We do not come back to Greville himself and his writing till the last chapter of all.

These diversions on Essex and Elizabeth are obviously important. The chapters on Elizabeth make up a considerable section of the whole work and in them Greville analyses her gifts of statecraft and pays her the tribute of his deep respect and admiration. At the end of his account of her, Greville tells the story of his frustrated attempt to obtain the materials for a full history of Elizabeth's reign. The long digressions on Essex and Elizabeth are Greville's substitutes for the history he was not allowed to write, but there are more motives at work in the framing of these sections than the wish simply to rescue from oblivion two studies from the projected history.

It is noticeable from the beginning of the book that reference to the past is edged with reference to the present, and though Greville acknowledges in the opening paragraphs that there are noble friends of his and 'many Honourable Magistrates' still living, the very first sentence has already struck a note of disappointment and disillusion. A few pages later, following his account of the friendship between Languet and Sidney, Greville adds a paragraph to explain why he has given so much attention to the topic. He has done so partly, he explains, to reinforce his claim that Sidney had 'extraordinary greatness' in him and also

> to bring the children of favor, and chance, into an equall balance
> of comparison with birth, worth, and education—and therein
> abruptly to conclude, that God creates those in his certain and
> eternal mouldes, out of which he elects for himself; where kings
> choose creatures out of *Pandoras Tun*, and so raise up worth,
> and no worth; friends or enemies at adventure. Therefore what
> marvail can it be, if these *Jacobs*, and *Esaus* strive ambitiously one
> with another, as well before as after they come out of such
> erring, and unperfect wombes? (*Life*, pages 10–11.)

It would be difficult to read this from the pen of any writer in the reign of James I without thinking at once of James's Scotsmen and his relations with Carr and later with Villiers.[18] Written by Fulke Greville, a respected servant of Queen Elizabeth, now supplanted at Court by James's favourites, it becomes a very sharp thrust at the quality both of the monarch and those men with whom he chose to surround himself. The same theme occurs in chapter III:

> Now let Princes vouchsafe to consider, of what importance it is to
> the honour of themselves and their Estates, to have one man of
> such eminence [the reference is, of course to Sidney]; not only as a
> nourisher of vertue in their Courts, or service; but besides for
> a reformed standard, by which even the most humorous persons
> could not but have a reverend ambition to be tried, and approved
> current . . . his very waies in the world did generally adde
> reputation to his Prince, and Country by restoring amongst us the
> ancient Majestie of noble, and true dealings: As a manly wisdome,
> that can no more be weighed down, by any effeminate craft,
> than *Hercules* could be overcome by that contemptible Army of
> Dwarfs. This was it which, I profess, I loved dearly in him,
> and still shall be glad to honour in the great men of this time:
> I mean that his heart and tongue went both one way, and so
> with every one that went with the Truth; as knowing no other
> kindred, partie, or end.    (*Life*, pages 34–5.)

God saw fit to remove Sidney from this life so that his worthiness should not be 'incorporated with our corruptions' but Greville's love of his prince and country leads him to pray that Sidney's 'worth, and way may not be fatally buried with him'. Other great men before Sidney's time and after have pursued honours for selfish ends. He did not, and the memory they leave behind them will be very different from his:

> when the pride of flesh, and power of favour shall cease in these
> by death, or disgrace; what then hath time to register, or fame to
> publish in these great mens names, that will not be offensive,
> or infectious to others? What pen without blotting can write the
> story of their deeds? or what Herald blaze their Arms without a
> blemish? And as for their counsels and projects, when they come
> once to light, shall they not live as noisome, and loathsomely
> above ground, as their Authors' carkasses lie in the grave? So as the
> return of such greatness to the world, and themselves can be
> but private reproach, publique ill example, and a fatall scorn to
> the Government they live in. Sir Philip Sidney is none of this

number; for the greatness which he affected was built upon true
Worth; esteeming Fame more than Riches, and Noble actions far
above Nobility itself. (*Life*, pages 37–8.)

There can hardly be a sharper example of the use of the ostensible
subject for devastating comment on the present. This rotund condemnation of mean-souled minions of contemptible governments damns
them on every count, temporal and spiritual, by contrast with Sidney,
and in the light of such passages, the descriptions of Sidney's life and
character take on a relative as well as an absolute significance.

The commentary, implicit and explicit, on the contemporary scene
is not limited to exposing James's choice of favourites by contrast with
the true nobility of Sidney. There are many comments on the ignoble
manners of the present: 'to manifest that these were not complements,
self-ends, or use of each other, according to our modern fashion but
meer ingenuities of spirit, to which the ancient greatness of hearts ever
frankly engaged their Fortunes' (pages 28–9), and: 'Here am I still
enforced to bring pregnant evidence from the dead: amongst whom I
have found far more liberall contribution to the honor of true worth,
than among those which now live; and in the market of selfness,
traffique new interest by the discredit of old friends; that ancient wisdome of righting enemies, being utterly worn out of date in our modern
discipline.' (*Life*, page 19.) There may be a personal reference here to
Robert Cecil against whom Greville felt particular bitterness. Certainly he was 'trafficking new interest' while Greville was discredited
and it was he who refused Greville the facilities he wanted for the
writing of his history of Elizabeth's reign, which would probably have
included a 'righting' of Essex.

There is yet another aspect of the political material of this work to be
considered before we can finally distinguish the unacknowledged
situations and characters which lie just beneath the surface. Sidney,
Elizabeth and Essex are ostensibly the dramatis personae: but there is a
second shadow cast on whom Greville's mind is continually running
as he recreates the past among the tensions and enmities of the em-
bittered present. There are two sequences of ideas in the *Life of Sidney*.
There is the thread which runs from the occasion of the writing – that
is, the publication of the works of Greville's youth, the writing which
he was inspired to do by the friendship and example of Sidney, and
which leads directly to the chapters containing the memorial to Sidney.

From his works again this thread of ideas leads to Essex as Greville recalls how he thought it best to burn his latest play, on the subject of Antony and Cleopatra, thinking it politically dangerous at the time of Essex's fall. There follows an account of and defence of Essex and this again leads on to a survey of the reign of Elizabeth. The thread is consecutive, if somewhat tenuous. But there is another sequence of associations, and here we have not a long-drawn-out thread but a pattern revolving round a few central points. The moral decline since the days of Elizabeth and the contrast between new style favourites and Sidney, true pattern of knighthood, have already been noticed as themes in the first part of the book. They recur in different guise in the chapters following the account of Sidney's death which constitute the second part of the book. Essex himself was a Queen's favourite and Greville thought him a worthy one. Essex had faults, acknowledged though not specified by Greville, and Sidney, in his account, had none: but they both represent ideal courtiers and, more generally, two types of virtue: one, Sidney's, contemplative and renunciatory, the other, Essex's, active, fully engaged in the affairs of the world and inevitably bruised by his contacts and preserving only a qualified virtue since action in an imperfect world can itself only be imperfect. The juxtaposition of these two has meaning within the scope of the *Life* because it gives examples of the two ways of good conduct, as Greville saw them, in court life, and it has meaning in a wider reference also, for Sidney and Essex typify basic ideas of Greville's – the imperfection of virtue in action, absolute virtue being possible only in total withdrawal.

But Greville has not done with the subject of favourites. He has described Essex's attitude towards Elizabeth: he describes also Elizabeth's attitude towards him. Even in the height of Essex's credit with her, Greville writes, she never allowed him to manipulate her power and so derogate from her authority and inflict a new tyranny upon her people. She never permitted 'the latitudes which some modern Princes allow to their Favourites, as supporters of Government, and middle wals between power, and the peoples envy' (page 176), but she 'published to the world, by a constant *Series* in her actions, that she never was, nor ever would be overloaden with any such excesses in her Person, or defects in her Government, as might constraine her to support, or be supported by a Monopolous use of Favourites; as if she would make any greater than her selfe, to governe Tyrannically by them.' (*Life*, page 179.)

A whole art of government is being reflected on here. The Elizabeth–
Essex situation is a transparency through which one sees the inept
figure of James, fooling with Robert Carr as later he did with Villiers,
squandering public money on his Scots, burdening the country with
his debts and rousing the finally implacable hostility of Parliament.

None of these points escapes Greville, and Elizabeth serves as the
pattern of all the virtues which James conspicuously lacked.

> She ever came in state, when she demanded aid from her
> House of Commons. Neither did she fetch, or force presidents
> from her Predecessors in those demands: but made her self a
> president to all Posterities, that the love of people to a loving
> Princesse is not ever curiously ballanced, by the self-pitying
> abilities of mankinde but their spirits, hearts, and states being
> drawne up above their own fraile selfnesse, the audit is taken after;
> and perhaps summ'd up with a little smart to themselves, wherein
> they glory.    (*Life*, page 173.)

The contrast between this state of affairs and the progressive acerbity
of the wrangling between James and his Parliaments could scarcely be
sharper. Elizabeth indeed knew how to use her Parliaments, not only
for the grant of money but 'withal, as Maps of orders, or disorders,
through her whole Kingdome' (page 187), and she was careful to bind
herself to her people by mutual trust and common interest: 'so as their
need and fears concurring with her occasions, made their desires and
counsels concurre too, and out of those equall, and common grounds
forced every man to believe his private fish-ponds could not be safe,
whiles the publique state of the Kingdome stood in danger of present,
or expectant extremities.' (*Life*, page 188.) She did not seek to govern
without Parliaments but respected and cherished them (how different
from her successor!) and Greville brings us back to the old theme –
'concluding that these two Honourable Houses, were the only judi-
cious, faithfull, and industrious Favourites of unincroaching Monarchs.'
(*Life*, page 191.)

Criticism of James is implicit in almost all the points which Greville
singles out to comment on in Elizabeth's handling of affairs. She was
thrifty in her household affairs (pages 183–6); James's notoriously bad
husbandry led to a number of projects for retrenchment in the royal
household. Elizabeth managed her navy providently and took care that

it should be well supplied and well-served (pages 198–203); under James conditions deteriorated so much that in 1608 and again in 1612–13 commissions were appointed to report on abuses in the government of the navy. Greville, of course, was specially interested in naval matters, having been Secretary to the Navy under Elizabeth (1598–1604), and he refers to his experience on page 201 when, describing a procedure, he comments, 'of which my self am witnesse, as being well acquainted with the use of it in my youth, but utterly unacquainted with the change since, or any reasons of it.' (The attention which Greville gives to these matters in this section of the *Life* suggests that this part at least was composed at a time when the management of the navy was in men's minds, i.e. probably 1608 or 1612–13.)

Proclamations and impositions also Greville takes every opportunity to refer to with disapprobation. Elizabeth (page 192) 'would have been as averse from bearing the envy of printing any new Lines of Taxe, Impositions, Proclamations or Mandats (without Parliaments) upon her ancient celestiall, or terrestriall Globes, as her humble subjects possibly could be, or wish her to be.' James in the first seven years of his reign put out more proclamations than Elizabeth had issued in thirty years. His penchant for governing by proclamation, independently of Parliament and the law, led to a famous constitutional pronouncement by four judges in 1610. They were called in to give an opinion on the King's rights in this matter and they formally declared that the King had no prerogative but that which the law of the land allowed him. In 1610 also the Commons were in a mood to demand that the King must resign all claim to lay impositions (customs and duties levied without Parliamentary consent), a long standing grievance since the early years of the reign. Government by proclamations and impositions 'which in our government is a confusion almost as fatal as the confusion of tongues' is one of the black marks which Greville scores against the French. (*Life*, pages 53 and 98.)

Above all, Greville stresses, the Protestant cause was the heart of Elizabeth's domestic and foreign policies and she was ever watchful to reduce the might of Spain, the Catholic power and natural enemy. Greville lays a good deal of stress on the Spanish danger and continually returns to it. The burden of William of Orange's conversation with him in 1577 as he reports it (pages 21–6) is the necessity of constant vigilance against the encroachments of Spain. The analysis of the state of Europe in chapters VIII and IX is directed to identifying the channels through which Spanish influence works and the means of combatting it. His accounts of Elizabeth's dealings with Spain culminate in a comment which again throws the view forward from the past to a less well-governed present. She kept the Spanish power down in her day and it might have been even further reduced had she lived longer or

> time not neglected her wisdom so suddenly, by exchanging that active, victorious, enriching, and ballancing course of her defensive Wars, for an idle (I fear) deceiving shadow of peace. In which whether we already languish, or live impoverished, whilst he growes potent, and rich, by the fatall security of all Christendom, they that shall succeed us, are likely to feele, and judge freely. (*Life*, page 210.)

The uncompromising anti-Catholic, anti-Spanish notes of Elizabethan patriotism, like many other things from the past which Greville stood by, were not in favour at the Court of James. He cherished schemes of putting an end to religious strife by marrying one of his children to a Catholic and he put out feelers for a Spanish marriage for the Prince of Wales. At Court, a party headed by the Earl of Northampton saw the restoration of Catholicism as the surest safeguard against democratic Puritanism and favoured a Catholic match, and James was inclined to relax penalties against Catholics at home when they made it possible for him. 'Abrupt and spirit-fallen toleration' Greville calls this kind of thing (page 51), and the Commons complained in 1610 that 'the laws are not executed against the priests, who are corrupters of the people in religion and loyalty'. James's attitudes must have seemed to Greville a criminal dalliance with danger and a betrayal of the past, especially after the murder of Henry IV of France in 1610 when Spanish aggression had once again become a real threat in Europe. The years 1610–11 were altogether particularly troubled ones. James dissolved Parliament in anger in February 1611 and at the same time, in deliberate defiance of opinion in the Commons, he made a grant of £34,000 to six of his favourites, four of them Scottish. On 25 March he conferred the title of Viscount Rochester in the English peerage on Robert Carr. To raise money, he sold baronetcies. The date of the Melbourne letter suggests that Greville had the writing of a history in mind in 1611 and his frustration over that may have combined with his sense of the follies of those years to produce the fierceness of his criticism of James, his ministers and his favourites in this part of the *Life*.

To the themes of moral degeneracy, favourites and their masters, and the decline from good government to the weak and wrong-headed which recur so inevitably in the *Life of Sidney*, these others must then be added: the danger of Spain and the necessity at all times of strengthening the Protestant alliance. These are the themes which are given extended treatment in chapter V, which details Sidney's objections to Elizabeth's proposed marriage to the Duke of Alençon, and chapters VIII and IX, which describe Sidney's diagnosis of the European situation in his day and his proposals for containing the Spanish. Chapter V is particularly interesting, for Sidney's own letter to the Queen can be set against it, written, as he told Languet, at the orders of those whom he was bound to obey and probably the result of conferences with Leicester and other senior members of his family. It is a good letter, arguing with restraint and dignity the disadvantages of the proposed match and attempting to persuade the Queen that the fears which he believes urge her to it are groundless. Greville's account of Sidney's views does not follow the letter at all. What we have in Greville, in fact, must be one of two things: a direct insight, obtained either through Greville's verbal memory or his possession of some sort of memorandum, into the ideas in Sidney's mind at the time of the composition of the letter; or a fabrication of Greville's based on the known views of his friend but with no claim to detailed authenticity. In support of the first possibility there is the suggestion in the text that Sidney made the points detailed here in conversation with Greville. Hints of this occur in the occasional insertions: 'as he said' (page 56), 'he willed me to observe' (pages 57 and 59), 'he briefly laid before me' (page 56); and it is quite likely on the face of it that Sidney would have talked over with Greville the subject uppermost in his mind in this way. Greville was out of England for some time in 1579 accompanying back to Germany Prince Casimir and Languet, both of whom had been on a short visit to England, but he returned before the end of the year. No doubt while he was away he heard rumours of what was afoot and perhaps on his return asked Sidney to bring him up to date with the arguments. If so the circumstances might have impressed the conversation on his mind, although thirty years or so is a long time to retain such detail. Greville may, of course, have made notes.

The question of source is more baffling in relation to chapters VIII and IX. If special circumstances had fixed Sidney's arguments concerning the Alençon marriage particularly firmly in Greville's mind and if, in addition, James's quest for another Catholic match encouraged him to sharpen up his recollection of what Sidney had said on the earlier occasion, no such circumstances seem to lie behind chapters VIII and IX. Chapter VIII gives, country by country, a detailed account of the international situation with particular reference to the Spanish menace, and is fairly lucid. Chapter IX, arguing closely that England should take the initiative in breaking the power of Spain, either by direct attack on Spanish territory and shipping, or indirectly through France, and assessing the probable consequences and reactions, is very obscurely written and extremely hypothetical. What purpose did Greville intend these analyses of a thirty-year-old situation to serve? They may perhaps show Sidney as a political analyst and statesman working out a line of policy: but chapter IX, with its reliance on many imponderables, could scarcely have much appeal to a practical politician at any time. It is possible that Greville here may be working on some notes of a gathering at Leicester House or Baynard's Castle – like the one at which the Alençon marriage letter was decided on – a sort of policy working-party drawn from the Leicester–Pembroke group, in which it was Sidney's task to throw out ideas and raise stimulating questions. A rough memorandum of Sidney's own may have come to Greville's hands, or some scribe's notes of what was said. This might account for the manner, which is often questioning, suggests the exploration of theoretic possibilities, and gives the impression of following a rapid sequence of thought. Perhaps Greville's decision to use this material was a late one and chapter IX never had a final revision at his hands.

Nowell Smith's edition seems to offer confirmatory evidence that this part of the book – chapters VIII and IX and perhaps also chapter X – were inserted later, in the fact that they interrupt the narrative and they put the chronology out. Chapter VII gives its brilliant account of Sidney's attempt to join Drake and chapter XI begins with his return to Court where he was 'instantly' made Governor of Flushing. But the last paragraph of chapter VII and the whole of the next three chapters suggest that after the failure of the Drake expedition he was busy formulating new plans and recasting his hopes of organizing a successful plantation overseas. In fact there was no interval. The events of chapter VII were followed by his 'instant' appointment to Flushing (as indeed Greville has said on page 76: the Queen's messenger to Plymouth offered him 'instant employment under his uncle, then going General into the Low Countries'). The colonization plans might possibly belong to an earlier period and may have been part of Sidney's plans for the Drake expedition or may date back to 1582 when Sidney was actively interested in Sir Humphrey Gilbert's plans for an American Commonwealth. The recently discovered Shrewsbury manuscript of the *Life*, not available to Nowell Smith, arranges the material differently and to some extent clarifies the situation. In this, the account of Sidney in the Netherlands (Nowell Smith, chapter XI) precedes the survey of the 'Map of the Christian world' (Nowell Smith, chapter VIII). The survey when it comes is introduced by the paragraph beginning on page 77 of Nowell Smith's edition: 'Whereupon, when Sir Philip found this . . .', which perhaps makes better sense if it is taken as referring to a period when Sidney was abroad. The Shrewsbury manuscript contains a part of the sentence omitted in the other texts. After 'active adventure(r)s abroad' it reads— 'And lastly sawe the Earle his unckle by misprision of this undertaken soveraignty not onely disgraced in person but in him all hope of future designe in those parts like to be totally buried'. This refers to Leicester's acceptance of the dignity of Viceroy which the Netherlands offered him and to Elizabeth's fury at his presumption. The Shrewsbury arrangement of the text puts Sidney's European thoughts in a period of disillusionment after he had arrived in the Netherlands, but it seems likely that Greville later put together with the original material recollections of Sidney's ideas and of discussions with him drawn from several periods in Sidney's career. The account in Nowell Smith's edition is fuller than that in the Shrewsbury manuscript, and that it is later seems to be established by the fact that the printed text of the *Life* includes the story of Greville's thwarting over his projected history, whereas the Shrewsbury manuscript does not have this.[19]

Whatever the explanation of its placing and content, the material of these chapters does not seem to be properly assimilated into the Nowell Smith text. As it stands this part of the book is not by any means the most readable, but the typical Grevillean lightning will flash out from even the obscurest sentence: 'these Tyrannicall encrochments doe carry the images of Hell, and her thunder-workers, in their own breasts, as fortune doth misfortunes in that wind-blown, vast and various womb of hers.' (*Life*, page 109.)

In many respects the situation presented by the *Life of Sidney* is very much like that with which the reader of *Caelica*, Greville's sonnet sequence, is confronted. Both works have Greville's close friendship with Sidney as a point of departure: both cover, whether in fact or in retrospect, a number of years; both draw into their orbit the results of Greville's broodings on state-craft and the ways of the world and, contrasted with these, the values of true religion. In the *Life of Sidney* we get a vivid re-creation of some of the experiences by which his conclusions were forged, and the work is warm with the love, admiration, anger, and contempt which inspired it. It is consequently a very revealing document but there should not be any mistake about what it reveals. It cannot be used as historical evidence about, for example, Essex, or Cecil, or even about Sidney, unless the motives which lead Greville to treat them as he does are properly recognized. He is not a dispassionate historian. The events and personalities of his lifetime fall into a pattern in his imagination, a pattern of moral, political, and religious significances, and it is according to the pattern so perceived that he organizes his material. The same pattern emerges over and over again in his works and a major difficulty in describing these is the isolating of particular parts so that the effect of the whole may be more fully seen and appreciated. The study of *Caelica* which follows in the next chapter will show the same elements assembled once more, but the pattern as it emerges is even more complex this time, and remarkably impressive. Greville's powerful but sometimes clumsy prose gives place to the wit, subtlety and economy of his lyric verse, and the result is one of his great achievements.

# 5 *Caelica* : Divine and human love

Only forty-one of the 109 poems which constitute the sequence *Caelica* are true sonnets and all these follow the English, not the Italian – and Sidney's – pattern. The rest consist of short poems in a variety of forms. Many of them are structures built of sonnet units, quatrains and six-lined stanzas, but there is also an example of rhymed sapphics, as well as *ottava rima*, poulter's measure, dactyls, and trochaics. In time, the composition of the sequence ranges from early days when Greville, Sidney, and their friend, Sir Edward Dyer, were 'a happy blessed Trinitie' writing poetry together in gay and friendly rivalry[1] to a later period when Sidney was dead and Greville's interests and the colouring of his imagination had grown more sombre. How late into Greville's life the composition of the *Caelica* poems extended no external evidence indicates. The probability that they were begun between 1577 and 1580 can be fairly well supported and a substantial number of them evidently belong to the period before Sidney's death in 1586.[2] Professor Bullough thought it likely that they were all written before 1600. More recently Professor Wilkes has put the latest of the *Caelica* poems into the group of compositions which he believes were the last Greville worked on and these he dates after the *Life of Sidney*. Precise dates seem unlikely to emerge but to read *Caelica* with a knowledge of Greville's other work and some familiarity with his characteristic modes of thought and his kind of language is to recognize it fairly confidently as a record of the living mind and experience of the man which, in effect if not in fact, spans his whole career as a writer. As the sequence develops it gathers a burden of reflections on man and on life and issues finally in sombre and powerful religious statements. There is no single situation on which Greville's thought and feeling are focused, but the poetry records instead his response to all kinds of emotional and intellectual stimuli. The sequence was not conceived as a whole but grew with Greville. To use a favourite metaphor of his own, it is a mirror which holds the image of his inner self. Though he could not have planned it from the beginning, he probably recognized in the end what it was, for the sonnets appear to follow a chronological arrangement. In the heavily revised scribal transcript in the Warwick manuscript Greville took the trouble to note that number LXXXIII was misplaced and should have come after number LXXVI. This suggests that the rest were arranged as Greville wanted them and since they do not follow any recognizable thematic scheme, it would seem that the order corresponds at least essentially to the order of composition.

The short lyric poems of *Caelica* cover many subjects and include many moods. Many of them are love poems, but this is not an adequate description. The reverent tone of some suggests that they may have been courtly poems addressed to the Queen. Number LXXXI would seem to fall clearly into this category but number I and others of similar tone might be taken equally well as being dedicated to some concept of Ideal Love or Heavenly Wisdom. By contrast, number L is a lively treatment of a coarse jest-book tale against women. The ambivalence of attitude to love runs throughout. Sometimes the lady is herself sexually cynical, sometimes she is chaste. Sometimes the lover holds love as an ideal, sometimes he is avowedly a pirate. Like Donne, Greville exercises his wit and ingenuity on the various approaches which his temperament suggests to the love relations of men and women, but there is nothing like Donne's sense of the mystic union of body and soul in *The Extasie* or his hymn of mutual love in *The Anniversarie*. Donne, reacting against the idealizations of his contemporaries, cocks a snook at neo-Platonic posturings with irreverent exuberance:

> Whoever loves and does not straight propose
> The right true end of love, is one that puts
> To sea for nothing but to make him sick

and at such points the tone of ruthlessly intelligent cynicism which characterizes many of Greville's poems chimes with his. For Donne the scale of experience runs from the frankest lust to the finest of feeling. Greville's range is different but he also surveys what appears to him as the comedy of sex behaviour and makes a series of sketches to illustrate it. He may see himself as an actor, or he may be an observer; the woman may be chaste and unobtainable, or she may prate of honour but be really loose. Sometimes she is unfaithful to him and he reproaches her, sometimes it is his love which is dead and she pursues him with a vain constancy. The names of the ladies change, even within the same poem. Myra, Cynthia, Caelica, all appear and may be the same woman or different ones or no real woman at all. In sonnet LVIII we hear how Caelica when she was young and sweet adorned her head with a golden wig but as she grows older she discards the gold and wears her own dark hair as if in mourning for her youth. The very oddness of this may tempt us to imagine that here we have a glimpse of some episode from life, but if so, so much sophistication has taken place in the treatment of it that it would be folly to attempt to pin the original down.

The whole poem runs as follows:

The tree in youth proud of his leaves, and springs,
His body shadowed in his glorie layes;
For none doe flie with Art, or others wings,
But they in whom all, save Desire, decayes;
Againe in age, when no leaves on them grow,
Then borrow they their greene of *Misseltoe*.

Where *Caelica*, when she was young and sweet,
Adorn'd her head with golden borrowed haire,
To hide her owne for cold; she thinkes it meet
The head should mourne, that all the rest was faire;
And now in Age when outward things decay,
In spite of age, she throws that haire away.

Those golden haires she then us'd but to tye
Poore captiv'd soules which she in triumph led,
Who not content the Sunnes faire light to eye,
Within his glory their sense dazeled:
And now againe, her owne blacke haire puts on,
To mourne for thoughts by her worths overthrowne.

The first two lines are an example of the pastoral imagery drawn evidently from appreciative observation which occurs pleasantly from time to time in *Caelica* and reminds us that Greville was a Warwickshire man; but this modulates soon into an aphorism in which 'Art' has its common, more or less pejorative sense in Greville. The final couplet of the first stanza acquires thus a double value, both literal and applied. The second stanza moves without preparation from the natural and moral laws of the first to the particular example of Caelica whose behaviour is quite opposite to that which these laws would imply. But Greville finds a rationale for this perversity too: she is in mourning for the decay of youth. The third stanza changes the ground again and the golden hairs are now thought of as the bonds by which she brought 'poore soules' into the captivity of desire where they suffered injury. Her black hair now is a token of mourning for reason overcome by her beauty, 'thoughts by her worths overthrown' – 'worths' being an equivocal, if not a positively ironical word in the context. The first stanza is non-committal, the second witty and ingenious, and the idea that she wore a wig to keep her head warm may even suggest playfulness, but the third stanza has a ring of something sharper and more dangerous about it: is the poem after all about the deceits of erotic love, and is Caelica, young and sweet, an emblem of corruption?

If to describe the poem in these terms seems to be to consider it too curiously, sonnet XLIV may be offered for consideration alongside it:

The *Golden-Age* was when the world was yong,
Nature so rich, as Earth did need no sowing,
Malice not knowne, the Serpents had not stung,
Wit was but sweet Affections overflowing.

Desire was free, and Beauties first-begotten;
Beauty then neither net, nor made by art,
Words out of thoughts brought forth, and not forgotten,
The lawes were inward that did rule the heart.

The *Brasen Age* is now when Earth is worne,
Beauty growne sicke, Nature corrupt and nought,
Pleasure untimely dead as soone as borne,
Both words and kindnesse strangers to our thought:

If now this changing World doe change her head,
*Caelica*, what have her new Lords for to boast?

The old Lord knowes Desire is poorely fed,
And sorrowes not a wavering province lost,
Since in the guilt-age *Saturne* rul'd alone,
And in this painted, *Planets* every one.

This begins by recalling directly Tasso's 'O bella età de l'oro' and a prelapsarian state of innocence. In those days words and thoughts were not at odds with each other and inner rectitude governed everything. Now in the brazen age everything is corrupted. So far, apparently, so good: the territory seems familiar enough though the expression is striking. But the last six lines bring the poem home to Caelica and in doing so complicate it very much. Professor Bullough writes (*Poems and Dramas*, i, pages 251–2): 'Greville's image is the fall of Saturn, Lord of the Golden Age, but in alluding to false Honour, he links it, as in other poems, with his mistress's changeability.' (Professor Bullough is taking the reference to 'false Honour' as being implicit in the echoes of Tasso since it is nowhere explicit in the poem.) 'Jupiter and his brothers overthrew Saturn and divided the world among them. Greville says that the world has degenerated under this divided rule. His allegory refers to i) the diversity of passions which afflict the modern lover; and ii) his many rivals to whom Caelica shows favour.' He goes on:

> Just as the astronomical universe would decay if rule passed from one deity to some of the lesser creatures, so the world of love is in decay owing to the rule of conventions, subterfuges, malice and inconstancy. This poem is a good example of Greville's complex thinking. He connects the Saturnian myth with his interest in astronomy, and with his political belief in the necessity of single rule. And he hints, through his general diagnosis, at his relations with Caelica, so that the last six lines are full of ambiguities.

This is ingenious, though not entirely convincing. The comment about complexity of thought is of course fully justified, and together with the astronomical and mythological references which Bullough distinguishes there appears to be a direct connection with sonnet LVIII which he does not recognize. Caelica, we remember, wore a golden wig when she was young but in the golden age of the world beauty was 'neither net, nor made by art'. The world now has changed its head, just as Caelica has changed hers by wearing her own darker hair. The governors of the world in its latter days have little to boast of since the world is degenerate and the new lovers of Caelica are no better off for she too is older and shares the degeneration of the world. Her supplanted lover knows he has not lost much: she was at best 'a wavering province'. There are other poems on ageing beauty and on a mistress's infidelity but the threads of allusion are everywhere tightly woven and the poems do not yield to gentle unravelling into biographical constituents. In number XLIV we have a serious treatment of the golden age theme with an undertone of theological meaning and a woman, who may be both a person and sexual love in general, or who may not be a woman at all, is seen to participate in the general decay and corruption of human nature and human activity.

One more example will serve to illustrate further this highly individual style of 'love-poetry'. This is number LXXI:

> *Love*, I did send you forth enamel'd faire
> With hope, and gave you seisin and livery
> Of Beauties skye, which you did claime as heyre,
> By objects and desires affinitie.
>
> And doe you now returne leane with Despaire?
> Wounded with Rivalls warre, scorched with Jealousie?
> Hence Changeling: *Love* doth no such colours weare:
> Find sureties, or at Honours sessions dye.
>
> Sir, know me for your owne, I onely beare,
> Faiths ensigne, which is Shame, and Miserie;
> My Paradise, and *Adams* diverse were:
> His fall was Knowledge, mine Simplicitie.
>
> What shall I doe, Sir? doe me Prentice bind,
> To Knowledge, Honour, Fame, or Honestie;
> Let me no longer follow Womenkinde,
> Where change doth use all shapes of tyranny;
> And I no more will stirre this earthly dust,
> Wherein I lose my name, to take on lust.

There are a number of Cupid poems in *Caelica* and this is one of the strongest-toned and most serious of them. The first two quatrains use the vocabulary of conventional love-poetry and the common legal image. Cupid's reply, in the third quatrain and the sestet, drastically changes the level on which the situation is being treated. The language becomes loaded with theological references. Though Cupid's faith was misplaced he wears the badges of shame and misery which may be the insignia in this world of true believers. He looked for a Paradise, but his was to be created by a woman, not, as Adam's was, by God. Adam fell through knowledge of good and evil but his fall was knowledge in another sense for through it he came to know the redemptive love of Christ. Cupid fell through simplicity, that is through unawareness that the woman could be so unkind as to reject him; but he was also simple, i.e. foolish, in that he misjudged what was worthy of faith and devotion. 'What shall I doe, Sir?' becomes the cry of the man profoundly disillusioned where he has set his heart. Love of women is not love but lust – as his master had said earlier without full awareness of the implications of what he said: '*Love* doth no such colours weare' – and he looks for other ideals to attach himself to, Knowledge, Honour, Fame or Honesty. We do not know how this poem stands chronologically in relation to the treatises *Of Humane Learning* and *Fame and Honour*. In the light of them, Cupid's plea for other worthier employment in pursuit of these ideals is ironical, for he is again attaching faith to what cannot sustain it, but the poem has considerable weight even without this added point and is a good example of how important the shifts of language are in *Caelica* as a way of creating a multi-dimensional record of experience.

There are of course simpler poems in the sequence though none is unequivocal, Number XL is, in the main, charming:

The *nurse-life* Wheat within his greene huske growing,
Flatters our hope and tickles our desire,
Natures true riches in sweet beauties shewing,
Which set all hearts, with labours love, on fire.

No lesse faire is the Wheat when golden eare
Showes unto hope the joyes of neare enjoying;
Faire and sweet is the bud, more sweet and faire,
The Rose, which proves that time is not destroying.

*Caelica*, your youth, the morning of delight,
Enamel'd o're with beauties white and red,
All sense and thoughts did to beleefe invite,

That Love and Glorie there are brought to bed;
And your ripe yeares love-noone (he goes no higher)
Turnes all the spirits of Man into desire.

Time the destroyer is also the ripener and Caelica, like the wheat which
nourishes and the beauty of the rose which delights, reaches a moment
of perfect development; but as the sun declines after noon, so does love
after the perfect ripeness of youth. The remorseless shadow of age when
physical beauty fades brushes the poem lightly but perceptibly and the
sonnet acquires a slight but characteristic Grevillean twist.

Of number XXII, Professor Bullough writes: 'One of the simplest and
perhaps the most praised of the poems, full of country customs and a
charming pastoral turn.' (*Poems and Dramas*, i, page 241.) It is certainly
an attractive poem:

I, with whose colors *Myra* drest her head,
I, that ware posies of her owne hand making,
I, that mine owne name in the chimnies read,
By *Myra* finely wrought ere I was waking:
Must I looke on, in hope time coming may
With change bring back my turne againe to play?

I, that on Sunday at the Church-stile found,
A Garland sweet, with true-love knots in flowers,
Which I to weare about mine arme was bound,
That each of us might know that all was ours:
Must I now lead an idle life in wishes?
And follow *Cupid* for his loaves, and fishes?

I, that did weare the ring her Mother left,
I, for whose love she gloried to be blamed,
I, with whose eyes her eyes committed theft,
I, who did make her blush when I was named;
Must I lose ring, flowers, blush, theft and go naked,
Watching with sighs, till dead love be awaked?

I, that when drowsie *Argus* fell asleep,
Like Jealousy o'rewatched with desire,
Was even warned modestie to keepe,
While her breath, speaking, kindled Natures fire:
Must I looke on a-cold, while others warme them?
Doe *Vulcans* brothers in such fine nets arme them?

Was it for this that I might *Myra* see
Washing the water with her beauties, white?
Yet would she never write her love to me;
*Thinks wit of change while thoughts are in delight?*
Mad Girles must safely love, as they may leave,
*No man can print a kisse, lines may deceive.*

This is a very pleasant little vignette of a country wooing but, like an anamorphic picture, it has another aspect too. The air of rural unsophistication is countered by the ironic reference to the feeding of the five thousand – how many lovers does Myra have? – and to the story of Mars and Vulcan, and is totally dispersed in the last stanza by the wicked suggestion that Myra was after all a calculating hussy who from the beginning took care never to put anything in writing.

The love or anti-love poems of *Caelica* bear clear evidence of a powerful and deep mind inherently distrustful of the seductions of the world and the flesh, turning for a time to explore with curiosity and often with irony the preoccupation with love which engaged Greville's friends and acquaintances and perhaps also – though never very deeply, one imagines – himself. The fusion of his cast of mind with a sharp wit produces the sardonic tone of much of *Caelica*. Of his own experiences we have little evidence. 'He came [to Court],' Naunton wrote, 'backt with a plentiful Fortune, which as himself was wont to say, was the better held together by a single life, wherein he lived and dyed a constant Courtier of the Ladies.'[3] A contemporary letter elaborates this: 'For Fulke Greville my wife knows he hath offered her courtesy already, and will again, the rather if she seek it, but he is not for her credit. Yet let her do as she please, he will but deceive her, as he hath done others of her sex. . . . It may be he will do my wife some pleasure. Let her take it. I never trusted him with a word of my mind or thought.'[4] This is not altogether reliable evidence concerning Greville's character since the writer of the letter was in trouble at the time (1588) and feeling generally bitter, but it is not impossible to imagine Greville as a rather cynical philanderer. Bacon preserves a saying of his in an anecdote of Greville at Court:

Sir Fulke Greville had much and private access to Queen
Elizabeth, which he used honourably and did many men good;
yet he would say merrily of himself 'That he was like Robin

Goodfellow: for when the maids spilt the milk-pans or kept any racket, they would lay it upon Robin: So what tales the ladies about the Queen told her, or other bad offices they did, they would put it upon him.'⁵

This may have been just a jest but it is not unlikely that Greville was unpopular with the ladies at Court. Certainly *Caelica* contains no sugared sonnets.

Some of Greville's poetry was being written at the same time as Sidney was composing *Astrophil and Stella*. A song of Cleophila (Pyrocles) in the old *Arcadia* describes the attitude to poetry which is projected in *Astrophil and Stella*. Why, if you must sing, Cleophila demands of his Muse, should it not be some pleasant tale of Venus and Adonis or Cynthia and Endymion:

> My muse what ails this ardour
> To blase my onely secretts? . . .
> 'Alas', she saith, 'I am thine,
> So are thy pains my pains too.
> Thy heated harte my seat is
> Wherein I burne, thy breath is
> My voice, too hott to keepe in.'⁶

'The singer is the song's theme' – there is no need to make a naïve biographical equation to see how this applies to *Astrophil and Stella*. Sidney is involved in what he writes because the love he is describing is an emotion he cannot reject as worthless despite its apparent conflict with the teachings of morality and religion. Because of the tensions he experiences in the pull of sympathies, 'The tunes be cryes, the words, plaints', and the twentieth century reader has a sense of intimate contact with a living personality in a situation which still transmits its drama. How different this is in tone and commitment from the poems of *Caelica* which treat of the themes of love will have been seen from the poems already quoted. To juxtapose a pair of anacreontic poems is to highlight more sharply the difference between the two friends' treatment of similar themes. This is *Astrophil and Stella*, number 8:

> *Love* borne in *Greece*, of late fled from his native place,
> Forc'd by a tedious proofe, that Turkish hardned hart,
> Is no fit marke to pierce with his fine pointed dart:

And pleased with our soft peace, staid here his flying race,
But finding these North clymes do coldly him embrace,
Not used to frozen clips, he strave to find some part,
Where with most ease and warmth he might employ his art:
At length he perch'd himself in *Stella's* joyfull face,
Whose faire skin, beamy eyes, like morning sun on snow,
Deceiv'd the quaking boy, who thought from so pure light,
Effects of lively heat, must needs in nature grow.
But she most faire, most cold, made him thence take his flight
To my close heart, where while some firebrands he did lay,
He burnt unwares his wings, and cannot fly away.

*Caelica* XII and XXXV may be connected with this, but number XI provides the most apt comparison:

*Juno*, that on her head *Loves* liverie carried,
Scorning to weare the markes of *Io's* pleasure,
Knew while the Boy in *Æquinoctiall* tarried,
His heats would rob the heaven of heavenly treasure,
Beyond the *Tropicks* she the Boy doth banish,
Where smokes must warme, before his fire do blaze,
And Childrens thoughts not instantly grow Mannish,
Feare keeping lust there very long at gaze:
But see how that poore Goddesse was deceived,
For Womens hearts farre colder there than ice,
When once the fire of lust they have received,
With two extremes so multiply the vice,
As neither partie satisfying other,
*Repentance still becomes desire's mother.*

Dr Ringler makes claims for the originality of Sidney's disposal of conventional materials in his *Astrophil and Stella* sonnet,[7] and it is a skilfully-turned poem. Greville's, beginning conventionally enough with love among the Gods, develops into a commentary on love in a cold climate which is both ironic and penetrating. The last line typifies many of Greville's gnomic 'sentences', with its abstract words laden with significance established by the poem and sinking deeply into the mind as a summary of experience and unsentimental reflection upon it.

The anacreontic poems do not provide the only instances of fairly obvious parallels between *Astrophil and Stella* and *Caelica*. Ward described *Caelica* XLVI as 'an exercise on the same theme as Sonnet 56 of *Astrophil and Stella*'.[8] Both poems are sonnets and the theme is that patience in love is an unprofitable virtue. Greville's version has some good lines:

> Patience, weake fortun'd, and weake minded Wit,
> Perswade you me to joy, when I am banish'd?

he begins, and concludes that in his present state when not only is he unrewarded but Myra favours a rival:

> The life of Patience then must be commotion;
> Since not to feele what wrong I beare in this,
> A senselesse state, and no true Patience is.

Sidney's is much more lively:

> Fy, schools of Patience, Fy, your lesson is
> Far far too long to learne it without booke:
> What, a whole weeke without one peece of looke,
> And thinke I should not your large precepts misse?
> When I might reade those letters faire of blisse,
> Which in her face teach vertue, I could brooke
> Somewhat thy lead'n counsels, which I tooke
> As of a friend that meant not much amisse:
> But now that I, alas, do want her sight,
> What, dost thou thinke that I can ever take
> In thy cold stuffe a flegmatike delight?
> No Patience, if thou wilt my good, then make
> Her come, and heare with patience my desire,
> And then with patience bid me beare my fire.

Greville never wrote with that sort of verve. With easy mastery of the form Sidney fashions his sonnet into a little dramatic *jeu d'esprit*, and the virtues of Greville's 'earth-creeping Genius' can hardly be recognized in the comparison. When Sidney is writing less vigorously, the merits of a companion poem by Greville show up more clearly. In

*Astrophil and Stella* 27 Astrophil defends himself against the charge that pride makes him unsociable in company by admitting that it is in fact ambition which makes him overlook everything but Stella. Greville's treatment of this theme is in *Caelica* LX:

> *Caelica*, you said, I doe obscurely live,
> Strange to my friends, with strangers in suspect,
> (*For darknessee doth suspicion ever give,*
> *Of hate to men or too much selfe-respect*)
> *Fame*, you doe say, *with many wings doth flye*
> *Who leaves himselfe, you say, doth living dye.*
>
> *Caelica*, 'tis true, I doe in darknesse goe,
> Honour I seeke not, nor hunt after Fame:
> I am thought bound, I doe not long to know,
> I feele within, what men without me blame:
> I scorne the world, the world scornes me, 'tis true;
> What can a heart doe more to honour you?
>
> Knowledge and fame in open hearts doe live,
> Honour is pure hearts homage unto these,
> *Affection all men unto Beauty give,*
> And by that Law enjoyed are to please:
> The world in two I have divided fit;
> My selfe to you, and all the rest to it.

Professor Bullough comments that 'the analytic, introspective quality of Greville's piece contrasts well with Sidney's simpler treatment' (i, page 259), and this is true, though the value of the comparison is limited for Greville is always analytic and introspective and the Sidney sonnet is one of his weaker ones.

The main interest of such comparisons lies in the evidence they offer of the close association in poetry which Sidney described as 'striving with my mates in song'. There must have been a good deal of give and take and exchanging of manuscripts between Sidney and Greville and Dyer at one time and ingenious competition in the treatment of similar themes and the handling of common patterns. Greville is not associated with the other two in Spenser's letter to Gabriel Harvey in which he speaks of Sidney's and Dyer's experiments in classical scansion. This may have been because during the years 1577–80 when

Sidney and Dyer were experimenting with classical measures Greville was out of the country a good deal, but he did make one experiment in rhymed sapphics, *Caelica* number VI, the form and subject of which suggest that it pairs with Cleophila's sapphics in the old *Arcadia*. These verses are not rhymed but Sidney uses rhyme in other sets of sapphics. Sidney's experiments were part of his endeavour to raise the status of English poetry to an equality with the best of the ancient and the modern world, but he probably also enjoyed 'the fascination of what's difficult' for its own sake and may have taken a pure aesthetic delight in striving for the precarious stilted beauty which these exotic pieces sometimes achieve. Greville writes with characteristic subtlety in *Caelica* VI but he was perhaps sceptical about the hopefulness of quantitative scansion as a prescription for English verse.

A clear example of interaction in the group is provided by *Caelica* LXXXIII and Dyer's poem 'A Fancy'. Greville's poem may be an imitation some years later of Dyer's complaint, but if Dyer's poem was not written till 1580, as is possible, he and Greville may have composed companion pieces simultaneously, deliberately taking some features of style and treatment in common.

Edward Dyer was eleven years older than Sidney and Greville, and had been writing poetry since his student days at Oxford when, according to Anthony à Wood: 'his natural inclination to poetry and other polite learning, as also his excellency in bewailing and bemoaning the perplexities of love were observed by his contemporaries.' He belonged properly to the poetic generation before Sidney's and Greville's but although he soon began to look old-fashioned, he had gifts which were ranked high by many, including Sidney. Much of what Dyer wrote is unidentified or lost, probably beyond recall, and some of the handful of poems ascribed to him are only doubtfully his. What we have or believe we have of Dyer may not strike us as very accomplished, but a genuine lyric gift which gleams momentarily in a line or a rhythm is evidently seeking for expression and there is a strong personal stamp on the poems. Sidney, who so triumphantly in *Astrophil and Stella* creates an individual and a world surrounding him, may have been particularly interested in Dyer's efforts to find accurate personal utterance in his poetry. Once even a Dyer poem has a moment of dramatic effectiveness such as occurs characteristically in *Astrophil and Stella*:

True hearts have ears and eyes, no tongues to speake:
They heare and see, and sigh, and then they breake.
(*The Lowest Trees have Tops*).⁹

Dyer's 'A Fancy' and *Caelica* LXXXIII are both written in poulter's measure; both lament lost favour and contrast their present woe-begone state with former happiness; and each concludes with a pun on the poet's name:

My song, if anie aske whose greivous Case is such,
Dy er thou let his name be knowne: his folly shewes to much.

and:

Let no man aske my name, nor what else I should be;
For Greiv-Ill, paine, forlorne estate doe best decipher me.

Apart from the general similarity of movement and theme in these two poems there are echoes of 'A Fancy' in other works of Greville's. Line 41: 'Then love, where is thy sauce, that makes thy torments sweete' is recalled in *Caelica* XVIII:

She saith, All selfe-nesse must fall downe before her:
I say, Where is the sauce should make that sweet?

and Dyer's line 33: 'In *was* stands my delight, in *is* and *shall* my woe' is echoed in the uncompleted epitaph for Sir Philip Sidney which Greville was composing in 1615:

feeding on tyms past:
Through is and shall make that which was to last.¹⁰

But comparison of the Dyer and Greville complaint poems serves chiefly to demonstrate once more how very individual Greville's manner and treatment are. His imagery has a far wider compass than Dyer's. Defining the situation which may qualify another to share his grief, he writes:

If from this heavenly state, which soules with soules unites,
He be falne downe into the darke, despaired warre of sprites;
Let him lament with me.

In this the phrase 'darke despaired warre of sprites' as a description of hell and internal conflict has considerable power. To pair with it there is an extended political image which, as Professor Bullough comments, recalls *Richard II*:

> Like as the Kings forlorne, depos'd from their estate,
> Yet cannot choose but love the Crowne, although new Kings
>     they hate;
> If they doe plead their right, nay, onely if they live,
> Offences to the Crowne alike their Good and Ill shall give.

As so often happens in Greville's work, religion and politics are taken as the two poles of human experience and every situation is placed in relation to them. It is impossible, consequently, to distinguish between 'light' and 'serious' pieces in *Caelica* because however trivial the topic in itself and however witty the treatment in its incidentals we are invariably reminded of the axis on which the world turns. The inexorable placing of every situation against the (to Greville) largest possible background is mainly responsible for the ironic edge and the equivocal tone of many of the poems, among them *Caelica* LXXXIII. The strong images and the subtlety of thought stand out in comparison with the Dyer poem, but so too does the greater sophistication on all levels:

> The worlds example I, a Fable every where,
> A Well from whence the springs are dried, A Tree that doth
>     not beare:
> I like the Bird in cage at first with cunning caught,
> And in my bondage for delight with greater cunning taught,
> Now owners humour dyes, I neither loved nor fed,
> Nor freed am, till in the cage forgotten I be dead.
> The Ship of *Greece*, the Streames and she be not the same
> They were, although Ship, Streames and she still beare their
>     antique name.
> The Wood which was, is worne, those waves are runne away,
> Yet still a Ship, and still a Streame, still running to a Sea.
> She lov'd and still she loves, but doth not still love me.

This is more fluent, more accomplished and more freely imaginative

than Dyer. It also shows Greville making use of rhetorical figures
which are unusual in his work and demonstrating a striking dexterity
in his employment of them.

So far purely literary connections between the lyrics of the three
men have been considered, but it is possible that there is a more intimate
relationship between the two sonnet sequences *Astrophil and Stella* and
*Caelica*. Professor Bullough comments that 'at times he [Greville]
seems almost to be giving his friend the lie direct' and Dr Ringler takes
the point a little further: 'Some of Greville's poems to Caelica are
ironical commentaries on certain of the poems to Stella.' Pointing out
that *Caelica* LXXIII–V deal with the same situation as the eighth song of
*Astrophil and Stella*, he adds that Greville 'attributes the lady's refusal
to a prudential fear of scandal rather than higher considerations, and
also indicates that she did not really reciprocate the affection of her
suitor.'[11] The suggestion implicit in these comments that *Astrophil
and Stella* and *Caelica* form in part a dialogue is worth some consideration.

Stella and Caelica are both names which associate the ladies with the
heavens, and Miss Frances Yates has suggested that they derive from
Sidney's and Greville's interest in Giordano Bruno's *nuova filosofia*.
This may be so, though Miss Yates's further suggestion that both
sonnet sequences are to be read in the light of *De Gli Eroici Furori* as
spiritual autobiographies or 'philosophical love poetry' pushes the
case for Bruno's influence too far and makes too little of other considerations.[12] Nevertheless, the names are evidently a pair and so are
the names of the lovers, Astrophil who woos Stella, and Philocell who
is named as Caelica's suitor in two poems which will be considered in
a moment. If we adopt as a temporary hypothesis the idea that Sidney
wrote love poems and Greville in friendly mockery wrote anti-love
poems we find that some poems or groups of poems seem to lend
themselves particularly well to commentary in this vein, for example,
*Caelica* LVI and the second song of *Astrophil and Stella*. Both poems
treat of an unguarded moment. Astrophil finds Stella asleep. Awake,
she obliges him to suppress his desire, but he kisses her in her sleep and
then regrets that he has not done more. Greville, or Philocell, goes to
his mistress's room at night (she is here called Cynthia but the various
women's names in *Caelica* appear to be interchangeable) but while
he stands thinking of the pleasures to come, she runs away. Both
poems are composed in trochaic rhythm, divided into quatrains of

seven-syllable lines. Sidney writes as if he is recording the immediate present:

> Have I caught my heav'nly jewell,
> Teaching sleepe most faire to be?
> Now will I teach her that she,
> When she wakes, is too too cruell.

He plans gleefully to discover 'What No her tongue sleeping useth' and then is abashed by his own temerity – '*Love* feares nothing else but anger.' The tone is ingenuous though nothing else in the poem is innocent. The song comes immediately after sonnet 72 in which Sidney speaks of Stella's decree that his desire should be banished – 'but yet alas how shall?' – and sonnet 73 which follows is an attempt to brazen out the situation. Stella is angry with him:

> my Starre, because a sugred kisse
> In spirit I suckt, while she asleep did lie.
> Doth lowre, nay chide; nay threat for only this:
> Sweet, it was saucie *Love*, not humble I.
> But no scuse serves.

The lover of *Caelica* in the same situation makes no attempt to gloss it over and offers no excuses. Greville strikes the note of uninhibited sensuality from the beginning:

> All my senses, like Beacons flame,
> Gave *Alarum* to desire
> To take armes in Cynthia's name,
> And set all my thoughts on fire.

Jove and Venus shine in Cynthia's heavenly eyes, showing that 'desire is divine'. He gazes with relish upon the 'milken way' of her naked body, an image which Sidney also uses in Pyrocles's praise of Philo-clea's nakedness in *Arcadia* and again in the fifth song of *Astrophil and Stella*. His mortification when Cynthia escapes him is tinged with self-mockery:

> There stand I like *Articke* pole,
> Where *Sol* passeth o're the *line*,

> Mourning my benighted soule,
> Which so loseth light divine.
> There stand I like men that preach
> From the Execution place,
> At their death content to teach
> All the world with their disgrace.

But the moral is serious. It is flatly anti-romantic in its use of overt sexual imagery and its dismissal of worship from afar as a waste of time. It may also be loaded with particular significance in its reference to the 'Love-desiring heart' which seeks in 'the stars' for satisfaction. Love is natural and earthy, not ethereal, and Sidney (perhaps?) over-estimates both love and Stella:

> He that lets his *Cynthia* lye,
> Naked on a bed of play,
> To say prayers ere she dye,
> Teacheth time to runne away:
> Let no Love-desiring heart,
> In the Starres goe seeke his fate,
> Love is onely Natures art,
> Wonder hinders Love and Hate.
> *None can well behold with eyes,*
> *But what underneath him lies.*

In Sidney's poem, desire repressed and denied puts the lover in a false position and he is caught between awe of the beloved and his need for physical satisfaction. Greville's poem discounts the awe as inappropriate and puts the whole situation firmly on an unideal basis.

Morris Croll draws attention to some similarities between Sidney's eighth song and *Caelica* LXXV. The time of the year is the same in both; so is the setting and the long silence between the lovers. Their dialogue, when they speak, follows the same pattern, the ardour of the man being restrained in Sidney's poem by Stella's nice care for her honour, and in Greville's, by Caelica's contempt. The metrical form of the poems is also the same, seven and eight syllable trochaic lines rhyming in pairs. Ringler notes that Greville's poem and the two preceding ones all deal with the same situation and his comment on the attitude they embody has already been quoted.

*Caelica* LXXIII is Myra's explanation to her lover of why, having once loved him and promised constancy, she now rejects him. All the evidence suggests that Myra, Caelica, and Cynthia are variant names for the same woman[13] and if this is so the Myraphill who is addressed in LXXIII must be the same person as Philocell in LXXIV and LXXV. Myra's explanation is that she was young and inexperienced when she vowed fidelity, but now she knows better. She and her lover have been parted and '*Nature and Love no* Vacuum *can endure*'. She is heartless and unscrupulous. Numbers LXXIV and LXXV might be alternative treatments of a common theme. In LXXIV Caelica and Philocell meet after absence. She has grieved and been faithful during their separation and shares his emotion when they meet again. But love is linked inseparably with shame and any encouragement she gives him is instantly cancelled by her fears for her honour. And he hesitates to overcome her scruples, for his is:

> true love that feares, and dare
> Offend itselfe with pleasing Care,

and he does not urge his love. Greville's comment is reminiscent of number LVI though somewhat gentler:

> But silent Love is simple wooing,
> Even Destiny would have us doing.
> Boldnesse never yet was chidden,
> Till by Love it be forbidden.

Finally Myra (the name has changed in the course of the poem)[14] leaves her still frustrated lover and only she knows what the outcome of it all will be. In number LXXV Caelica and Philocell again meet and this time, though

> Paine of all paines, Lovers feare,
> Makes his heart to silence sweare,

yet in the end desperation overcomes fear and he pleads for her love. She rejects him with contempt. At the end of number LXXIV when the lover has not dared to push the situation to a conclusion, it is possible to give Caelica/Myra the benefit of any doubt about the sincerity of her feelings, though Greville does not appear to be very sanguine about the situation. In LXXV, Philocell speaks and Caelica's response is quite unambiguous. Bearing in mind our hypothesis that these poems have some direct relation to *Astrophil and Stella* and serve as commentary on Sidney's attitudes, we notice that Philocell is 'Poore, but not of poorest minde' and he is afraid that Caelica will hold this against him. Sidney's resources, we know, were much overstrained by his life as a courtier and he died heavily in debt. Greville himself had money. More striking is the way in which Philocell reinforces his plea with an appeal to his past conduct:

> Deare, if ever in my dayes,
> My heart joy'd in others praise:
> If I of the world did borrow,
> Other ground for joy or sorrow:
> If I better wish to be
> But the better to please thee;
> I say, if this false be proved,
> Let me not love, or not be loved.
> But when Reason did invite
> All my sense to Fortunes light;
> If my love did make my reason,
> To it selfe for thy selfe treason;
> If when Wisdome shewed me
> Time and thoughts both lost for thee;
> If those losses I did glory,
> For I could not more lose, sory;
> *Caelica* then doe not scorne
> *Love*, in humble humour borne.

All these protestations can be paralleled in Astrophil's appeals to Stella:

> *Stella* thinke not that I by verse seeke fame,
> Who seeke, who hope, who love, who live but thee;
> Thine eyes my pride, thy lips my history:
> If thou praise not, all other praise is shame.
>
> (*Astrophil and Stella* 90.)

I do not envie *Aristotle's* wit,
Nor do aspire to *Caesar's* bleeding fame,
Nor ought do care, though some above me sit,
Nor hope, nor wishe another course to frame,
But that which once may win thy cruell hart:
Thou art my wit, and thou my Vertue art.

                              (*Astrophil and Stella* 64.)


   one worse fault, *Ambition*, I confesse,
That makes me oft my best friends overpasse,
Unseene, unheard, while thought to highest place.
Bends all his power, even unto Stella's grace.

                              (*Astrophil and Stella* 27.)

Greville's lines

   If those losses I did glory,
   For I could not more lose, sory

are a direct echo of the final couplet of *Astrophil and Stella* 18[15] and the
whole of Greville's account of the reproaches of reason seems to be
related to this poem of Sidney's:

With what sharpe checks I in my selfe am shent,
When into Reason's audite I do go:
And by just counts my selfe a banckrout know
Of all those goods, which heav'n to me hath lent:
Unable quite to pay even Nature's rent,
Which unto it by birthright I do ow:
And which is worse, no good excuse can show,
But that my wealth I have most idly spent,
My youth doth waste, my knowledge brings forth toyes,
My wit doth strive those passions to defend,
Which for reward spoile it with vaine annoyes.
I see my course to lose my selfe doth bend:
I see and yet no greater sorrow take,
Then that I lose no more for *Stella's* sake.

In Greville's poem Philocell's pleadings receive a cold answer for

Caelica is unmoved. She warns him that if he persists in loving her she will not reward him but:

> Your owne will must be your hire.
> And desire reward desire.

This is very much the situation which Stella tries to impose upon Astrophil. Philocell presses her further and Caelica speaks her full mind. She acknowledges that she accepted Philocell's devotion but she sees no reason why that should bind her to him. He must simply cancel the memory of her favours in the past. She may love someone perhaps, but not him:

> My delight is all my care,
> All lawes else despised are,
> I will never rumour move,
> At least for one I doe not love.

There is a long coda to this story, in which Greville, addressing an audience of ladies, comments dryly on the behaviour of Caelica in particular and of women in general:

> Shepheardesses, when you change,
> Is your ficklenesse so strange?
> Are you thus impatient still?
> Is your honour slave to will?
> They to whom you guiltie be,
> Must not they your errour see?
> May true Martyrs at the fire
> Not so much as life desire?

He hints at the subsequent development of the situation: Philocell continues to be abused by Caelica and jealousy of a rival is added to his woes. But in defiance of all reason, and in spite of scorn, despair, her ingratitude and inconstancy, he goes on loving her. It is a story, Greville points out, of a man's faithfulness and woman's inconstancy.

*Caelica* LXXV is not of course in the least *like* the eighth song of *Astrophil and Stella.* There are resemblances in form and the lover's plea to his mistress is the common theme, but Sidney's poem is personal, intimate and tender and the woman and her feelings are fully and sympathetically realized. The situation is moving and has even some tragic dignity because of the genuine depth of feeling which leads the lovers to this impasse. Greville writes as the detached observer of a comedy of sex relations. He sees in it some pathos, some absurdity, some cruelty, some shame, and he treats it partly as *exemplum*, an up-to-date version of Scoggin's jest about the unfaithfulness of women, with the sensitive renaissance gentleman as victim instead of the coarse-minded husband. His detachment is not quite complete for he is moved to protest in oblique fashion in the final section and to linger over the sufferings of Philocell and his tenacious love.

*Astrophil and Stella* 18 is echoed in *Caelica* LXXV as well as the eighth song and the same sonnet is again in Greville's mind when he composes *Caelica* XLI. XLI is a poem about the folly of expecting or practising constancy in love. The first two stanzas dismiss as hopeless a devotion like Philocell's:

Alas poore soule, thinke you to master *Love*,
With constant faith. . . .

The last three stanzas make a sonnet, and the opening echoes the opening of *Astrophil and Stella* 18:

When Honours Audit calls for thy receipt,
And chargeth on thy head much time mispent;
Nature corrupted by thy vain conceipt,
Thy Reason servile, poore, and passion-rent.
What shall be thy excuse, what can'st thou say?

But whereas Sidney goes on to defy reason and regret only that he cannot forfeit more for Stella's sake, Greville cannot believe the world well lost for a love about whose real nature he is utterly cynical:

What shall be thy excuse, what can'st thou say?
That thou hast erred out of love and wonder?
No hereticke, thou *Cupid* doest betray
And with religion wouldst bring Princes under;
By merit banish Chance from Beauties sky,
Set other lawes in Womens hearts, than will;

Cut Changes wings, that she no more may flye,
Hoping to make that constant, which is ill;
Therefore the doome is, wherein thou must rest,
*Myra* that scornes thee, shall love many best.

Professor Bullough, noticing the echoes of *Astrophil and Stella* 18, suggests that Greville's poem may have been written in rivalry with it. It is possible that what we have in these poems where the connection between *Astrophil and Stella* and *Caelica* seems particularly close is a purely literary game, or a trial of skill. This is not difficult to believe of some of the poems where everything depends on the twist given to similar material, but it is a less acceptable account of the poems which have just been discussed in which what is involved is not simply a different fashioning of literary matter but a wholly different reading of experience, with an admonitory note sounding through Greville's words as he plays Apollonius to Sidney's Lycius, ensnared by the Lamia of romantic love.

The hypothesis advanced earlier that Sidney wrote love poems and Greville in friendly mockery wrote anti-love poems is shown on this reading to be only partially satisfactory. The dialogue between the two sequences appears in fact to have two phases: one, the earlier, where the parallels derive from the friendly rivalry of the time referred to in the *Two Pastoralls*; and the second, in which the exchanges become more serious as Greville looks on with misgiving while Astrophil woos. Probably Sidney never saw the darker poems, but he is hardly likely to have been ignorant of his friend's views:

Your words my friend (right healthful caustiks) blame
My young mind marde, whom *Love* doth windlas so,
That mine owne writings like bad servants show
My wits, quicke in vaine thoughts, in virtue lame:
That *Plato* I read for nought, but if he tame
Such coltish gyres, that to my birth I owe,
Nobler desires, least else that friendly foe,
Great expectation, weare a traine of shame.

(*Astrophil and Stella* 21.)

This sounds very like Greville. He read Sidney's writings with particular care and was just the man to dispense 'right healthful caustiks'.

As a friend of the Sidney family, none knew better than he what was expected of the son of Sir Henry and Lady Mary Sidney, and as the companion of Sidney's journey to the Emperor and to William of Orange he could speak with particular authority of the 'great expectation' he had roused. The friend appears again in *Astrophil and Stella* 69. Stella has confessed that she loves Astrophil and there can be no doubt of her sincerity:

> For *Stella* hath with words where faith doth shine,
> Of her high heart giv'n me the monarchie.

He rejoices and he particularly calls on his friend (who has doubted?) to rejoice with him:

> My friend, that oft saw through all maskes my wo,
> Come, come, and let me poure my selfe on thee;
> Gone is the winter of my miserie.

This again may well be Greville, the intimate friend who feels for him and shares his pain and his rejoicing. He may also be the friend of sonnet 14 whose 'rhubarb words' predict the ill consequences of desire:

> saying that Desire
> Doth plunge my wel-formed soule even in the mire
> Of sinfull thoughts, which do in ruine end.

The mature Greville, much aware of the mire of sinful thoughts in the map of human experience, may have shown himself quite early in Greville's career as one young man admonished another that the course he was following would lead to no good.

Many of the poems in *Caelica*, then, subject romantic love and the desires of the flesh to sceptical and disenchanted commentary. Many also employ a theological language which imparts an ironic edge or serves to place their situations in a perspective which at once diminishes them. When we turn from the love poems to the specifically religious poetry in the latter part of the sequence, the change is not so very great and the religious poems may be seen to offer not so much a contrast to the preoccupations of the earlier lyrics as a development of some aspects of them according to deeply-engrained temperamental characteristics. *Caelica* is altogether a very personal work. How true this is of the religious poems can readily be appreciated if they are seen side by side with other poems in which Greville treats similar themes.

Religion and the church are treated more or less extensively by Greville in three works: *A Treatise of Monarchy*, section 6: 'Of Church'; *A Treatie of Humane Learning*, stanzas 80–93; and *A Treatise of Religion*. Of these, the church section of *Of Monarchy* and the stanzas from *Of Humane Learning* have much in common with each other. In both Greville is concerned with religion as an instrument of state:

> *Religion*, by whose name the Scepter gaines
> More of the world, and greater reverence breeds
> In Forrayners, and homeborne subjects too,
> Then much expence of bloud or wealth can doe.
>
> (*Of Monarchy*, stanza 202.)

In both he distinguishes powerfully between 'Gods true religion' and the ceremonies and institutions of the visible church, but he is predominantly concerned with the visible church. Though it is but the 'shadow' of the true church, though its rites and teaching are 'superstition' and its practices are 'hypocrisies built on passion', yet, debased as it is, it nevertheless exercises a powerful hold on men's minds, and kings must take care not to let the mitre usurp their sway. The 'sacred avarice' of a church which thirsts for secular power can hardly be withstood unless it be checked at an early stage, for the church has not only armies but other weapons too:

> Power for a pensile, conscience for a table,
> To write opinion in of any fashion,
> With witts distinctions, ever merchantable,
> Betwene a princes throne, and peoples passion
> Upon which text shee raiseth, or pulls downe
> All, but those objects, which advance her Crowne.
>
> (*Of Monarchy*, stanza 216)

Kings must therefore control the power of the church and they must take care also to see that good order is maintained in church government and that theological disputations be not allowed to disturb the minds of the people. When all this is done, it is no more than giving decent order to the 'superstitious spheare' of the church in the world. This is worth doing:

> For though the World, and Man can never frame
> These outward moulds, to cast Gods chosen in;
> Nor give his Spirit where they give His Name;
> That power being never granted to the sinne;
> Yet in the world those *Orders* prosper best,
> Which from the *word*, in seeing varie least.
>
> Since therefore she brookes not Divinity,
> But Superstition, Heresie, Schisme, Rites,
> Traditions, Legends, and Hypocrisie;
> Let her yet forme those visions in the light,
> To represent the Truth she doth despise;
> And, by that likeness, prosper in her lies.
>
> (Of Humane Learning, stanzas 87–8.)

In *Of Humane Learning* Greville's main preoccupation is with man's vain affectation of knowledge, and the pride of theologians –

> Dreaming to comprehend the Deity
> In humane reasons finite elevation   (Stanza 82.)

– is used as a telling example. *Of Monarchy* is focused on the arts of kingship. But the point of view, the preoccupation with the management of the outward church is the same in both poems. The later poems of *Caelica* and the *Treatise of Religion* are similarly linked, but this time the common area is their concentration on the unseen church:

> All outward Churches ever knowe him thus,
> They beare his name, but never runne his race
>
> (Of Religion, stanza 62.)

but Greville is now concerned with those:

> who of that Church would be,
> Which (though invisible) yet was, is, shall
> For ever be the state and treasurie
> Of Gods elect, which cannot from him fall.   (Stanza 95.)

In the attaining of true religion, he writes, 'all rests in the hart', and whereas the lyrics of *Caelica* take particular aspects of personal experience as their material, *Of Religion* builds up a larger framework into which the personal record can be set.

The main points which Greville wishes to make in *Of Religion* relate to the insufficiency of human endeavour to redeem man from a state of sin, and the munificence of God's gift of grace.

> Prince of earth let man assume to be,
> Nay more, of man let man himselfe be God,
> Yet, without God, a slave of slaves is he;
> To others, wonder; to himselfe a rod;
> Restlesse despayre, desire, and desolation,
> The more secure, the more abhomination.    (Stanza 6.)

The ancient world thought that with its stoic ideal it had achieved virtue, but this was a delusion:

> Under this maske besides no vice is dead,
> But passion with her counterpassion peas'd;
> The evill with it selfe both starv'd and fedde,
> And in her woes with her vayne glories eas'd:
> The worcke and tooles alike, vayne flesh and blood,
> The labour great, the harvest never good.    (Stanza 38.)

Only through the grace which is offered as a gift beyond the resources of human nature can man be saved:

> It is a light, a guifte, a grace inspired,
> A sparcke of power, a goodness of the good,
> Desire in him, that never it desired,
> An unitie where desolation stood;
> In us, not of us; a spirit not of earth,
> Fashioninge the mortall to immortall birth.    (Stanza 3.)

To attain it we need faith:

> this word *Faith*, implies a state of minde,
> Is both our wooinge, and our mariage ringe;

The fyrst we meet, and last, but *Love*, we finde;
A given hand that feeleth heavenlie thinges;
And who beleive indeed God, heaven, and hell,
Have past, in that, cheife lets of doeinge well.   (Stanza 55.)

But many men, aware of their sin, are nevertheless unwilling to submit
themselves to the spiritual transformation which true faith requires and
instead they construct religions in their own image. Here lies the origin
of the outward churches which at best, as *Of Monarchy* and *Of Humane
Learning* show, can only hope to conceal their hollowness with a show
of superficial decency:

For when the Conscience thus Religion fashions
In blinde affections, there it straight begetts
Grosse superstition; when in wittie passions
It moulded is, a lustre there it setts
On harts prophane, by politique pretense;
Both buying shadowes with the soules expence.   (Stanza 17.)

God's true religion is thus translated to 'bottomless hypocrisie' and
takes on the character of the ruling passion which motivates it: fear, or
politic ambition. From these various kinds of hypocrisy:

strange inundations flowe,
To drowne the sea-marckes of humanitie,
With massacres, conspiracie, treason, woe,
By sect and schisme prophaning Deitie.   (Stanza 33.)

The marks of true religion are quite different from this. The 'heavenly
change' transmutes pride to meekness, atheism to zeal, lust to con-
tinence, anger to charity (stanza 44), and the knowledge of God brings
about a reorientation of the man's whole outlook:

And even this sacred band, this heavenlie breath,
In man his understanding, knowledge is;
Obedience, in his will; in conscience, faith;
Affections, love; in death it selfe, a blisse;
In bodie, temperance; in life, humilitie;
Pledge to the mortall of eternitie.   (Stanza 47.)

These values, Greville insists, are not the values of the world, and men should not delude themselves that they could ever become so. Secular power, human law, and the outward church are bound to reject them. Human arts dissolve to nothingness in the light of the glory of God. The religious man will acknowledge the inevitable corruption of the things of this world and will not seek after impossible reformations:

> Mixe not in functions God, and earth together;
> The wisdome of the world, and his, are two;
> One latitude can well agree to neither;
> In each men have their beinges, as they doe:
> The world doth build without, our God within;
> He traffiques goodnesse, and she traffiques sinne.    (Stanza 98.)

The final stanza is a summary of the conclusions that the poem reaches:

> Then man! Rest on this feelinge from above,
> Plant thou thy faith on this celestiall way.
> The world is made for use; God is for love;
> Sorrows for sinne; knowledge, but to obay;
> Feare and temptation, to refine and prove;
> The heaven, for joyes; Desire that it may
> Finde peace in endlesse, boundlesse, heavenly things;
> Place it else where, it desolation bringes.

The poem is written with a directness and urgency rare to Greville. The point of view is made perfectly plain and the didactic intention is obvious in the method of question and answer which is adopted and the use of such phrases as 'the reason is. . . .' The exhortatory tone is also strong: 'Then man! pray, and obtaine . . .', 'Then judge, pore man! . . .', 'Then man! learne by thy fall. . . .' The unmistakable personal commitment to the subject-matter produces vigorous and also beautiful expression, particularly in the stanzas which describe the works of grace.

Some of the poems in *Caelica* fit readily into this framework. Stanza 4 of *Of Religion* links the Fall of Man and the Fall of the Angels; the Angels fell by pride and we were infected by their sin. Men, unlike the angels, may be redeemed by Christ. *Caelica* CII deals at greater length with the problem of the origin of evil and Greville exclaims in wonder at the fact of the Fall:

> Yet is there ought more wonderful than this?
> That *Man*, even in the state of his perfection,
> All things uncurst, nothing yet done amisse,
> And so in him no base of his defection;
> Should fall from God, and breake his Makers will,
> Which could have no end, but to know the *Ill*.

Man was deceived into sin by the fallen angels –

> Sin, then we knew thee not, and could not hate,
> And now we know thee, now it is too late.

The way back to God as a personal experience is described in *Caelica* xcvi. In youth, the poem begins, we seek only pleasure:

> Sense, Desire and Wit,
> Combine that Reason shall not rule the heart.

But the primrose path leads only to a prospect of vice and man comes to a realization of his proper state:

> By which true mappe of his mortality,
> Mans many Idols are at once defaced,
> And all hypocrisies of fraile humanity,
> Either exiled, waved, or disgraced.

At this point, in 'the depth of fatall desolation' there 'springs up the height of his Regeneration':

> *For God comes not till man be overthrowne;*
> *Peace is the seed of grace, in dead fleshe sowne.*

The imagery of death and rebirth is, naturally enough, common in *Of Religion* too.

> What living death, what strange illumination
> Must be inspir'd to this regeneration?

Greville asks in stanza 41, and in 104 he reflects the situation of *Caelica*
XCVI when he speaks of the intermediate state, when man realizes the
futility of his life of the flesh but sees no way to improve his condition.
The *Caelica* poem describes it as a

> confused sphere . . .
> With equall prospect over good or ill;
> The one unknowne, the other in distaste,

and in *Of Religion* it is, less metaphorically,

> this fight, wherin the man despayres
> Between the sinne, and his regeneration.

The falseness of men's professions is rebuked in *Of Religion* stanza 70
and in *Caelica* XCVII, and the vanity of human learning in *Of Religion*
stanza 7 and *Caelica* LXXXVIII and CIII. The repudiation of the idea of
man's self-sufficiency which led to the dismissal of heathen virtue in
*Of Religion* finds an echo in *Caelica* LXXXVI where Greville contemplates the state of man and proposes two alternatives, either simply to
endure the pains and sorrows which cannot be remedied, or the higher
way which is to 'forsake thy selfe, to heaven turne thee', when the
burden of sinful human nature will be lightened. But more important
than particular points of similarity between the poems is the way in
which the *Caelica* lyrics take up and expand in a purely personal way
aspects of situations which are more generally treated in *Of Religion*.
The false values of the world are the subject of a group of four poems,
numbers XCI, XCII, XCIII, and XCIV.

> Rewards of earth, Nobilitie and Fame,
> To senses Glorie, and to conscience woe,
> How little be you, for so great a name?

– the theme runs through the group and is treated with a sad clear-
sightedness. Number XCIV combines what may be a reference to his
experience as Treasurer of the Navy (from 1598 to 1603), if not as
Chancellor of the Exchequer (from 1614 to 1621), with one of those
details from the life of the countryside which sometimes come so
refreshingly in the work of this statesman-courtier:

Men, that delight to multiply desire,
Like tellers are that take coyne but to pay,
Still tempted to be false, with little hire,
Blacke hands except, which they would have away:
*For where power wisely Audits her estate,*
*The* Exchequer Mens *best recompense is hate.*

The little Maide that weareth out the day,
To gather flow'rs still covetous of more,
At night when she with her desire would play,
And let her pleasure wanton in her store,
Discernes the first laid underneath the last,
Wither'd, and *so is all that we have past*:

Fixe then on good desires, and if you finde
Ambitious dreames or feares of over-thwart;
Changes, temptations, bloomes of earthly minde,
Yet wave not, since earth change, hath change of smart.
*For lest Man should thinke flesh a seat of blisse,*
*God workes that his joy mixt with sorrow is.*

Almost all these later poems of *Caelica* are remarkable for the vigour
and vividness of their language and the variety and aptness of their
imagery. Writing single-mindedly, without irony and without
equivocation, Greville shows a powerful command of language and
of the characteristic verse forms built up of cross-rhymed quatrains and
couplets. The most impressive of all these striking poems are those
which speak of the sense of sin. Two of them, numbers xcviii and
xcix, are directly personal:

Wrapt up, O Lord, in mans degeneration;
The glories of thy truth, thy joyes eternall,
Reflect upon my soule darke desolation,
And ugly prospects o're the sprites infernall.
Lord, I have sinn'd, and mine iniquity,
Deserves this hell; yet Lord deliver me.

Thy power and mercy never comprehended,
Rest lively imag'd in my Conscience wounded;

Mercy to grace, and power to feare extended,
Both infinite, and I in both confounded;
Lord, I have sinn'd and mine iniquity,
Deserves this hell, yet Lord deliver me.

If from this depth of sinne, this hellish grave,
And fatall absence from my Saviours glory,
I could implore his mercy, who can save,
And for my sinnes, not paines of sinne, be sorry:
Lord from this horror of iniquity,
And hellish grave, thou wouldst deliver me.

The subtlety of thought and the power of language here yield nothing
to Donne, and the poem which immediately follows it strikes a note of
assurance of his own personal salvation which is not heard in Donne's
poetry:

Down in the depth of mine iniquity,
That ugly center of infernall spirits;
Where each sinne feeles her owne deformity,
In these peculiar torments she inherits,
Depriv'd of humane graces, and divine,
Even there appeares this *saving God* of mine.

And in this fatall mirrour of transgression,
Shewes man as fruit of his degeneration,
The errours ugly infinite impression,
Which beares the faithlesse downe to desperation;
Depriv'd of humane graces and divine,
Even there appeares this *saving God* of mine.

In power and truth, Almighty and eternall,
Which on the sinne reflects strange desolation,
With glory scourging all the Sprites infernall,
And uncreated hell with unprivation;
Depriv'd of humane graces, not divine,
Even there appeares this *saving God* of mine.

For on this sp'rituall Crosse condemned lying,
To paines infernall by eternall doome,

I see my Saviour for the same sinnes dying,
And from that hell I fear'd, to free me, come;
Depriv'd of humane graces, not divine,
Thus hath his death rais'd up this soule of mine.

The picture of each man's own individual hell in the first stanza and
the state of utter desolation in the second are set in dynamic contrast to
the refrain with its repeated 'Even there appeares this *saving God* of
mine.' In the third stanza one word changes the refrain. 'Depriv'd of
humane graces, *not* divine' comes with great dramatic force and prepares for the situation of the last stanza where the redeemed soul par-
takes of the fruits of the vicarious atonement: 'Thus hath his death
rais'd up this soule of mine.' The recognition of man's ineluctable
captivity to sin, Greville writes in stanza 2, 'beares the faithlesse downe
to desperation', but the acceptance of Christ's sacrifice by the faithful
will save them. The same combination of ideas occurs in *Of Religion*.
The 'true antidotes against dispayre', we are told, consist in the
knowledge that:

> our *Christ* can of his loose none,
> Which unto us makes grace and merit one.   (Stanzas 53 and 54.)

Greville has been often described as a Calvinist and it is very plain
that his outlook is ultra-Protestant. He allows nothing to the visible
church as a medium of spiritual truth and sees it as nothing but an
arm of political power either for qualified good or for downright evil.
The life of the spirit is entirely within and comes from a man's personal acceptance of faith and from a direct experience of the redemptive power of Christ owing nothing to any mediation of priest or
church. In the rigour of his insistence on man's state of sin and his
stern opposition of worldly and spiritual values he has a good deal in
common with Calvin's thought. Whether or not he accepted the
Calvinist doctrine of predestination is less easily decided. The emphasis
in the two *Caelica* poems just discussed and in *Of Religion* is largely on
God's mercy made freely available, if only man will believe, through
Christ. It is true, as Greville points out, that the Bible gives two sensational examples of unexpected effects of sin and grace in the stories
of Judas and the thief on the cross: 'Vice rays'd to heaven, perfection
fal'n to hell,' but such examples God has deliberately made few 'Least

hope or feare should over-worke in anie.' (*Of Religion*, stanza 71.) Mankind has no capacity to understand the workings of God, and human knowledge is but folly in comparison with true wisdom: Greville makes these points time and again. It is not to be expected consequently that God will judge as the world judges or that His judgement will be governed by the outward appearance of virtue. But Greville takes no pleasure in contemplating damnation. The sort of paradox in which Browning's Johannes Agricola delighted, whereby a man can live a saintly life and yet be eternally damned and another can sin as he pleases and yet be unable to forfeit his salvation, has no intellectual or other attractions for Greville. On the nature of election he seems to take advantage of some of the subtleties of distinction which Calvin himself used in developing his ideas in the last edition of the *Institutes of the Christian Religion*. Calvin distinguished two, or even three, sorts of election,[16] and Greville also seems to have in mind two, one general, one specific. The general sort is that which is available to all who believe and to whom salvation through Christ then becomes available. These are the men such as himself who, as he describes their situation in *Caelica* xcviii and xcix quoted above, are at first committed to the world, then enter a state of spiritual destitution when they become aware of the ugliness of sin and the futility of their purely human gifts, and who are rescued from this state when they suffer the death of the old life and are reborn in Christ. The second kind of the elect are a special band:

> that little flocke, Gods owne elect,
> (Who livinge in the world, yet of it are not)
> God is the wealth, will, Empire they affect;
> His Lawe their wisdome, for the rest they care not:
> Amonge all flouds this Arck is still preserved,
> Stormes of the world are for her owne reserved.
>
> (*Of Religion*, stanza 111.)

In *A Treatie of Humane Learning* these specially elect are deliberately excluded from those whom Greville is addressing, for they have not been misled by the follies of the world and stand in no need of his correction:

> Yet here, before we can direct mans choice
> We must divide *Gods Children* from the rest;

Since these pure soules (who only know his voice)
Have no *Art*, but *Obedience*, for their test:
A mystery betweene God, and the man,
Asking, and giving farre more than we can.   (Stanza 64.)

The mass of men do not share this innate purity but their salvation must
be hard-won in a continual struggle with sin. They do not easily distinguish by God-given perception between the things which are
Caesar's and the things which are God's and must always labour to
separate the claims of God from the seductions of the world, the flesh,
and the devil.

The *Caelica* poems make it quite clear that Greville counts himself
among the first class of the elect and not the second. He is not a 'pure
soul' but one upon whom the pressures of the world bear heavily.
His involvement with the affairs of the world is evident even in the
midst of the religious poems of *Caelica*, where political themes still
have their place. There are several poems here which have no specifically
religious reference but which contemplate instead the corruptions of
power. But his own condition and the state of man at large are brought
together in two magnificent poems, one a general confession of sin, the
other an appeal to Christ to 'fill up time and come' and cleanse the sins
of the world. The first is number xcvii:

Eternall Truth, almight, infinite,
Onely exiled from mans fleshly heart,
Where ignorance and disobedience fight,
In hell and sinne, which shall have greatest part:
When thy sweet mercy opens forth the light,
Of Grace which giveth eyes unto the blind,
And with the Law even plowest up our sprite
To faith, wherein flesh may salvation finde;
Thou bidst us pray, and wee doe pray to thee,
But as to power and God without us plac'd,
Thinking a wish may weare out vanity,
Or habits be by miracles defac'd.
One thought to God wee give, the rest to sinne,
*Quickely unbent is all desire of good*,
True words passe out, but have no being within,
Wee pray to *Christ*, yet helpe to shed his blood;

For while wee say *Believe*, and feele it not,
Promise amends, and yet despaire in it,
Heare *Sodom* judg'd, and goe not out with *Lot*,
Make Law and Gospell riddles of the wit:
We with the *Jewes* even *Christ* still crucifie,
As not yet come to our impiety.

This is a very hard-hitting description of frail humanity's desire to enjoy the fruits of salvation without paying the price for it. Stopping at the half-way stage in the hard path to regeneration is a temptation to which mankind is very prone and in *Of Religion* Greville has accounted for the 'outward churches' by it. To think that lip-service is enough is a comfortable but dangerous delusion. As *Caelica* LXXXIX puts it:

If this be safe, it is a pleasant way,
The Crosse of Christ is very easily borne;
But *sixe dayes labour makes the Sabboth day*,
*The flesh is dead before grace can be borne.*
*The heart must first beare witness with the booke,*
*The earth must burne, ere we for Christ can looke.*

It is the sin of society as a whole that by taking refuge in priestly half-truths it has come to deny the living reality of God:

*Syon* lyes waste, and thy *Jerusalem*,
O Lord, is falne to utter desolation,
Against thy Prophets, and thy holy men
The sinne hath wrought a fatall combination,
Prophan'd thy name, thy worship overthrowne,
And made thee living Lord, a God unknowne.

Thy powerfull lawes, thy wonders of creation,
Thy Word incarnate, glorious heaven, darke hell,
Lye shadowed under Mans degeneration,
Thy Christ still crucifi'd for doing well,
Impiety, O Lord, sits on thy throne,
Which makes thee living Light, A God unknown.

Mans superstition hath thy truths entomb'd,
His Atheisme againe her pomps defaceth,

That sensuall unsatiable vaste wombe
Of thy seene Church, thy unseene Church disgraceth;
There lives no truth with them that seem thine own,
Which makes thee living Lord, a God unknown.

Yet unto thee, Lord, (mirrour of transgression)
Wee, who for earthly Idols, have forsaken
Thy heavenly Image (sinlesse pure impression)
And so in nets of vanity lye taken,
All desolate implore that to thine owne,
Lord, thou no longer live a God unknowne.

Yet Lord let *Israels* plagues not be eternall,
Nor sinne for ever cloud thy sacred Mountaines,
Nor with false flames spirituall but infernall,
Dry up they mercies ever springing fountaines,
Rather, sweet Jesus, fill up time and come,
To yeeld the sinne her everlasting doome.

The language which Greville finds for his themes gives compressed and powerful utterance to long held and deeply pondered ideas which have become a part of the nature of the man who writes and which issue consequently with the whole force of character and conviction behind them: 'That sensuall unsatiable vaste wombe / Of thy seene Church' uses repeated s sounds and modulations of u, v, and w to give striking aural effect to a definitive summary of his view of the church in the world, and repetition and illiteration similarly reinforce the subtler 'false flames spirituall but infernall', which describes the damnable effects of sin. The poem is a highly skilled structure, with its ringing prophetic denunciation counterpointed in the first three stanzas with the note of direct and intimate address to God. The last two stanzas present a change from denunciation to pleading, but their tone is not identical for stanza 4 asks for God's pity to the faithful who suffer in his name, 'all desolate' upon this earth, but stanza 5 has a richer orchestration of words and its images are triumphant.

In the face of the varied accomplishment of *Caelica* it is difficult to know what value can be given to the term 'plain style' which is sometimes offered as a quasi-technical description of Greville's way of writing. He is not, as the quotations will have made apparent, deficient in imagery, and he has a highly-developed range of rhetorical techniques which enables him to employ, for example, both sophisticated irony and the biblical power of some of the religious poems. That the remarkable individual quality of *Caelica* has not been fully appreciated is due not to 'plainness' of style but rather to the fact that the poetry is so close-textured and so rich with interwoven strands of thought and experience that it does not yield much to impressionistic reading and may be quite misjudged because of this. A recent attempted commentary by D. L. Peterson in his book *The English Lyric from Wyatt to Donne* is vitiated by confusion over 'plain style' and also by oversimplification of Greville's material and attitudes. The attempt to read the sequence in isolation from Greville's other work is largely responsible for the inadequacy of Dr Peterson's commentary on the substance of the poems, for *Caelica* illustrates with abundant clarity the vital integrity of Greville's work and its intense personality. Greville had no time for art as display or as *jeu d'esprit*, but the poetry that he came to write in the first place under Sidney's influence and impelled by Sidney's example, he forged in the end, through his successive revisions, into a record of a strong and pre-eminently independent mind's encounters with life.[17] The cross-references between work and work and between work and life are consequently numerous and complex, and no description of his work which does not take account of this situation can hope to do it any kind of justice. The reward of the endeavour to read *Caelica*, in particular, fully is to find that its complexity is not obscurity, and that its intellectuality does not result in thought-bound crabbedness of style and imaginative thinness, but that, on the contrary, this sequence is one of the most varied, accomplished, dynamic and deeply interesting pieces of writing which the whole of the period produced.

# 6   Political poetry

The important part played in Greville's life by his political activity is obvious and the importance of political themes in his writing is no less so. The *Life of Sidney* is in large measure a political tract and there are political poems in *Caelica*. The treatises *Of Monarchy* and *Of Warres* indicate their material by their titles and a study of them at this point may fill out the picture of Greville's attitudes and opinions which has already emerged. *Of Monarchy*, in particular, also offers a fresh view of Greville as a writer, partly through what he says of his intentions in the treatise and partly through the style, or styles, of the poem itself. The poem is divided into fifteen sections, the first five treating of the origins of monarchy and the dangers of too strong, or too weak, rule. The last three compare monarchy with government by aristocracy or democracy. In between Greville gives a section each to church, laws, nobility, commerce, crown revenue, peace, and war. He analyses, prescribes, and exemplifies, sometimes drawing his illustrations from ancient history, sometimes from myth, and sometimes from the contemporary world. Section 9: 'Of Commerce', for example, begins by telling how the gods took pity on man and taught him handicrafts and established the beginnings of trading between nations. Greville then goes on to point to the prosperity of Venice, 'That famous merchant common-wealth', and to draw lessons from Dutch practice. He makes specific recommendations concerning an import-export policy and such matters as avoiding the concentration of trade in any one centre to the disadvantage of the rest of the country. He advocates the controlling of exchange:

the type of merchants polecie,
Wherby he rayseth or letts fall all thinges;
And though inferior, byndes or looseth Kinges.    (Stanza 417.)

He insists that prosperity at all levels of the community is the best
means of ensuring loyalty and peaceful government, for it is a mistake
to believe that poverty is 'the best bonde of subjection' (stanza 421).
From its mythological beginnings this section develops into a commentary on contemporary situations which stems from considerable
attention to the topic in hand and to the study of evidence bearing on it.
'Of Commerce' offers some of the most straightforward and detailed
practical advice in the poem but in its range of material from general
to particular it is fairly typical.

Greville's comments on the treatise *Of Monarchy* occur on pages
152–5 of the *Life of Sidney* (Nowell Smith's edition). He is writing of his
own work and singles out *Of Monarchy* for special attention. 'Let me
beg leave of the favourable Reader,' he writes, 'to bestow a few lines
more in the story of this Changling, then I have done in the rest', and
he goes on to explain that in the first version of the poem it was divided
into three parts and that he intended to use these as choruses between
the acts of his tragedies. This, as he has already explained (pages 150–1)
was his original intention for all his treatises (at least for all those which
had been written when he was composing this part of the *Life of Sidney*:
whether or not this included all that we now have is discussed in
the Appendix); but later on he changed his mind about this and rearranged the treatises, removing them from the tragedies. This rearrangement, he says, has taken place in his old age (if the *Life* was
composed between 1610 and 1614, Greville would then be between
fifty-six and sixty years of age) and, he continues, 'then did I (like an
old, and fond Parent, unlike to get any more children) take pains rather
to cover the dandled deformities of these creatures with a coat of many
seames, then carelesly to drive them away, as birds do their young
ones'. But when he came to work on *Of Monarchy*, his customary caution gave him another pause:

Yet againe, when I had in mine own case well weigh'd the
tendernesse of that great subject; and consequently, the nice path
I was to walke in between two extremities; but especially the
danger, by treading aside, to cast scandall upon the sacred

foundations of Monarchy; together with the fate of many
Metaphysicall *Phormio's* before me, who had lost themselves in
teaching Kings, and Princes, how to governe their People: then
did this new prospect dazzle mine eyes, and suspend my travell
for a time.

This remarkable piece of analytical autobiography then continues:

But the familiar self-love, which is more or lesse born in every
man, to live, and dye with him, presently moved me to take
this Bear-whelp up againe and licke it. Wherein I, rowsing my
selfe under the banner of this flattery, went about (as a fond
mother) to put on richer garments, in hope to adorne them.
But while these clothes were in making, I perceived that cost
would but draw more curious eyes to observe deformities. So
that from these checks a new councell rose up in me, to take away
all opinion of seriousnesse from these perplexed pedigrees;
and to this end carelesly cast them into that hypocriticall figure
*Ironia*, wherein men commonly (to keep above their workes)
seem to make toies of the utmost they can doe. And yet againe,
in that confusing mist, when I beheld this grave subject (which
should draw reverence and attention) to bee over-spangled with
lightnesse, I forced in examples of the Roman gravity, and
greatnesse, the harsh severity of the *Lacedemonian* Government:
the riches of the *Athenian* learning, wit, and industry; and like a
man that plaies divers parts upon several hints, left all the
indigested crudities equally applied to Kings, or Tyrants: whereas
in every cleere judgement, the right line had beene sufficient
enough to discover the crooked; if the image of it could have
proved credible to men.

This extraordinary story needs careful commentary. Perhaps first to
be noticed should be the tenacity with which Greville clings to his
work. The half-playful comparisons of his attachment to it to a parent's
fondness for a child reflect the evident truth that his work was important to him. He sees very clearly what the dangers may be of handling
the theme he has chosen but all the same, man of affairs and experience
as he is, he is not willing to destroy his poem. The third and last of his
tragedies, a play dealing with the story of Antony and Cleopatra,

Greville had thrown into the fire fearing that it was 'apt enough to be construed, or strained to a personating of vices in the present Governors, and government' (page 156). This was a sacrifice to the pressure of the times which Greville was evidently not willing to repeat and the passage about *Of Monarchy* shows him trying to protect himself against possible disaster and at the same time preserve his poem. It also shows him deliberately taking up various stylistic modes and adopting finally an ambiguity which it will devolve on the 'cleere judgement' of qualified readers to see through. The care which he takes over these matters and his anxiety to insure himself against attack seem to suggest that he was not at this time thinking of reserving his works until after his death although later in the *Life*, after his frustrated attempt to gain access to state papers for the writing of his history, he speaks of his writing in terms which reflect a decision not to publish in his own lifetime: 'these Pamphlets, which having slept out my own time, if they happen to be seene hereafter, shall at their own perill rise upon the stage, when I am not.' (*Life*, pages 219–20.)

This seems to be a piece of evidence that the composition of the *Life* was spread over some time and it serves to make even more knotted the very complicated textual history of *Of Monarchy*. This is dealt with at large in the Appendix: here it is sufficient to note that there are a few references in the poem which point to dates: stanza 406 considers what Queen Elizabeth would have done 'if she had lyv'd' and stanza 214 refers to the excommunication of Venice in 1606. Stanza 102 may point to the truce between Spain and Holland effected in 1608 but it could refer to events of the 1570s. The allusion to the 'late' Henry IV of France in stanza 434 must have been written after Henry's death in 1610. Stanza 166 has a reference to Jesuit equivocation which may have been prompted by the trial of Father Garnet.[1] The reference to the arts used by sheriffs at election times in stanza 297 may be a side-glance at Sir Thomas Lucy's attempt to deprive Greville of his seat in Parliament in 1601. Themes which are prominent in the *Life* recur in the poem: anti-Catholicism, the misgovernment of French princes, the necessity of the right use of Parliaments, the evils of impositions and monopolies, the need for the monarch to give an example of frugality and good economy. The sections on commerce and crown revenue seem to glance particularly at James's notorious extravagance and improvidence.

All this evidence indicates that Greville was working on the treatise during the first decades of the seventeenth century. But if his plays were written by 1600–1, as they seem to have been, and if some, or some parts, of the treatises were originally intended to serve as choruses to the plays, as Greville says they were, parts of *Of Monarchy* may also have been written in the 1590s. There is a good deal of sea imagery in the poem and several references to the importance of naval power:

> *England*, this little, yet much envied *Ile*,
> By spreading fame and powre many wayes,
> Admitt the worlde at her land conquests smile,
> Yet is her greatnes reverenc'd by Seas,
> The *Ocean* beinge to her both a wall,
> And engine to revenge her wronges withall.   (Stanza 411.)

The interest in the navy and the evidence of observation of the sea might very well belong to the nineties when Greville was Treasurer of the Navy and also gaining practical experience in preparing ships for the Islands Voyage and in expectation of a Spanish invasion. Yet this evidence, like the rest, is not conclusive for the date of writing since Greville is still deeply interested in naval affairs, when he writes the *Life of Sidney* (see pages 198–203), and in January 1613 he was being 'sought violently' by the King to be one of the Commissioners for the reformation of the Navy.

It is impossible to assign parts of the poem to various periods of Greville's life through a study of the style in spite of what look like clear pointers in the account of the poem in the *Life of Sidney* since it was evidently revised, added to and rearranged very extensively. The form throughout, with a few irregularities, consists of a six-lined stanza composed of a quatrain and a couplet. The syntactical divisions vary, the quatrain-couplet pattern being the most common but grouping by threes, or three two one, three three, two two two, etc., occur. The imagery can be sharply witty as in stanza 10:

> All lawes like Cobwebbs, catching little flies,
> But never great ones, without Princes eyes.

and once or twice it has an unexpected poetic richness as when Greville describes the Catholic threat to Europe:

> Lye not *France, Poland, Italie* and *Spaigne*
> Still as the snow doth, when it threatens more   (Stanza 214.)

or when, in a mythological account of the beneficent providence of the gods, he tells how Pallas:

> of her lovinge father did obtaine
> *Castor* and *Pollux*, as two savinge lights,
> To calme the stormes, which hidden doe remayne
> In furrows of the Oceans face, who spights
> To have his deepe complexion without leave
> Ploughd upp by those, that venture to deceave.   (Stanza 367.)

Most of the images, like the references to mythological or historical examples, are illustrative. The sea imagery is often striking, as here, where it perfectly carries Greville's meaning:

> Soe that without the guide of clowde or fire,
> Man since sailes fatall straights of hope and feare,
> In ebbs and floodes of travelling desire.   (Stanza 49.)

The chief obstacle to the reading of the poem is Greville's use of abstract words in elliptical constructions:

> Whence from inferiors, visions fitted be,
> Deceiving frailtie with her owne desire;
> Ease is made greatnes, trust a liberty,
> A point of craft for power to retire,
> To worke by others held a soveraigne state,
> Resting as God, whoe yet distributes fate.   (Stanza 92.)

Some of the difficulty, though not all, and not the strain on the attention, is removed by familiarity with the connotations of Greville's abstractions. He tends to use the same words over and over again and they rapidly become charged with moral judgements. The reader learns to recognize them and to make the right associations and to accept them as constituting a kind of shorthand system by which Greville is enabled to make his points extremely economically. Thus 'supersition', 'vision', 'idol', 'opinion', 'passive' or 'unactive', 'shadow', 'wit' and all compounds with 'self' are invariably pejorative, whereas 'active' and 'real' as well as more obvious laudatory words carry much stronger meaning in Greville's work than is common. Once the language is learnt much of the poem takes on the character of forceful and pithy statement. Though there are passages of 'Of Commerce', for example, or 'Of Croune Revenue' where the verse seems to add little if anything to the matter, yet one does not read long without coming upon a strong phrase, a penetrating thought or a well-adapted image. It is not to be expected, from the nature of the subject matter, that the poem should make gripping reading in the mid twentieth century, but as an attempt to use verse for the exposition and analysis of political themes it is very interesting, not least so in its use of traditional poetic devices to enliven and enrich the treatment of the main subject. Such are the pictures of the golden age which introduce the first and other sections, and the mythology of the stars with which 'Of Nobilitie' opens, in order to illustrate how differences of degree are part of universal nature. Greville deliberately, with full awareness of what he is doing, calls imagination to the help of reason, and since he is a man of intellectual power and also deeply experienced in the practical bearings of his subjects, the poem represents a remarkable attempt to extend the scope of poetry. This is not merely didactic verse for the poem is exploratory and analytical rather than simply instructive and in the qualities of its language, its imagery and its illustrations it makes a bid to touch the imagination as well as the intelligence.

When Samuel Daniel wrote his poem *Musophilus*, subtitled 'a generall defence of learning', in 1599, he invoked Greville's 'learned judgement' to support him in this attempt to write a poem of 'discourse'. He refers only, in the last lines of his poem, to Greville's 'judgement', not to his example, and he goes on, in fact, to claim that his own enterprise is unique. His muse has been encouraged by Greville and now

Is made so bold and ventrous to attempt
Beyond example, and to trie those waies,
That malice from our forces thinkes exempt:
To see if we our wronged lines could raise
Above the reach of lightnesse and contempt.

It would seem that *Of Monarchy* had not yet taken shape as anything like a poem of discourse for if it had Greville would surely have shown it to Daniel. When he did so shape it, Greville made of it something less readily appealing than *Musophilus*, Daniel's warm personal testament of faith in the values of literature, but *Of Monarchy* should be seen, nevertheless, as making a case in its own way for the value and the effective power of poetry.

Another poem of Daniel's offers a closer comparison with Greville's work. Daniel's verse epistle to Sir Thomas Egerton was published in 1603 and congratulates Egerton on his appointment as Lord Keeper of the Great Seal of England. Its subject is the law and Daniel here, as in his pastoral drama *The Queenes Arcadia*, of 1605, is much concerned about lawyers' malpractices which stir up rather than settle contention. A large part of the corruption which he observes is, he believes, due to the obscurity of legal language and to its being in a foreign tongue so that the law is wrapped up:

> in strange confusednesse,
> As if it liv'd immur'd within the walls,
> Of hideous termes framd out of barbarousnesse,
> And forraine Customes, the memorials
> Of our subjection, and could never be
> Deliv'red but by wrangling subtiltie.

Egerton, he trusts, will be the guardian of equity, protecting the weak and the innocent from the oppressions of the law and ensuring honest practice in the courts. He adds that:

> this is that great blessing of this land,
> That both the Prince and people use one Barre,
> The prince, whose cause (as not to be withstood)
> Is never badde but where himselfe is good.

Section 7 of *Of Monarchy* is also about laws. Greville begins, characteristically, by contrasting a primal state of natural law enforced by conscience with the laws of human societies as they now are:

> Falling from lawes of heav'n like harmony,
> To mans lawes, which but corrupt reason be.    (Stanza 242.)

He then takes up some of the specific criticisms which Daniel also makes and which are indeed the common coin of criticism of the time: that laws cause division and contention and that law tends to support the stronger party. He is less sanguine about the relation between monarchy and law than Daniel was, calling law 'a Maister peece of power' by which men are obliged to conform to 'Crowne opinions':

> Whoe simply prize not good, nor punish synne:
> But whatsoever doth withstand their will,
> That barr, as if by nature it were ill.   (Stanza 245.)

Thus it was a capital offence to say that Nero did not sing well and Greville adds ironically:

> Whether by law men roote or rayne take,
> Sure am I scepters it doth sacred make.   (Stanza 250.)

It is because law is such a powerful instrument of state-craft that Greville thinks it useful to set down 'some generall directions' and this he proceeds to do, stating as the first principle that:

> the true grounde indeed of human lawes,
> Ought to be that lawe, which is ever true,
> His lighte that is of everie beinge cause.   (Stanza 257.)

Laws ought, he agrees with Daniel, to be in a readily intelligible language. To allow otherwise is to adopt the practice of the Roman church by which 'poore sowles' are 'forc'd to pray' in a foreign language. Laws should also be unambiguous so that exposition does not depend on the judges. He goes on to consider such matters as the conduct of trials, the desirability of setting up provincial courts and, 'above all', as he says, the necessity of 'cherishing' Parliaments as the supreme law-makers and the medium which 'joynes with content a people to a throne' (stanza 288). This section, 'Of Lawes', is the longest in the poem and its subject was fraught with dangers, as this comment by a modern historian makes plain: 'The political thinking of most Englishmen at this time moved within the limits of two conceptions, of the sanctity of kingship and of the rule of law. It was the attempt to define these general principles more closely and to bring them into some practical relation with each other that produced the Stuart Revolution'.[3]

Greville must have been well aware of the thorny nature of the ground he walked on. He argues that kings should maintain and observe the law, but he adds that in doing so they will ultimately get their own way the more easily. Perhaps this is an example of his use of 'that hypocritical figure *Ironia*' which he says in the *Life* he adopted as a measure of protection lest he should be called to account for unacceptable doctrine. At the end he confesses that what he has written could be a prescription for either a tyrant or a good king but he dare not speak out more distinctly:

> If I without distinction doo sett downe
> Theis humble precepts, in a common style,
> Their difference beinge not plac'd in the Crowne,
> But crafte or truth to governe, or beguile;
> Let him that reads in this, and in the rest,
> Each cruditie to his fayre ends digest.   (Stanza 321.)

Though the uneasiness which Greville speaks of in the *Life* makes itself felt in this section, he nevertheless ranges widely and argues closely making abundant use of illustrations drawn from history and mythology and also from observation and experience. Laws must be clearly set down and ordered or else they will be 'rocks, not sea-markes' (stanza 288); laws are useful rules for guidance as a man wishing to write or draw may find it helpful to rule lines on his page (stanza 260); and there is a neat and vivid comment: 'People like sheepe and streames goe all one way.' (Stanza 298.)

Daniel's poem is perhaps the most austere of his works for the law is not a subject which readily lends itself to the sympathetic treatment in which he excels. Like Greville he argues his points in detail but his eight-lined stanzas, often consisting of a single sentence, do not have the firm hard impact of Greville's and the richer harmony of the language, together with the looser form and syntax, do not urge the intelligence to engage so strenuously with what he has to say. The last stanza, nevertheless, is a good example of the humane, undogmatic but firm moral judgement which characterizes Daniel's best work and which rouses respect for the poet and the man:

> All glory else besides, ends with our breath,
> And mens respecte scarse brings us to our grave:

But this of doing good, must out-live Death,
And have a right out of the right it gave:
Though th'act but few, th'example profiteth
Thousands, that shall thereby a blessing have.
The worlds respect growes not but on desarts,
Power may have knees, but Justice hath our harts.

This note of faith in human virtue is not in Greville's compass and the comparison of his poem with Daniel's at a point where their material is closest brings out clearly some essential differences between the work of the two men in this kind of writing. Greville is unremittingly intellectual and his stern world-view disciplines everything. The lines of Daniel's argument are more blurred but even the unresponsive subject he has in this poem acquires some warmth from the impress of his own sensitive personality.[4]

The basis of Greville's attitude towards the political matter treated in *Of Monarchy* is illustrated by a passage in section 4, 'Cautions against these Weake Extremities'. Greville has been writing in the previous section about 'weak minded tyrants' and he begins the new section with the question of:

How to prevent, or stay those declinations,
And desperate diseases of estate.

Many brave and great men in such bad times have seen no alternative but to 'retire away, and yield the sterne of government to fate' and their despair may be thought reasonable:

But graunt such spiritts were to be excus'd,
As by oppression or necessitie,
Disgraced lyve, restrayned, or not us'd,
As part themselves of publique miserie;
Yet whoe are free, must labour and desire
To carry water to this common fire.    (Stanza 110.)

History offers examples of those who have

Even in the crossest course of evill tymes,
With passyve goodness woonne against the winde
10—F.G.

and there is comfort to be drawn even from the very instability of human affairs since times are always likely to change. Ultimately divine power has the revolutions of time in its governance and so the imperfections of kings and of people alike must be accepted as part of the human condition. To hold on and work for better things is a nobler part than that of Seneca or Cato.

This would stand quite well as a statement of Greville's political philosophy under James and it demonstrates Greville's characteristic attitude towards the business of the world. He does not disdain to work with imperfect or even mean tools for, as he writes in stanza 115, true perfection is divine 'And noe where ever brought to passe with less,' but in this world the disease and the cure often exist side by side and it is foolish, perhaps even culpable, to neglect the cure because of distaste for the disease. This attitude informs the whole of *Of Monarchy*. When he considers the institution of monarchy, the church, the laws and all the rest of his topics, Greville begins from the premise that all have declined from some ideal state and that the work to be done is to make the best of a bad job. The attitude produces, of course, a fundamental irony of the kind typified in section 5 by the discussion of 'pleasing vices'. Some faults in a king are more acceptable than others:

Ill chosen vyces vanish in dispaire,
Well chosen still leave something after faire.   (Stanza 149.)

Vices themselves may be 'arts of tyranny' if the king has the skill to control them (stanza 156). But the moral stance is never for a moment seriously in doubt, and Greville sums it up in one of the last stanzas:

And though the ways of witt be infinite,
Not to be cast in anie mould or art;
Like shaddowes, changing shape with everie light,
Ever and never, still the same in part:
Yet by this Modell, wiser men may see,
That there is choice even in the vanitie.   (Stanza 662.)

The framework in which Greville's ideas are set distinguishes him essentially from Machiavelli although on individual points they have a good deal in common, as Croll pointed out in his study and as Napoleone Orsini has more recently shown in his book *Fulke Greville tra il*

*Mondo e Dio* (Milan, 1941). The common ground is only part of the total area of Greville's thought and not ultimately the most important.

The direction of his thinking being as it is, it is to be expected that Greville's respect for monarchy will be much qualified. *Of Monarchy* opens in fairy tale style. Once upon a time, Greville begins, there were good kings and 'Kinge, and people seem'd conjoyn'd in one' but this golden age is long past:

> Whereby the sway of many years are gone,
> Since any Godhead rul'd an earthly throne.

But men are not strong enough to live without a governor and so they created kings to rule them. Kings once created have seized more and more power to themselves but men have no right to complain of this for it was by their choice that it became possible. Greville refers (stanza 25) to I Samuel viii which tells how the Israelites came to Samuel and demanded that he give them a king:

> And the Lord said unto Samuel, Hearken unto the voice of the people in all that they say unto thee: for they have not rejected thee, but they have rejected me, that I should not reign over them. . . . Now therefore hearken unto their voice: howbeit yet protest solemnly unto them, and shew them the manner of the king that shall reign over them.

Samuel does as he is bid and prophesies to the people that the king will tyrannize over them and deprive them of their wealth and seek only his own selfish ends: 'And ye shall cry out in that day because of your king which ye shall have chosen you; and the Lord will not hear you in that day'. This is the opening of *Of Monarchy* and it is radical enough for any taste. But Greville stops short of revolution. In the final sections of the poem he compares the relative merits of aristocracy and democracy as alternative forms of government and concludes that monarchy is preferable because more efficient, but the basis of his rejection of violent political action lies deeper than that, on the grounds which section 1 proceeds to set out:

> Let each then knowe by equall estimation,
> That in this fraile freehold of flesh and blood,

Nature it self declines unto privation,
As mixt of reall ill and seeming good . . .
Now if considered simply man be such,
Cast him into a throne, or subjects mould,
The function cannot take away this tuch,
Since neither what hee ought, or can, or would.    (Stanzas 27 and 28.)

Since men have fallen from obedience to God ('they have rejected me' – Samuel), human corruption is inescapable whatever the form of society, and the sensible course is to make a reasoned assessment of the situation, not to expect too much, either of the governor or the governed, and to attempt to ensure that their mutual relations are settled on as sound a foundation as possible. This is not easy, for in the course of history the situation has deteriorated:

Yet since election did resigne to birth,
True worth to Chance, brave industry to blood,
Nature to art, and force commaund the earth,
That natyve Commerce which wrought mutuall good
Twixt Crownes and men, was soone exil'd from hence,
And wee like beasts, left noe rights but in sence.    (Stanza 35.)

The Church has been called in to fortify the power of the throne and teach men that kingly power has a divine sanction and can do no wrong. 'True religion' teaches no such thing but, Greville reflects, man's self-will is so inordinate that perhaps even the restraints imposed by worldly power and the church have some value in controlling his worst excesses.

It is from this beginning that Greville proceeds to his discussion of monarchy. He is concerned throughout with balancing the authority of the king and the welfare of the people and with considering the means by which stability and prosperity can be achieved. As he writes in stanza 513:

that indeed is not true monarchie,
Which makes Kinges more then men, men less then beasts:
But that which worcks a perfect unitie,
Wheare Kinges as heads, and men as members rest,
With mutuall ends lyke twynns, each helpinge other,
In service of the common wealth, their mother.

It follows from his view of the general instability and corruption of human affairs that he is willing to face frankly the possibility that all his prescriptions for alleviating the consequences of mortal frailty may fail. Thus, with a touch of sardonic humour, he concludes his 'Cautions against Weake Extremities' with:

> Lastly, if these milde cautions faile to stay
> These frailties, which disease-like turne and tosse,
> And soe for that change every where make way,
> Which change unguided, still begetteth losse:
> Then hee whoe cannot take, must taken be,
> Such sharpe points hath frayle mans supremacie.    (Stanza 145.)

The conclusion of 'Stronge Tyrants' originates in the same attitude of mind but is couched in more sombre terms:

> But if pow're will exceed, then lett mankinde
> Receave oppression, as fruites of their error;
> Let them againe live in their duties shrinde,
> As their safe haven from the windes of terror,
> Till he that rais'd powre, to mowe mans synnes downe,
> Please, for pow'rs owne synnes, to pluck of her Crowne.

Whether or not it was lawful to depose a bad king was a question which much concerned political thinkers of the time, especially on the continent, and Sidney and Greville were well aware of the lines of argument.[5] But Greville's thought is relevant to this political debate only up to a point. He sees monarchy as a social, not a divine institution, and he treats it purely pragmatically, but since he does not believe that human society is capable of real improvement under any political dispensation, in the last analysis his advice in political extremities is to wait for the bad times to pass.

As his other works do, *Of Monarchy* refers back inexorably to a religious view of the sinfulness of man. In the foreground of the picture he paints there are the figures of princes and nobles and the preoccupations of statecraft, but the sense of perspective is never lost and Greville remains ready to cast the whole world aside for the higher truths. This is stated explicitly in section 12, in which Greville insists that true religion requires that no compromise be made with Roman Catholicism, whatever temporal advantages that may seem to offer:

Her [Religion's] name beinge deerer farr, then peace, and wealth,
Hazerde for her, of freedome, life, or goods
Welcome, as meanes to everlastinge health,
Hope with noe mortall powre to be withstood:
So much of greater force is conscience,
Then any lower vision of the sense.   (Stanza 545.)

Others, of course, including Greville's heir, Robert Greville, and
his Cambridge lecturer, Isaac Dorislaus, were not prepared to make the
same move from the political to the religious plane of argument and
became active opponents of Charles I in the great crisis of the monarchy
in the seventeenth century. Though Greville himself stopped short, his
free-thinking on political matters was always likely to encourage
others to translate radical ideas into action and *Of Monarchy* remained
explosive matter throughout the seventeenth century. It was not published with the edition of Greville's work which appeared in 1633,
but it appeared in 1670 together with *Of Religion*. The treatise *Of
Religion* had been intended for inclusion in *Certaine Learned and Elegant
Workes* of 1633, as appears from an entry in Herbert's records, but *Of
Monarchy* is not included in the list of works given there. *Of Religion*
was omitted in 1633 perhaps because of his hostility to the 'outward
church'. Laud, who may have been responsible for suppressing it, had
also been the recipient of Dr Wren's report on Dorislaus's 'dangerous'
lectures at Cambridge in 1627 and the publication of *Of Monarchy*
would probably not then have been allowed, even if it were contemplated. As late as 1681, the poem caused some astonishment—'Sir
*Fulk Grevil . . .* hath a Poem lately Printed for Subjects Liberty, which
I greatly wonder this Age would bear', Richard Baxter wrote in his
'Epistle to the Reader' in *Poetical Fragments*, and though this comment
misrepresents the real tenor of the poem, it shows what aspects of
Greville's thought were likely to be most readily seized upon, especially
in troubled times.

In section 12 of *Of Monarchy*, Greville treats the theme of war. He
derives war, inevitably, from 'mans error' and then, this being understood, proceeds to distinguish the causes which may be alleged for
going to war. These are protection of rights and self-defence. He
recommends the maintenance of discipline and a good navy as means to
ensure military success.[6] One of the last poems of *Caelica*, number
cviii, treats the same theme and asks why states that make war and are

victorious should have more honour than peaceful states, since war and conquest 'sin In blood, wrong liberty, all trades of shame'. The answer Greville gives is that peace breeds idleness, and idleness breeds mischief in the state. Conquest, on the other hand, excites the imagination as do all great actions: 'To dye resolv'd though guilty wonder breeds.' Greville himself is sceptical about the heroism which proceeds from vanity: such sacrifices, he suggests, are not productive of new life. The poem is a very subtle and condensed treatment of both political and moral ideas, one of the very impressive *Caelica* poems in which Greville has found a language capable of expressing his full mind with the greatest economy and effectiveness.

He writes about war again in *A Treatie of Warres* and the difference between this and the 'Of Warre' section of *A Treatise of Monarchy* is the same as that between *A Treatise of Religion* and 'Of Church'; that is to say, whereas the topics are treated in *Of Monarchy* primarily as aspects of government, in the treatises *Of Warres* and *Of Religion* it is their absolute values which are considered. The *Treatie of Warres* begins by extolling the benefits of peace (Greville is taking a different point of view here from that in the *Caelica* poem) and then contrasts these with the destructive, barbarous character of war. States are fond of war because they increase their empires by it, but it is also true that they are ruined by it. The Turks and the Catholics glorify war and all its ugly passions are disguised as virtues. Peoples suffer through the wars their governors lead them into but they are not themselves guiltless. War is a punishment of the 'common staines of our Humanity':

> in man the humour radicall
> Of Violence, is a swelling of desire;
> To get that freedom, captiv'd by his *fall*.  (Stanza 25.)

When we lost the image of God at the Fall, we took on the devil's, and since then men show greater vitality and ingenuity in works of destruction than of creation. Rather unexpectedly, Greville chooses as an example of this the greater popularity of satire than lyric or epic. War is a punishment of men's sin, but God uses it also to produce the flux and transitoriness which are characteristic of mortal affairs. Nothing in the world will endure: here we have no abiding city. So states, like men, decline and fall:

For *States are made of Men, and Men of dust,*
*The moulds are fraile, disease consume them must.*   (Stanza 47.)

The state of man is full of discords and war is its symbol:

All prove God meant not Man should here inherit,
A *time-made* World, which with time should not fade;
But as *Noes flood* once drown'd woods, hills, and plain,
So should the fire of *Christ* waste all againe.   (Stanza 48.)

Greville is prepared to allow that there are holy wars but even these
are to be waged with clemency and moderation. After all this, his
clear-sightedness compels him to admit that war does gain temporal
advantages and that it is only to be expected that the powerful will use
their power. So that, he concludes:

only they
Whose end in this World, is the World to come,
Whose hearts desire is, that their desires may
Measure themselves, by Truths eternall doome,
Can in the *War* find nothing that they prise,
Who in the world would not be great, or wise.

With these I say, *Warre*, Conquest, Honour, Fame,
Stand (as the World) neglected, or forsaken;
Like Errors cobwebs, in whose curious frame,
Fleshe only joyes, and mournes; takes and is taken:
In which these dying, that to God live thus,
Endure our conquests, would not conquer us.   (Stanzas 59–60.)

The other kind of men, who 'serve the World to rule her by her Arts',
who make the sword the judge of right and wrong, and who seek
after fame and power are wanderers in a 'wildernesse of evils' in which
'None prosper highly, but the perfect devils.' (Stanza 63.) It is the fault
of the Christian church that it belongs neither to one party nor the
other:

God and the World they worship still together,
Draw not their lawes to him, but his to theirs,

Untrue to both, so prosperous in neither,
Amid their owne desires still raising feares:
Unwise, as all distracted Powers be.
Strangers to God, fooles in humanitie.   (Stanza 66.)

Greville finishes his poem with a couplet which firmly places war in the context of his whole thought:

*Since States will then leave warre, when men begin*
*For Gods sake to abhorre this world of sinne.*

Professor Bullough thinks that the *Treatie of Warres* was earlier than *Of Monarchy* because of the number of references there are in the poem to the Turks. The Turkish problem, he says, was the dominant problem in Europe before the Peace of Zeitva-Torok in 1606 and he adds that he suspects that the poem was originally intended as a chorus to *Mustapha*. Professor Wilkes, who argues that only *Of Monarchy* had been written by the time of the *Life of Sidney*, of course puts the *Treatie of Warres* later, and takes it as demonstrating the reorientation of Greville's ideas in later life, away from the specifically political interests of earlier years towards a religious *contemptus mundi*. He points out that the Chorus Secundus of *Mustapha*, where Professor Bullough find similarities with the treatise, was added in revisions and was not part of the original version of the play so that similarities do not point firmly to an early date for the treatise.[7]

Neither chronology has really convincing evidence to support it. Both rest on assumptions about the nature of Greville's 'development' in the course of his career which have not been proven. Professor Bullough thinks that as he grew older Greville wrote a more prosaic style and as an elder statesman wrote *Of Monarchy* to embody the teachings of his experience. Professor Wilkes takes quite a contrary view. It is difficult to subscribe to either when the close interrelation of the 'Of Warr' section of *Of Monarchy* and the *Treatie of Warres* has been observed. For although the emphasis is different, the tissue of thought in both is the same, only certain parts of the pattern are given greater prominence in one than in the other. It may be that a greater or lesser amount of time elapsed between the two poems, but to suppose this is not by any means necessary. Only the 'pure souls' whose:

life is death, their warre obedience,
Of crowns, fame, wrongs, they have no other sense

(*A Treatie of Warres*, stanza 51.)

are free of the double vision which sees absolute virtue and practical
expediency simultaneously, and Greville was not one of these and
never thought that he was.[8]

# 7  The Plays

Ever since Lamb wrote of *Alaham* and *Mustapha*, Greville's two surviving plays, that 'their author has strangely contrived to make passion, character and interest, *of the highest order*, subservient to the expression of State dogmas and mysteries,' the political background of Greville's plays has been fully recognized. Comment, with the notable exception of Peter Ure's article on Greville's dramatic characters,[1] has tended to stop at that point, but as this study has been demonstrating throughout, Greville's meaning is rarely confined to one level alone and to describe the plays as political parables is certainly an oversimplification.

The natural point of departure for a consideration of the plays is the relevant passage in the *Life of Sidney*. Greville's account of his own work begins in chapter XIV. 'The workes (as you see),' Greville writes (page 150),

> are Tragedies, with some Treatises annexed. The Treatises (to speake truly of them) were first intended to be for every Act a Chorus: and though not borne out of the present matter acted, yet being the largest subjects I could then think upon, and no such strangers to the scope of the Tragedies, but that a favourable Reader might easily find some consanguinitie between them; I preferring this generall scope of profit, before the self-reputation of being an exact Artisan in that Poeticall Mystery, conceived that a perspective into vice, and the unprosperities of it, would prove more acceptable to every good Readers ends, then any bare murmur of discontented spirits against their present

Government, or horrible periods of exorbitant passions among equals.

After this comes the account of the successive revisions of the *Treatise of Monarchy* which has already been discussed, and then Greville returns to the plays:

> Lastly, concerning the Tragedies themselves; they were in their first creation three; Whereof *Antonie* and *Cleopatra*, according to their irregular passions, in forsaking Empire to follow sensuality, were sacrificed to the fire. The executioner, the author himselfe. Not that he conceived it to be a contemptible younger brother to the rest: but lest while he seemed to looke over much upward, hee might stumble into the Astronomers pit. Many members in that creature (by the opinion of those few eyes, which saw it) having some childish wantonnesse in them, apt enough to be construed, or strained to a personating of vices in the present Governors, and government.

The fall of Essex at this time brought home to him, he says, how readily men, as well as books, could be misinterpreted, and so, ever cautious, he burnt his play. There follows his strongly-worded defence of Essex, 'this gallant young Earle', and after that three whole chapters on the Queen, a substantial section of the whole book. After this very considerable interruption, chapter XVIII resumes the account of the tragedies. It seems likely that the Essex and Elizabeth pages were added to an original manuscript at the time when Greville was smarting with anger at Cecil's refusal to allow him access to state papers (see the Appendix). If the historical matter were removed from the text as we now have it the resumed discussion of the tragedies in chapter XVIII would follow on quite naturally from the point where it broke off in chapter XIV.

'Now to return to the Tragedies remaining,' Greville goes on (page 221),

> My purpose in them was, not (with the Ancient) to exemplifie the disastrous miseries of mans life, where Order, Lawes, Doctrine, and Authority are unable to protect Innocency from the exorbitant wickednesse of power, and so out of that melancholike

Vision, stir horrour, or murmur against Divine Providence: nor
yet (with the Moderne) to point out Gods revenging aspect
upon every particular sin, to the despaire, or confusion of
mortality; but rather to trace out the high waies of ambitious
Governours, and to show in the practice, that the more audacity,
advantage, and good successe such Soveraignties have, the more
they hasten to their own desolation and ruine.

He further distinguishes his own work from that of Greek and Latin
drama and from modern Italians:

for the Arguments of these Tragedies they be not naked, and
casuall, like the Greeke, and Latine, nor (I confesse) contrived
with the variety, and unexpected encounters of the Italians, but
nearer Level'd to those humours, councels, and practises, wherein
I thought fitter to hold the attention of the Reader, than in the
strangeness, or perplexedness of witty Fictions; In which the
affections, or imagination, may perchance find exercise, and
entertainment, but the memory and judgement no enriching at
all; Besides, I conceived these delicate Images to be over-
abundantly furnished in all Languages already.

It is interesting that his description of the 'witty fictions' which he
has eschewed brings to his mind Sidney's *Arcadia*. In *Arcadia* Sidney
dealt in such things, and Greville can only regard the romance as
marginal to Sidney's more serious work, though even here, he claims:
'his end . . . was not vanishing pleasure alone, but morall Images, and
Examples, (as directing threds) to guide every man through the confused *Labyrinth* of his own desires and life.' Though these 'delicate
(though inferior) Pictures' of his friend were too delightful to be suppressed, yet Greville thinks that no one else should seek to do further
work of the same kind. As for himself:

For my own part, I found my creeping Genius more fixed upon
the Images of Life, than the Images of Wit, and therefore chose
not to write to them on whose foot the black Oxe had not
already trod, as the Proverbe is,[2] but to those only, that are
weather-beaten in the Sea of this World, such as having lost the
sight of their Gardens, and groves, study to saile on a right course

among Rocks, and quick-sands; And if in thus ordaining, and
ordering matter, and forme together for the use of life, I have
made those Tragedies, no Plaies for the Stage, be it known, it
was no part of my purpose to write for them, against whom so
many good, and great spirits have already written.

But he that will behold these Arts upon their true Stage, let
him look on that Stage wherein himself is an Actor, even the
state he lives in, and for every part he may perchance find a
Player, and for every Line, (it may be) an instance of life,
beyond the Authors intention, or application, the vices of former
Ages being so like to these of this Age, as it will be easie to find
out some affinity, or resemblance between them, which whosoever readeth with this apprehension, will not perchance
thinke the Scenes too large, at least the matter not to be
exceeded in account of words.

Lastly for the Stile; as it is rich, or poore, according to the
estate, and ability of the Writer, so the value of it shall be
enhanced, or cried downe, according to the grace, and the
capacity of the Reader, from which common Fortune of Bookes,
I looke for no exemption.

The plays date back to Greville's early life. Frustrated in his attempts
to engage in service overseas, he decided to do as Sidney did, express
himself on paper if not in action and so 'to steale minutes of time from
my daily services, and employ them in this kind of writing'. Greville's
last attempt to see service abroad was in 1587 and he was denied the
Queen's presence for six months as a punishment for it. It may have
been during this time, or soon after, that the writing of the plays began.
    The actual events on which the play *Mustapha* are founded occurred
in 1553 when Solyman II, the great Turkish ruler whose career of
conquest struck fear throughout Western Europe, murdered Mustapha,
his son and heir. Professor Bullough has deduced from his study of
the sources that 1588 is the earliest date by which all the material used
by Greville in *Mustapha* was available.
    The story of *Alaham* is again an Eastern one and full of cruelty. This
time a son, ambitious for the throne, first blinds his father and then
kills him, sending him, together with a sister and a brother, to be
burnt alive. Ludovico di Varthema's *Itinerary*, which provides the

foundation for the story, was first published in 1510 and went through many editions. Bandello used the Alaham tale from it and it was translated into English from the French of Belleforest in 1577.

The reference to the provocative Antony and Cleopatra play confirms that all three dramas were in existence before 1600-1. *Antony and Cleopatra* (if it was called that) was burnt because of the situation created by 'the Earle of Essex then falling' and Greville's description of it as a 'younger brother to the rest' must mean that the other plays had been written earlier. In 1609 an edition of *Mustapha* was published by Nathaniel Butter. This is a bad edition, based on a version of the play of which two manuscripts survive, one at Cambridge, and one in the Folger Library. The play also exists in a much-revised version in the Warwick manuscripts and, again with some differences but closely related to the Warwick version, in the 1633 folio. Copies of *Alaham* exist only in the Warwick manuscripts and the folio and these are virtually the same. There may, of course, have been other versions of both plays which preceded the copying at Warwick and which have not survived. The volumes of the Warwick manuscripts which contain *Mustapha* and *Alaham* cannot have been copied till after 1610 as Professor Bullough has demonstrated (*Poems and Dramas*, i, page 31) so that we are once again faced with a familiar situation in considering the date of Greville's work: that we have a time range in which we can fairly confidently put the inception and perhaps the first completed version of a work, but the only *terminus ad quem* which is certain is Greville's death in 1628. The folio text of both plays includes corrections which may very well have been made in the last few years of Greville's life when he had retired from the chancellorship of the Exchequer.

As Greville says, the plays were not intended for the stage. After Sidney's death, his sister, the Countess of Pembroke, attempted to create, by encouragement and example, a body of English neo-classical drama which would observe the unities and depend on the resources of rhetoric rather than of action for the treatment of its moral and political themes. In doing so she probably thought that she was working in the spirit of those pages in the *Apologie for Poetry* where her brother reproaches the contemporary theatre with crudity and lack of literary sophistication. Lady Pembroke herself translated a play concerned with the Antony and Cleopatra story, *Marc-Antoine*, by the sixteenth-century French dramatist Robert Garnier, and Daniel composed a companion play, *Cleopatra*, at her behest. Kyd translated *Cornélie*, another play of Garnier's, and Sir William Alexander between 1603 and 1607 composed plays which are fully characteristic of the French Senecan school. Greville's plays are characteristic of nothing but his own remarkable personality, but in form and mode they belong to this same movement. They are Senecan and *Alaham* is full of echoes of *Medea*. The action of both is full of blood and terror but the method of development is through static dialogue and the reports of messengers. There is no attempt at individualization of characters. They are the images of concepts but they have no life as people. Nevertheless, in sheer handling of the situations, the plays show a considerable amount of skill. One kind of revision which Greville made of his earlier version of *Mustapha* was a rearrangement of the order of the scenes. The play hinges on the question whether Soliman will give ear to evil counsel, believe unjustly that his son, Mustapha, is plotting to supplant him, and have him killed, or whether he will resist the wiles of Mustapha's stepmother, in particular, who wants Mustapha disposed of so that her own son, Zanger, can succeed. In the early versions, Greville had aimed at illustrating the conflicting ideas in Soliman's mind by immediate contrast between the good and evil characters: so, in act II, he gave the first two scenes to the attempts of Camena (Soliman's daughter) to persuade her father of Mustapha's good faith and the last two to the plots of Rossa and her accomplice, Rosten. Act III has a similar structure. The later versions give up this effect of swift transition from Soliman's good to his evil geniuses so as to achieve sharper climaxes and to put back the account of Mustapha's murder to the last act instead of allowing it to come, as it did, too early, in the middle of act IV. In general the reordering of the scenes makes for a tauter dramatic structure and shows Greville successfully taking thought for dramatic effectiveness.

Though some main plot points get obscured in *Alaham* in the smoke of the funeral pyre which consumes Alaham's father, sister, and brother, other moments emerge very strongly with a ferocious power. Act III scene iv shows Hala alone with the nurse, having heard how her lover Caine has been trapped and executed by her husband, Alaham. In the previous scene the news has been given her by Alaham and she has been forced to dissemble her rage in his presence. Now, Alaham being gone, she gives the rein to her fury: 'Rage then unprisoned be!' she exclaims, and invoking Rage as a spirit, she bids it 'prey abroad; swell above all respect'. The nurse has one of Hala's children with her, and the child becomes gradually inwoven with Hala's thought as, all her being concentrated on hatred and revenge, she seems to pursue a rapt colloquy with the spirit of Rage.

Scorn'st thou to make examples out of him?

she demands, projecting her own feeling that to kill Alaham would not be satisfaction enough for her hatred:

Hast thou found out his children? They are mine,
Proud horror! Do'st thou chuse the innocent?
False conqueror of nature! do'st thou move
A womans spite to spoyle a mothers love?
Rage! shall we strive which shall give other place?
Well! on. So that (like ruine) I may fall,
And ruine him; take children, me and all.

The cumulative power of the scene up to this point is immense and the starkness of the climactic lines increases the horror as the bounds of normal restraint are broken down and a human being is given over wholly to domination by a demonic passion.

Act V, scene iii, between Hala and Alaham, makes some comparable effects. A little earlier Alaham has been congratulating himself on the success of his schemes to get rid of his father, the old King, and his brother and sister. He has been disturbed in his rejoicings by noise of lamentations and a messenger has entered to tell how the people have been roused by the sight of Alaham's kindred going to their deaths and that Alaham's newly-won position is in danger. Alaham is wearing a crown and mantle prepared for him by Hala and impregnated with poison. At the messenger's news, some stirrings of conscience and the poison begin to work in him at the same time. His dead father, brother, and sister seem to be racking him and he cries out:

Where is my wife? There lacks no more but shee:
Let all my owne together dwell with me.

Scene iii opens as Hala enters and picks up his cry:

*Wife*! Is that name but stile of thy remorse?
Must I goe where thy silly parents be?
Thou yet but feel'st thy selfe: thou shalt feele me.

This grim promise is amply fulfilled in the scene as Hala taunts her husband and torments him with her intention to murder their child. Alaham pleads with her to spare the child but it adds to his anguish that he knows she will refuse and that his pleas and distress will only increase her enjoyment. All her concern is that he should be fully conscious when she murders the child and the moment of climax, like that of the earlier scene just discussed, is presented in language so bare that its shocking effect is all the greater. She bids pity glance aside:

Cast hence your eyes, These works are but for two!
For him, that suffers; and for me, that doe.

Alaham dies and Hala curses mortality that may so soon be extinguished and limits the scope of vengeance:

Flesh is too brittle mould for brave excesse.

Then she discovers that it is Caine's child that she has killed instead of, as she intended, Alaham's:

Who did this deed? None answers, It was I.

Again the use of bare statement at a moment of particular intensity creates a powerful effect. In the last part of this final speech of Hala's she prepares to die and unite herself in hell with those furious passions which mortal life is too feeble to sustain – 'Flesh is too weake, it hath satietie.' Peter Ure describes this as a 'terrible passage, so powerfully written that it almost justifies French Senecanism'. Its qualities do not stand alone in the play for as the analyses above have suggested Greville more than once unleashes a power in his writing before which the reader quails.

Two other moments in the play have great force, though of a rather different kind. Both occur in scenes involving Celica, Alaham's sister, for whom there is no original in Greville's source. The first is in act IV, scene iii when Zophi, her weak-minded brother, blinded and terrified, comes upon her and not knowing who she is begs her as a stranger for help in escaping from Alaham. She answers at first cynically:

> Fly unto God: for in humanity
> Hope is there none.

but with a sudden change of tone she goes on with something approaching tenderness:

> Reach me thy fearfull hand:
> I am thy sister.

The other occurs in the following scene with Alaham when she defies him to draw from her the secret of her father's whereabouts. Alaham orders his men to search for the old King, and she bursts out:

> Seeke him amongst the dead, you placed him there:
> Yet lose no pains, good soules, goe not to hell;
> And but to heaven, you may goe everywhere.

These lines with their pent-up anger and irony are fine in their context and have an amplitude and authority which make one of the triumphs of Greville's use of plain language for striking effect in these plays.

The dialogue in both plays is written in five-foot lines which may be rhymed or unrhymed, the rhymes sometimes occurring in couplets and sometimes in alternate lines.[3] It involves a high proportion of *sententiae*. In the opening scene of *Mustapha*, for example, Soliman is considering what attitude he should take in face of his fears that his son is a dangerous rival, and Rossa is urging him that the only safe course is to have Mustapha killed at once. The following lines are italicized in just over three pages of Professor Bullough's edition:

> *love . . .*
> *Is it which governes every thought of ours.*
>
> *Many with trust, with doubt few are undone.*
>
> *Monarch . . .*
> *Must (like the Sunne) have no light shine, but his.*

*Strength knowes what strength can weld.*

*For love, and Empire, both alike take pleasure,*
*Part of themselves upon deserts to measure.*

*But love is onely that which Princes covet;*
*And for they have it least, they most doe love it.*

*Yet these all-daring spirits are rarely knowne,*
*That upon Princes graves dare rayse a Throne.*

> *few in number are Time presents children;*
*Where man ends, there ends discontentments empire;*
*Novelty in flesh hath alwaies had a dwelling.*

*Old age is Natures Poverty, and scorne.*

> *Corrupt occasion still preferreth*
*The wisdome, that for selfe-advantage erreth.*

*The wicked wrestle both with Might and Slight.*

*Wrong is not Princely; and much lesse is feare.*

> *Heavy Princes doubting is.*

*It mortall is if Kings see cause to feare.*

*Order alone holds States in Unity.*

There is a good deal of political emphasis in these aphorisms and in this they reflect one of the major preoccupations of the plays. In the *Life of Sidney* Greville described his intention to 'trace out the high waies of ambitious Governours, and to show in the practice, that the more audacity, advantage, and good successe such Soveraignties have, the more they hasten to their owne desolation and ruine.' The plots of the plays can readily be described in these terms. Soliman presumes upon his power and authority to have his son murdered and so causes a popular revolt in which the state is in danger of overthrow; Alaham enacts multiple murders to satisfy his ambition for the throne and he also overreaches himself and brings about disorder in the state and his own ruin. Many other political points are made: *Mustapha* illustrates the dangers of government by a tyrant, *Alaham* the perils of a state ruled over by a weak king (Alaham's father). The vulnerability of kings, who need someone to relieve them of the burden of their loneliness but who can never be sure whether the devotion offered them is genuine or deceitful, is illustrated by Soliman's relations with Rossa and Alaham's with Hala. Some of the choruses reinforce the political points with their commentary on affairs of state.

When Greville writes in the *Life of Sidney* that the reader who wishes to see these plays on their true stage may 'look on that Stage wherein himself is an Actor, even the state he lives in' and goes on that 'for every part he may perchance find a Player, and for every Line (it may be) an instance of life, beyond the Authors intention, or application,' he may be hinting that specific references to contemporary affairs are contained within the generalized political reflections. Some attempts have been made to identify these[4] but the evidence is very doubtful. It is an interesting fact that the character of Mahomet, which has been built up as strong and wise, drops out of *Alaham* at an early point in the play without further reference being made to him, whereas in Varthema it is Mahomet who kills the usurping Alaham and restores order to the State. It has been suggested that Greville composed an early version of the play which followed the source and in which he intended the character of Mahomet to represent Essex clearing corruption from the State and assisting the old Queen to grasp the reins of government. On this hypothesis, Greville recast the ending when Essex came to a bad end in 1601.

It could have been so but it is an unlikely story to found on flimsy evidence. If Essex is to be brought in, there might be a better case for seeing something of him in the other play, in the figure of Mustapha who has powerful enemies at Court and is brought, innocent, to his death. But these speculations are no more than diversions and are not necessary or helpful to the reading of the plays. Situations which justly represent human behaviour can always be translated into contemporary terms: as Greville says, 'the vices of former Ages being so like to these of this Age, as it will be easie to find out some affinity, or resemblance between them.' There has been some attempt also to see in the revisions of *Mustapha* hostile reactions by Greville to James's claims to Divine Right. A comparison of the 1609 version with the later text does not offer much evidence to support this. It is true that the political issues are stated rather more strongly in the revised version, with a sharper contrast between the absolutist position taken by Soliman and the moral and political rebellion against it, but this does not necessarily imply a change of viewpoint. The play as a whole is fuller and firmer in the revision and all the situations become more pointed. The revised play is a much better one than the earlier version, and this is enough fully to account for such differences as there are in the presentation of political issues.

When the political references of *Alaham* and *Mustapha* have been thoroughly exhausted, the more interesting part of the two plays still remains. The plots and characters are the images through which Greville projects his thoughts on the whole range of human activity and the *sententiae* of *Mustapha* demonstrate as clearly as the passionate scenes of *Alaham* that political material is only a part of the total meaning compressed within the elliptical dialogue and jetting out from time to time in the violent action. A psychology of human behaviour is contained in *Alaham* and the play begins, appropriately enough from Greville's point of view, in hell. The ghost of one of the old kings of Ormus rises to speak the prologue and it is from hell's deepest, darkest centre that he comes:

> Nor from the lothsome puddle *Acheron*,
> Made foule with common sinnes, whose filthie dampes
> Feed *Lethes* sinke, forgetting all but mone:
> Nor from that fowle infernall shaddowed Lampe,
> Which lighteth *Sisiphus* to rowle his stone:
> These be but bodies plagues, the skirts of hell;
> I come from whence deathes seate doth death excell.
> A place there is upon no centre placed,
> Deepe under depthes, as farre as is the skie
> Above the earth; darke, infinitely spaced:
> *Pluto* the King, the Kingdome, miserie.
> The Chrystall may Gods glorious seate resemble;
> Horror it selfe these horrors but dissemble.

The state of the inmates of this lowest circle of hell is one of 'depriving, not tormenting doome.' They are in the grip of eternal sin which is the absence of God. The particular sins which have doomed them to this desolation are atheism, pride (the primal sin), hatred of mankind, and hypocrisy, and the sinners thus condemned are those who are great on the earth, kings by birth or by nature. Among them are tyrants who have corrupted authority, 'Councell'd out of the feares of wickednesse', and who, because they are 'Cunning in mischiefe, prowd in crueltie', become in hell the furies who torment the weaker ghosts, those 'Whose soules, entising pleasure only lost.' The weaker kings, whose kingdoms suffered because of their lack of firmness, are also damned but they do not stay in hell for they must go back into the world to tempt the living. The ghost who speaks the prologue is one of these. In his lifetime he let authority slip from him to his pashas and they killed him, for 'Subjects growing full is Princes wane.' As punishment for the disorder he brought to the state by his weakness, he comes back to earth to ruin his posterity, 'That have their sinnes inheritance from me.' Dwellers in hell have not thrown off their knowledge of the world, and here Greville combines a neo-Platonic view of the interrelation of body and soul with the Calvinist doctrine of election. None come to hell, he says:

> but spirits overgrowne,
> And more embodied into wickednesse:
> The bodie by the spirit living ever;
> The spirit in the body joying never:
> In heaven perchance no such affections be;
> Those Angell-soules in flesh imprisoned,
> Like strangers living in Mortalitie,
> Still more, and more, themselves enspirited,
> Refining Nature to Eternity;
> By being maids in earths adulterous bed.

The ghost come from hell retains knowledge of his kindred only to ruin them and his mission on earth is to sow evil wherever he can by craft and deception. The reigning King, 'weake both in good, and ill', will perish by Alaham:

> whom he know'th ill,
> Yet to beware lackes active constantnesse,
> A destinie of well-beleeving wit,
> That hath not strength of judgement joyn'd with it.

Alaham, the son, 'overborne with error infinite', will find his plots recoil on himself. Hala, his headstrong, proud wife, in the end:

> In prides vainglorious martyrdom shall burne.

Zophi, the eldest son, will be the victim of pitiless 'wit'. Caine, a shifting and uncertain character with no better guide than 'Change for his wisdome; and chance for his ends', will come to disaster. Celica, who appears good, will not escape defilement, for in her insistence on martyrdom with her father she is tainted by pride. The judgement here is severe:

> *Celica* (because in flesh no seedes are sowne
> Of heavenly grace, but they must bring up weedes)
> Death in her fathers murder she affects,
> Seduc'd by glory; whose excesse still feedes
> It selfe, upon the barren steepes of mone.
> For humane wit wants power to divide,
> Wherby affections into error slide.

As for Heli, the priest, Greville's summary of him is typical of his view of the outward churches and their ministers:

> *Heli* the priest; who teaching from without,
> Corrupted faith, bound under lawes of might;
> Not feeling God, yet blowing him about,
> In every shape, and likenesse, but the right;
> Seeking the world; finds change there joyn'd with chance,
> To ruine those whom error would advance.

The comment on Mahomet is as subtle and far-reaching as those on Celica and Heli but this picture of an honourable man striving to correct the corruptions of the world and becoming contaminated by the stuff he works in and confused about the nature of duty is not reflected in the treatment of the character in the play itself. Mahomet's part, as has been remarked, is somewhat truncated. The analysis of the prologue applies much more fully in fact to the character and situation of Achmat in the other play:

> *Mahomet*, with honor faine would change the tide
> Of times corrupt; here stopping violence,
> There countermining craft, and pleading right;
> But reason sworne in generall to sense
> Makes honor, bondage; justice, an offence:

Till liberty, that faire deceiving light,
Turnes mischiefe to an humor popular,
Where good men catch'd in nets of dutie are.

There is a remarkably sophisticated use of language in these character
sketches. The pregnant phrases succeed in establishing subtle discrimi-
nations against a large background of moral ideas. The device itself,
an anticipatory prologue offering sketches of the actors to appear, may
seem clumsy and archaic (Jonson used it for special effect in *Every Man
out of his Humour* and Daniel adapts the idea in his masque *The Vision
of the Twelve Goddesses*) but Greville's prologue is far more than a
formal introduction. Its vision of hell and analysis of the ways by
which sin infects the human heart indicate the nature and dimension
of the play's action.

The first three choruses have the same function, and if the prologue
looks at first glance like a piece of rusty Senecan machinery, the
choruses seem a throw-back to the medieval allegorizing world. The
first chorus is 'Of good Spirits', the second 'Of Furies: Malice; Crafte;
Pride; Corrupt Reason; Evill Spirits', and the third is 'A dialogue; of
Good and Evill Spirits.' The archaic form is again deceptive for the
spirit of a later age informs it and in these choruses Greville raises and
contemplates questions concerning the ultimate sanctions of morality.
The first chorus is written in rhymed couplets of poulter's measure but
the strong intellectual engagement gives force and urgency even to this
unhappy measure. Why, the good spirits ask, are their efforts to protect
the good and frustrate the evil so ineffectual in the world? The evil
angels appear to triumph although good comes from God and evil is
merely the state of spiritual deprivation. Why then does the victory
go to the worser party:

Showes *Truth* lesse glorious in the earth, than her ill picture *Lies?*

Since there can be no comparison between the real power of the good
angels and the fallen, the dominance of evil in human affairs must be
due to the nature of men:

The object then it is, from whence this oddes doth grow,
By which the ill o'erweighs the good in every thing below.
And what is that but Man? A crazed soule, unfix'd;

Made good, yet fall'n not to extremes, but to a meane betwixt:
Where (like a cloud) with windes he toss'd is here and there,
We kindling good hope in his flesh; they quenching it with feare.

One of the ploys of the evil spirits is to delude men about the nature of
right and wrong by misusing the names:

Calling the Goodnesse, weake; Patience, a lacke of sense,
Or seeming not to feele, because it dares make no defence.
True Pietie in Man, which upward doth appeale,
They doe deride, as argument of little strength, much zeale.

Prosperity on earth they preach as the only creed.

The chorus then applies these reflections to the situation of the play.
Alaham has accepted the guidance of the evil spirits and pursues his
path of wickedness to gratify his ambition. But the chorus sees how,
even as he lays his plots, Hala is deceiving him with Caine and how,
also, Alaham's actions against the King his father are teaching the
people to abandon the reverence which belongs to a throne, and that
he is thus sowing the seeds of future disorder. The dismay with which
the good spirits contemplate the situation is not without some comfort:

So that our griefe and joy is in this Tragedy,
To see the ill, amongst her owne, act unprosperity;
The corne fall to the ground, the chaff in sives remaine,
Which of the corne was once, and yet cannot be corne againe.

The ugliness of the evil spirits is exposed and the power of good
remains ultimately unshaken and unshakeable. Even so, the chorus concludes pessimistically, men will still fail to choose the right path:

in mans muddy soule, the meane doth not content,
Nor equally the two extremes; but that which fits his bent.
This makes some soare, and burne; some stoope, and wet their wings;
And some againe commit excesse, even in indifferent things. . . .
So in mans choice, suppose his ends indifferent:
The good, and ill, like equall wayes; yet will the worst content.

By the end of act II Alaham and Hala, each seeking to make use of

the other, have between them brought Caine to the point of agreeing
to kill Mahomet, his friend and fellow-pasha, but when he attempts to
do it he is shamed by Mahomet into confessing his intention and re-
penting of it. The chorus of Furies, at the end of the act, is concerned
with this situation and Malice, Craft, Pride, and Corrupt Reason
debate impatiently in heroic couplets about the cause of this hitch in
their evil plans. Craft suggests that they defeat their own ends by
making mankind cherish fame. Malice is surprised at this suggestion,
for Fame:

> breaks Religions bounds, and makes him ours,
> By forming his God out of his owne powers:
> For if by Conscience he did leave, or take;
> On that smooth face we could no wrinckle make.

All the same, Craft replies:

> fame keepes outward order, and supports.
> For shame and honour are strong humane forts.

After this exchange, Craft and Malice quarrel about their own efficacy
as mischief-makers. Craft accuses Malice of having only one weapon,
violence, and since few men are really given to this, Malice has only
small success. Craft on the other hand can find apt material everywhere:

> The *Christian* Church from me is not exempt;
> Lawes have by me both honour and contempt;
> By me the *Warre* upholds her reputation;
> And *lust*, which leaves no certain generation;
> *Envy*, that hates all difference of degree;
> And *self-love*, which hath no affinity.

Craft sums up its claims:

> I am the mould, and Majesty of hell.

Pride takes up the argument and claims that greater evil than anything
achieved by Craft is done in the name of honour which is a concept

born of Pride. The claims of all the other Furies are dismissed by Corrupt Reason which speaks next and describes the others as 'but the Carriers . . . of my rich store.' It is Corrupt Reason which breaks 'the banks of dutie, honour, faith,' and in the minds of men weighs equally with the truth. Since Right Reason was forfeited at the Fall, Corrupt Reason has given birth to all the other sins. Yet it warns the others that they can never hope for absolute success:

> Be it mans weaknesse that doth interrupt,
> Or some power else that cannot be corrupt;
> Or be there what there may be else above,
> Which may, and will maintaine her owne by love.

The voice of Corrupt Reason is too reasonable for the evil spirits. They believe that men have reached a stage of depravity in which they can do without the masks of Justice, Religion, Honour, and Humbleness with which, in the past, they sought to conceal their desires. These, even though they are but false images of the realities, have nevertheless exercised some restraint on men's activities and now there is no need for them:

> Wrong needs no veile, where times doe tyrannize;
> And what, but lacke of heart, is then unwise.

This is the grimmest diagnosis of the human situation in all Greville's works for here men, painted elsewhere as self-deceivers ever, are envisaged as having cast off even so much decency as hypocrisy amounts to and to be ripe for transformation to beasts.

This is not an account which Greville accepts. If it were left to men alone, there might be little to prevent such total corruption as the evil spirits envisage, but Corrupt Reason has enough glimmerings of the truth to know that his destiny is not in the hands of man alone. Something 'above' prevents the final degradation and the last words of the evil spirits contain a hint that they themselves do not intend:

> This time is ours: What need we haste?
> Since till time ends, our raigne is sure to last.

The good spirits have already contrasted Eternity with Time and evidently we are meant to see the evil spirits' boast as unconsciously ironic.

In the chorus to act III, written again in poulter's measure, there is a confrontation between the good and evil spirits. By this time in the action of the play, Caine is dead by Alaham's orders and Hala has invoked the spirit of Rage to assist her in executing a dreadful vengeance. The funeral pyre is about to be constructed in which the old King and Celica and Zophi are to burn. The priest has lamented the unhappy and helpless state of the priesthood in the world, and the scene is everywhere black. In the chorus the ill spirits taunt the good and jeer at their achievements even in the prelapsarian state of innocence. Sinlessness produced only:

> A lasy calme, wherein each foole a pilot is:
> The glory of the skilfull shines, where men may go amisse.

Their advice to the good spirits now is to: 'strive no more to carry men against affections streames.' They point to the characters of the play and assure the good spirits that they have no hope of influencing them. We only, the evil spirits claim:

> We only make things cheape, or deare, as *Lords* of life, and death.

In their reply, the good spirits rest on the belief that though evil may prosper in the world this triumph is merely a delusion, an aspect of temporal experience which to 'reall beings' is quite insignificant:

> Then play here with your art; false miracles devise;
> Deceive, and be deceived still; be foolish, and seeme wise;
> In peace erect your Thrones; your delicacie spread,
> *The flowers of time corrupt soone spring, and are as quickly dead.*

With the beginning of act IV, the old King, Celica and Zophi come upon the stage and though they are not free from weakness, they recognize a moral law and they are free of the dire sins of Alaham and Hala. Their deaths stir the people to revolt against Alaham, and the end of the play shows him expiring in agony and Hala, demented, dying and going to hell. Evil has destroyed itself, the good have had a kind of triumph, and the view of the good spirits may be said to have been justified – that evil will prove to the good, in the end:

> but like those *showres of raine,*
> *Which, while they wet the husbandman, yet multiply his gaine.*

These three choruses of *Alaham* provide a reading of human experience. Greville looks full in the face of the problem of evil, accepts
the triumph of sin in the world and does not flinch from it. He poses
in extreme terms in his play two of the basic situations of human life,
sexual lust and lust for power, and by means of the choruses he provides a vast background for the action and decisions of the individual
lives. With this in mind, we can see for what they really are such in-
trusions of the supernatural in the play as Alaham's vision in act IV,
scene ii and Hala's invocation of Rage and her conjuring of hell. At
these points the spiritual ambience of human activity is made overt
and the scenes should be recognized as statements of a reality, rather
than, what at first they may appear, pieces of intense metaphorical
writing devised for merely exciting effect.

The fourth chorus of *Alaham* is in the six-lined stanza form of the
treatises and is a political one, 'Of People'. The action is sharpening
towards its climax here. Alaham has captured his father, sister, and
brother and is about to send them to their deaths. At their execution
disorder will break out and a voice will cry:

> *Revenge, and Liberty.*
> Princes! Take heed; *Your glory is your care;*
> *And Powers foundations, Strengths, not vices, are.*

The chorus prepares for this political débâcle, defining the art of
government as the maintenance of balance between the latent, but
dangerous power of the people and the power of the Crown. If the
kings overstep the bounds of decorum, the people will revolt:

> *Nor can the Throne, which Monarchs doe live in,*
> *Shaddow Kings faults, or sanctifye their sinne.*

The final appeal is to God:

> Kings then take heed! Men are the *bookes of fate,*
> Wherein your vices deep engraven lye,
> To shew our God the griefe of every State.

The moral and the political are closely inwoven here and the fourth chorus serves to bring to bear on the events of the plot the reflections on good and evil in the lives of men which have been the material of the preceding choruses.

It will be plain from what has been said that to describe *Alaham* as a political play is inadequate. This is true also of *Mustapha*. The same motives of action as in *Alaham* are the springs of the plot in this play: sexual love (Soliman's enslavement to Rossa) and ambition (Rossa's determination to put her son on the throne). A striking difference from *Alaham*, however, is that the non-political implications of the action are worked out in the scenes of the play, and the choruses are to a large extent concerned with the political aspects of the situation. This reverses the technique of *Alaham*.

*Mustapha*, as has been noted earlier, underwent an extensive revision, virtually a rewriting, at some time in Greville's career. The early version is that represented by the text of Butter's 1609 quarto (Q) and the Cambridge manuscript (C).[5] The rewritten version is extant in the Warwick manuscripts (W) and the 1633 folio (F). C and Q represent a simpler version of the play than W and F, and though the essential structure remains the same, WF develops very much more fully one aspect of it and by doing so changes the balance of the play.

Of the main characters, Rossa, Soliman's wife and stepmother to Mustapha, is the least affected by the revision. The material of some of her scenes is rearranged but her character and her situation are not changed and she remains a type of single-minded ambition, willing to use craft and violence alike to bring about her ends and killing even her own daughter in order to strengthen her case with Soliman. She has affinities with Hala, a figure dominated by passion and impatient of any restraint. Her last speech, like Hala's, is full of horror, despair, and a kind of fiendish exultation. Greville found literary precedent for the type in Medea but did not think it untrue to life, as he explains in the *Life of Sidney*. It is not 'malice, or ill talent to their Sexe,' he says (*Life*, page 222), which has caused him to draw Rossa and Hala:

> But as Poets figured the vertues to be women, and all Nations
> call them by Feminine names, so have I described malice, craft,
> and such like vices in the persons of Shrews, to shew that many
> of them are of that nature, even as we are, I meane strong in
> weaknesse; and consequently in these Orbes of Passion, the weaker

Sexe commonly the most predominant; yet, [he adds] as I have not made all women good with *Euripides*, so have I not made them all evill with *Sophocles* but mixt of such sorts as we find both them, and our selves.

Plenty of melodramatic action centres on Rossa in all versions of the play but in WF a different kind of interest is brought into greater prominence and to appreciate this involves an appraisal of the roles of Soliman, the Beglerbie, Achmat, Heli, and Mustapha himself and the changes that are made in the presentation of these in the revised version.

The character of Soliman is generally strengthened in the revision, so that his speeches become more sinewy in style and substance and the conflict in his mind between the arguments for and against the killing of Mustapha is sharpened. There are two alterations which are of particular importance. Act I, scene ii of CQ contains an elaborate account by Soliman of a vision of the goddess of creation which has as its point the coexistence of reason and passion in man. Soliman comments that he recognizes this divided nature in his own experience, for he is distracted by many emotions, affection for Mustapha and jealousy of him, fear of doing wrong and fear of suffering wrong, and Reason is unable to make any order out of this chaos. 'Truthe mee thinckes,' he confesses helplessly:

> speakes both with him and against him,
> And as for Reason that shoulde rule these passions
> I finde her so effeminate a power
> As shee biddes kill to save, biddes save, and doubte not,
> Keepinge my love and feare in equall ballance
> That I with reason maye thinke, reason is
> A glass to shewe, not helpe what is amisse.

There is nothing of this in WF. Instead, at this point of the play, there is what appears at first sight to be a very surprising speech by Soliman in which he comments on the instability of human nature, easily influenced as it is by fluctuations of feeling and circumstance, and draws from this the lesson that a king, of all men, should be on his guard against unworthy influences. He goes on to analyse the situation between himself and Mustapha with penetrating shrewdness. Rosten, the husband of his daughter Camena, is, Soliman says, at the bottom of the trouble. Rosten has for years been working to set father and son against each other in order to seize power for himself. Now he has contrived Mustapha's summons to his father's presence and intends that one shall be the death of the other. Both will be ruined and Rosten will have the crown at his own disposal. Soliman's insight into the means which have been employed to divide him from his son and the motives at work is unerring. He only fails to see that Rossa is at least as deeply implicated as Rosten.

The second important change has a bearing on this speech of Soliman's and its meaning in the play. The vision of creation in CQ has been eliminated but WF has a supernatural revelation of its own. Soliman describes it in act IV, scene i. He has been to the church to pray for guidance in the confusion of advice and feeling which besets him. His prayers have been answered in only too plain a manner and he is thoroughly dismayed. He has received with horror the instruction that:

> *Safetie, Right, and a Crowne,*
> *Thrones must neglect that will adore Gods light*

and he has been bidden submit to the will of God and in disaster leave revenge to Him. He has seen the image of himself in a celestial glass and the truth of things presented is very different from what he had conceived it:

> My wrongs, and doubts, seeme there despayres of Vice;
> My Power a Turret, built against my Maker;
> My danger, but disorders prejudice.

The vision is too much for Soliman:

> This Glasse, true Mirror of the *Infinite*,
> Shewes all; yet can I nothing comprehend.

It would teach him that his empire, the whole world itself, is but a shadow and he is incapable of assimilating this knowledge:

> I that without feele no Superior power,
> And feele within but what I will conceive,
> Distract; know neither what to take, nor leave.

Soliman, in fact, is spiritually destitute. Wherever he looks, within or without, his view is bounded by worldly self-interest. The supernatural revelation throws him into turmoil but there is only one way of action open for such as he:

> If God worke thus, *Kings must looke upwards still,*
> *And from these Powers they know not, choose a will.*
> Or else beleeve themselves, their strength, occasion;
> Make wisdome conscience; and the world their skie:
> So have all Tyrants done; and so must I.

This is a new scene in WF. The creation vision in CQ embodies only part of its significance. The mixture in man of reason and passion which it describes is of course an important point, and it is brought out in the revised version by Soliman's new speech in which he analyses Rosten's part in the conspiracy against Mustapha but fails to see, because he is blinded by his infatuation with her, that Rossa is an active agent in the plot too. It is passion in both versions which determines Mustapha's fate, for the political arguments for and against him are fairly evenly balanced in the pleas of Rossa on the one hand and of Achmat, who counsels clemency, and Camena, on the other. It is Rossa's action in killing Camena, her daughter, allegedly because she has been conspiring with Mustapha, which tips the scales in Soliman's mind and sets him on a course of bloodshed. Where the WF scene goes beyond this is that it shows a man not merely confused by human weakness but making a deliberate choice of the things of this world in defiance of a divine revelation which instructs him to repudiate these and abide by a higher law. Soliman thus is not only a fallen man but a lost man who hardens his heart in selfishness and sin.

The extension of the field of reference and the deeper exploration of the implications of the experiences presented are characteristic of the revised version of the play. They can be seen again in the treatment of the roles of the Beglerbie and Achmat. The Beglerbie is a high military officer and Achmat a councellor of state, and both are aware of the conspiracy against Mustapha and of Mustapha's innocence. Their reactions to the problems posed by their awareness are studied by Greville. Act I, scene ii opens in all versions with a soliloquy by the Beglerbie just before he makes his report to Soliman and Rossa that Mustapha has obeyed the summons to come to his father. This first speech is shorter in WF than in CQ but the gist of both is adequately expressed in the first eleven lines which WF retains. In CQ the Beglerbie has one more brief speech in this scene and that is all. In WF he has much more to do. Soliman questions him carefully about Mustapha's reception of the command to come to him and about his son's deportment in general and manner of keeping court. The Beglerbie answers fully and, it would appear, scrupulously, but in fact his speeches are subtly ambivalent. He praises the son with the apparent expectation that these praises will be grateful to the father's ears but in such a way that what he says will be fuel to the jealousy already in Soliman's mind. All versions show that the Beglerbie knows very well what he is doing. He enters reproaching himself for folly in allowing himself to be distracted by 'divers thoughts' which unsettle him and break 'Natures peace'. It is not for him, he argues, to attempt to dispute the rights and wrongs of things:

Nor doe thou see that which thou dar'st not speake.

His philosophy is simple:

Power hath great scope; she walkes not in the wayes
Of private truth: Vertues of common men
Are not the same which shine in Kings above,
And doe make feare bring forth the workes of love.
Admit that *Mustapha* not guilty bee;
*Who by his Prince will rise, his Prince must please;*
And they that please judge with humility.

In lines added in WF he comments on Soliman and Rossa who are waiting to hear his news and observes:

In Rossa's face behold desire speaketh,
*He keepes the lawes, that all lawes for me breaketh.*

The effect of these revisions of the Beglerbie's part in this scene is to give a demonstration of his time-serving corruption rather than simply to state his attitude, as in CQ. 'Knowledge a burden is, obedience ease,' he says in CQ, and WF actually shows how he chooses to shuffle off the responsibilities of knowledge and serve instead the unjust demands of power. In doing so he contributes to Soliman's dilemma, and tyrant and flatterer become companion pictures of that ultimate state of sin in which, with full knowledge of what he chooses, the man says: 'Evil, be thou my good.'

The one and only scene in which Mustapha appears, act IV, scene iv in WF, act III, scene v in CQ, shows also an important extension of the Beglerbie's part in the revised version. The scene in WF opens with a speech of thirty-one lines by the Beglerbie which is not in CQ at all. He begins with general reflections on the unhappy state of kings who will be betrayed where they most trust and on the equally unhappy state of the subject who creates his own misery by giving power to the 'Idol' he himself has made. Soliman is the type of the one, the Beglerbie himself of the other, for he is being used to destroy Mustapha:

> That Courts should have no great hearts innocent.

This looks like a stirring of repentance on the part of the Beglerbie but he at once recalls himself to his former resolution:

> But stay: why wander I thus from my ends?
> New counsells must be had when Planets fall:
> *Change hath her periods, and is naturall.*
> The Saint we worship is *Authoritie;*
> *Which lives in Kings, and cannot with them die.*
> *True faith makes Martyrs unto God alone:*
> *Misfortune hath no such oddes in a Throne.*

Mustapha, 'this Foot-ball to the Starres', then enters with Heli, the priest, and the Beglerbie stands aside to listen to their conversation and take advantage of whatever transpires. If Mustapha were to defy Soliman a revolt might prosper; if not, the Beglerbie is sure of Soliman's favour:

> Whether he get the Crowne, or lose his blood,
> The one is ill to him; to me both good.

The language throughout this speech has a double reference. On one level it reveals the corruption of courts and courtiers, the ruthlessness and amorality of the power game. On another, the language of the speech defines the situation as another episode in the struggle between the forces of religion and anti-religion in the play. Man is frail, his 'wit' is perverted, he worships an 'idol' of his own creating, true worth ('merit') will not advance him but he must prostitute himself to gain the favour ('grace') of this idol. This false religion, nevertheless, which has authority as its saint and demands martyrdoms on the altar of power, is the one that the Beglerbie is determined to accept. This speech, with its witty, ironic, and, at bottom, deadly serious use of *double entendre* is one of the brilliances of the revised play and exemplifies perfectly the way that extra meaning is folded into the treatment of its situations.

Achmat's first entry is in act II, scene i and, like the Beglerbie in act I, scene ii, he introduces himself with a discussion of what his attitude should be to the situation at Court. His position in the empire as Soliman's pasha is mighty and, to all appearance, enviable but to Achmat himself it is one of anguish:

Even I thus rais'd, this *Solymans* belov'd,
Thus caried up by fortune to be tempted,
Must, for my Princes sake, destroy Succession,
Or suffer ruine to preserve Succession.
Oh happy Men! that know not, or else feare
This second slippery place of Honors steepe,
Which we with *envy* get, and *danger* keepe.

Achmat sets out the situation absolutely plainly. Mustapha has been brought to court on false pretences with the intention of murdering him when he gets there. To say this is to be a traitor to the prince. To conceal it is to be guilty. To attempt to dissuade Soliman from his purpose is to run a great risk. Yet Achmat concludes that he must attempt it:

while none dare shew Kings they goe amisse,
Even base Obedience their Corruption is.

He dismisses all unworthy fears:

I first am Natures subject, then my Princes;
I will not serve to Innocencies ruine.
*Whose Heaven is Earth, let them beleeve in Princes.*

The contrast with the Beglerbie as the revised play presents him is very striking and the WF treatment of the material of acts IV and V brings out more fully what is involved in Achmat's stand for truth, just as the enlargement of the Beglerbie's role brings out more than in CQ the implications of his capitulation to power. All the climactic moments of the play are, in WF, kept back for the last act: the account of Mustapha's death, Zanger's suicide, Rossa's confession, the revolt of the people, Achmat's choice between fanning revolt or attempting to save Soliman for the sake of the stability of the State. In CQ this material is spread over acts IV and V and one effect of the change in WF is to concentrate attention more fully on Achmat. He is given a long and effective speech in Act V, scene iii, in which he sees and rejoices in the prospect of a just retribution overtaking Rossa, Rosten and Soliman and urges the people on in their rebellion:

> Proceed in Furie: *Furie hath Law, and Reason,*
> *Where it doth plague the wickednesse of Treason.*

But this, he realizes, is the wrong course. The people are not fit governors. He must, at risk to himself, endeavour to save the Crown and with it the prosperity of the State.

In this debate and decision of Achmat's there is, of course, a great deal of political content, but that is not all. The contrast with the Beglerbie, so fully worked out in the revised version, has been concerned mainly to distinguish between the man who is without moral scruple of any kind because he believes in no higher power and regulates all his actions by worldly self-interest, and the man who does believe in moral absolutes, believes that they are reflected in the ultimate order of things, and is prepared to sacrifice himself, if need be, rather than betray them. But a man like Achmat is subject to dilemmas of a very acute kind, for absolute righteousness is rarely translatable into action in this world. Thus at the end he must choose between saving Soliman, who has shown himself to be an unfit ruler, and allowing the State to fall into anarchy. It is a choice of evils and in the dilemma which confronts him Achmat's state is something similar to that of Camena, Rossa's daughter, who, torn between her love for her brother Mustapha and her duty to her mother and to Rosten, her husband, finds how beset by contrary temptations and dangers all moral choice is to those who have bound themselves with ties in this world.

The Beglerbie and Achmat and, to some extent, Camena stand in contrast to each other, but Mustapha stands sharply distinguished from them all. Mustapha appears in person in only one scene and in WF this scene is prefaced by the Beglerbie's speech of anti-religious cynicism which has been described. Mustapha's interlocutor in this scene is Heli, a priest, who enters before Mustapha and like Achmat, the Beglerbie, and Camena, reveals his state of mind in a soliloquy. His first words inveigh against Mahomet and his monarchal law which supports the tyranny of kings. Priests like himself have made themselves the tools of tyrants and delivered the innocent, like Mustapha, up to slaughter. His inmost mind is laid bare in the stress of the moment and he cries:

> People! Beleeve in God: we are untrue,
> And spirituall forges under Tyrants might.

To Mustapha, explaining the cause of his excitement, he speaks of:

> the self-accusing Warre,
> Where knowledge is the endlesse hell of thought.

Like Soliman himself and the others in the play, Heli is aware of the conspiracy against Mustapha and has lent himself to it though he knows that Mustapha is innocent. He has chosen the line of least resistance, but unlike the Beglerbie, he is capable of remorse and his conscience will not let him rest. Before it is too late he is determined to enlighten Mustapha as to the danger he is in and urge him to resist his father's will.

Mustapha enquires the grounds of the accusations against him and sighs over the condition of the world:

> *Good World, where it is danger to be good.*

He asks Heli, as a priest, what he should do and Heli replies:

> No man commanded is by God to die,
> As long as he may Persecution flie.

Mustapha rejects the idea of flight but Heli urges him more strongly to save himself, surround himself with his soldiers, and kill Rossa.

The idea that he should cause division in the kingdom for the sake of protecting himself is utterly abhorrent to Mustapha. He embraces death much rather:

> *Heli*! even you have told me, Wealth was given
> The wicked, to corrupt themselves, and others:
> Greatnesse, and health, to make flesh proud, and cruell.
> Where, in the good, Sicknesse mowes downe desire;
> Death glorifies; Misfortune humbles.
> Since therefore Life is but the throne of Woe,
> Which sicknesse, paine, desire, and feare inherit,
> Ever most worth to men of weakest spirit:
> Shall we, to languish in this brittle Jayle,
> Seeke, by ill deeds, to shunne ill destinie?
> And so, for toyes, lose immortalitie?

Heli tries desperately to argue him out of his resolution and persuade him to rebel. To give up life for abstract beliefs to him seems a folly:

> What is the world to him that is not there?

he cries, and Mustapha replies:

> Tempt me no more. Goodwill is then a paine,
> When her words beat the heart, and cannot enter.
> I constant in my counsell doe remaine,
> And more lives, for my owne life will not venture.

In act V, scene ii, his death at the hands of stranglers on his father's orders is reported:

> Mustapha, in haste to be an Angell,
> With heavenly smiles, and quiet words, foreshowes
> The joy and peace of those soules where he goes.
> His last words were; *O Father! Now forgive me;*
> *Forgive them too, that wrought my overthrow:*
> *Let my Grave never minister offences.*
> *For, since my Father coveteth my death,*
> *Behold, with joy, I offer him my breath.*

In revising this scene from the original, Greville cut down long speeches of Mustapha's and made Heli's contributions to the argument more vigorous. The result is to bring out very sharply the worldly view of the priest who clings to life and the world as the greatest good and to show how, in a crisis, he utterly discounts the other-worldly values which he preaches. Mustapha, on the other hand, is prepared to suffer evil rather than commit it, and willingly renounces the here and now since he believes absolutely in a world beyond. His farewell to Heli:

> *Thinke what we wille: Men doe but what they shall*

might in a different context be interpreted as fatalism but in the setting of this play the meaning must be that men are in the hands of God and must resign themselves to Him. Reminiscences of Christian phraseology recur in Mustapha's words, as when he bids Heli, as Christ Satan, 'Tempt me no more', and when at the moment of death he asks the forgiveness of his 'father', and forgiveness also for his persecutors. Mustapha, in fact, in spite of the Mohammedan setting of the play, is a Christian saint, one who lives so much in the light of spiritual things that the world has no hold on him. He is quite free of the anguish of divided loyalties which afflicts Achmat and Camena, the best of the other characters, for they have given hostages to the world and he has given none. They can attain consequently only qualified goodness: absolute purity is reserved for him.

Two small but significant changes from the earlier text establish the faultlessness of Mustapha as he appears in WF. The more important of them occurs in act II, scene iii, where Camena tries to convince her father of Mustapha's loyalty to him. In WF she speaks of the 'ugly works of monstrous Parricide' and the sort of person who might be drawn to them, and she contrasts Mustapha with the picture she has painted:

> Compare now *Mustapha* with this despaire:
> Sweet Youth, sure Hopes, Honor, a Fathers love,
> No infamie to move, or banish feare,
> Honor to stay, hazard to hasten fate:
> Can horrors worke in such a Childes estate?

The comparable passage in CQ is quite different. In that Camena is willing to concede that Mustapha's behaviour may not have been beyond reproach and to make excuses for it:

> But pardon mee, my Lorde, admitte it soe
> That Mustapha in wanton youthes conceate
> Had wandered from the course he owghte to goe
> Yett thinke what frayltie is, and what the bayte.

WF makes no such suggestion but on the contrary emphasizes that Mustapha's life is beyond reproach.

The second alteration affects Mustapha's rejection of Heli's advice to fly from Soliman's anger. It is shameful to fly, Mustapha answers, it indicates guilt and fear, it means the abandoning of friends, gives the victory to tyrants, and is dishonourable:

> Death! doe thy worst. *Thy greatest paines have end.*

CQ and WF have the same ideas so far, though worded differently, but whereas WF ends the speech on this exalted note, CQ goes on:

> Besides where can man hide these cowarde feares?
> But feares, and hopes of power will then reveale,
> For kinges have manye tongues and manye eares.

The cumulative effect of such details is considerably to reduce the effect of high, unassailable virtue created by WF.

There are, then, three possible and apt descriptions of *Mustapha*: one, that it traces the high way of an ambitious governor and shows how he overreaches himself and brings trouble to himself and to the State; two, that it is about the havoc wrought by the schemes of a passionate and ambitious woman: both these accounts are given or suggested by Greville himself; three, it studies what happens when men are confronted with a straight choice between God, on the one side, and the world and the flesh on the other. *Mustapha* is not a drama of tragic errors. All the protagonists act in full knowledge of what they do and the issues involved. In observing their alignment, there is no allowance to be made for ignorance or mental incapacity. There are the damned, like the Beglerbie and Soliman, who have no compunction in choosing the world. There are the weak, like Heli, who would like to appease their consciences, but who, in the last analysis, are not capable of the spiritual effort to rise to the challenge facing them. There are the good men and women like Achmat and Camena, who struggle to act justly but are confused by their entanglement with the world. And there are the elect, the angel-souls, like Mustapha, whose spiritual nature is so refined and pure that they can unhesitatingly give themselves to God. Mustapha belongs to the Church invisible whose members are described in the *Treatise of Religion*:

> Fooles to the world these seeme, and yet obay
> Princes oppressions, wherat fooles repine;
> They knowe these Crownes, these theaters of clay
> Derive their earthlie power from power Divine:
> Their suffringes are like all thinges else they doe,
> Conscience to God, with men a wisdome too. (Stanza 66.)

The revised version of *Mustapha* is produced from the same line of thought as that from which the *Treatise of Religion*, the later poems of *Caelica*, and the *Treatie of Humane Learning* also come. They have in common a powerful sense of the contrast between worldly and other-worldly values and of man's fallen nature which leads him invariably to choose immediate selfish gain rather than spiritual riches. It may be that at some point in his life Greville experienced a profound reorientation of his outlook. Sonnets LXXXIV and XCVI of *Caelica* seem to suggest this. If so, the situation most likely to have produced it was the death of Sidney when all Sidney's actual brilliance and his still greater promise of effectiveness on the European scene were suddenly cut short and Greville was prostrated by the blow. His attempt to come to terms with this frustration of hopes and plans as well as personal grief at the loss of the friend he loved can be seen in the *Life of Sidney* where he allegorizes Sidney's career and makes him an emblem of patient self-sacrificing virtue, an image to hold before men's eyes as a pattern of the good life lived in human flesh. Mustapha enacts a ritualized version of the same career, and if the trial and execution of Essex have contributed something to his story too this would not be inappropriate, for Essex is the second hero of the *Life*. As Greville saw him, Essex embodied virtue in action as Sidney embodied it in patience. (It follows from this that his career could not present the pattern of unsullied

virtue that Sidney's did and his connection with Mustapha must therefore be a subsidiary one.)

It accords better with the facts to put Greville's loss of faith in the
world's capacity to fulfil the aspirations of men early in his writing
career rather than late, for even in the *Treatise of Monarchy* the perspective is likely at any point to change and show the preoccupations of
policy and power in relation to eternal values. The same ideas that are
worked out more fully in the later versions are clearly behind the CQ
texts of *Mustapha*, as references to the Fall, and the nature of the
choruses, make plain. The real development in Greville's career as a
writer is not from a worldly to an other-worldly outlook but to a
way of writing in which he could present experience on several levels
at once. Some of the love poems of *Caelica* use a highly-charged
language which carries several possibilities at the same time, but much
of Greville's writing depends on contrast, the confronting of the 'false'
truths of men with the 'real' truths of God. In *Mustapha*, pre-eminently,
Greville evolved a form of multiple statement by which he could con-
vey an account of man's passional, political and spiritual nature
simultaneously. *Mustapha* is not better than some of the *Caelica* poems
but it is a literary work of quite remarkable depth and subtlety.


2

The unfinished prose work *A Letter to an Honourable Lady* is of considerable interest in relation to Greville's plays, The *Letter to an
Honourable Lady* purports to be addressed to the wife of an unfaithful
husband and it counsels her that the way of virtue is to submit to her
unhappy situation and to practise patience and resignation. Greville
illustrates the various points of his argument with examples drawn
from history, from the Bible, and from the poets, but his most extended illustration is from the story of Antony and Cleopatra. 'If you
desire,' he writes,

> an example of this obedience, which I urge you to, it may
> please you in that arch-story of love, to read the licentious
> affection of Antonie toward Cleopatra: where you shall see, that
> if his vertuous wife Octavia had striven to mark his dissolute-
> nesse: – Augustus was her brother and his competitor in the
> Empire; whereby right and strength, might with some possibility

have lifted up her ambition and revenge, from the barren grounds
of duty. If she had striven to please him with change, whom she
could not keepe from it; the pride of Rome did then manifest
variety of delights, and the servile instruments of Time and
Greatnesse, would soone have had an eye to their gaine and her
fortune. If she would have rowled the stone of Sysiphus, and
studied with merit to call backe his love; she was as yong, equall
in beauty, stronger in honour; but ever the same, which – she
knew – was not so pleasing to him, as the same in others.
Besides, she had the colour of estate to enammell all revenges
upon his ungratefullnesse. Notwithstanding, this worthy lady
would never yeeld to adventure her honour upon the dice of
Chance, nor vainly seeke to have power over him, that had none
over himselfe; but dividing her innocency from his errors with
the middle-wall of a severe life, she remained still his good angell
with Octavius; temper'd publike jealousies and all advantages of
private wrongs; and to be short, was content, when she could not
doe the workes of a well-beloved wife, yet to doe well, as
becomes all excellent women. In which course of moderation
shee neither made the world her judge, nor the market her
theater, but contented her sweet minde with the triumphs of
patience, and made solitarinesse the tombe of her fame; which
fame, as true to her worth, and envious to his lasciviousnesse;
hath multiplied her honour and his shame, to live – as you see –
many ages after them both. Where, if on the other side she had,
with her first thoughts, descended into the counsells of im-
patiency, pleaded distresse in teares, and wrongs in complaint;
who sees not that she had therein not only lost greatnesse of
reputation – the true shadow of great hearts; but stirred up
Murmur, which handles all things; but either never concludes
any, or at least concludes in the worst part? And so, perchance,
by overacting, might have brought her right and his errors into
an equall balance.[6]

This passage seems to stem from a well-considered and worked out
approach to the Antony and Cleopatra story and it is reasonable to
suppose that it was the approach which Greville adopted in his last
play. If so, that drama and *Mustapha* must between them have composed a diptych on the theme of selfless patience and humility. Perhaps

Cleopatra made a third towering passionate female figure alongside Hala and Rossa.

In the *Life of Sidney* Greville says that he destroyed his third play because it might have been thought to have dangerous political implications. The *Letter to an Honourable Lady* may offer some light on this too. It is based on the Senecan formula of couching moral teaching in the form of personal address to someone involved in a specific situation.[7] Greville makes use of this formula in characteristic ways. His comments on the situation of his unfortunate lady embrace not only personal morality – and he writes well about love and mutual trust in personal relationships as well as about the growth and nature of evil – but also political morality, for he compares the position of the wife in relation to her husband to that of a subject under a king, and this enables him to pass shrewd judgements on the ways of power and the psychology of kings and courtiers. He writes, for example, that the 'faults of Power' lie often undisclosed: 'selfelove covering them within and flattery without: under which two veyles the will of supreme Authority is many times stolen away; and the lion's skinne become the foxe's priviledge' (page 285).

Whether or not there is any significance in the coincidence that Greville here uses the same fable as Spenser in his politically loaded *Mother Hubberd's Tale*, it is easy to see how the parallel that Greville draws in the *Letter* between domestic and regal tyranny might lend itself to all sorts of development easy enough to be construed, as he says in the *Life*, as 'a personating of vices in the present Governors, and government'. As for the moral teaching which the *Letter* inculcates, Greville argues that 'nature' points to self-discipline as the best response to tribulations. This would accord with Seneca's stoicism, but Greville constantly invokes also the idea of Grace and lifts the discussion from the plane of ethics to that of religion. He contrasts human power and divine power in a fine passage at the beginning of chapter 4:

> For as the two authors [i.e. God and worldly rulers] differ in the disproportion of infinite good and finite evill; so doe their workings within us. The one makes faith a wisedome, the other infidelitie a freedome: the one giving abilitie to walke over the deepe sea of God's commandements, which while they seeme impossible prove easie; the other drowning weake faith in the shallow dews of

mistrust, vanity, selfenesse and other such irregular humours, as while they seeme easie, prove impossible.

In chapter 6 Greville sets out the gains to be expected from winning one man and winning the world, and contrasts both with the spiritual blessings won by the worship of God. Against these all the prizes that the world can offer are nothing:

> For in the one we worke with our owne strengths, which are but weaknesses: in this with His, that is omnipotent; in the first with flattering promises, that will deceive; in this with Him that is greater than all things, and onely equall with His word; as whose each part is of His owne essence, indivisible, infinite, and eternall.

In the *Letter to an Honourable Lady* we may well have, then, what is virtually a prose draft of Greville's *Antony and Cleopatra*, or to put it perhaps more accurately, a first working out of the ideas which clustered round the story as he understood it. In personalizing his theme of patient suffering in the implied story of the honourable lady he has already half dramatized it, and the fact that the *Letter* breaks off unfinished may indicate a realization that he could work all the moral, political, and religious implications into a more effective pattern if he activated the half-formed images within the framework of a verse drama.

It is possible that the play preceded the *Letter* and that the *Letter* is an attempt to salvage something of the play, in which case the *Letter* was written after 1601, but this seems unlikely. There is a casual reference to the Duc de Guise in chapter 5 which would seem to suggest that the date of composition was nearer to the time of the Duke's assassination on 23 December 1588, and it is easier to see the *Letter* crystallizing into a typical Grevillean play than to envisage a play relaxing into the discursive prose of the *Letter*.

The composition of Greville's *Letter* may be connected with Daniel's poem, *A Letter from Octavia to Marcus Antonius* which was published in 1599, and this poem is, in its turn, connected with a verse epistle which Daniel addressed to the Lady Margaret, Countess of Cumberland, in 1603. Daniel's *Letter from Octavia* is dedicated to the Countess of Cumberland who was, like Octavia and Greville's honourable lady, an ill-used and neglected wife. The *Letter* reflects the situation after Octavia has laboured once to reconcile Antony and Octavius, but Antony has gone back to Egypt and deserted her for Cleopatra. She writes to beg him to return to her, to assure him of her loyalty to him and to promise her forgiveness if he will come back. The poem does not set out to impart a moral lesson but Daniel's intention, as he says in the dedication to the Countess of Cumberland, is to realize sympathetically how Octavia may have felt:

> And made this great afflicted Lady show,
> Out of my feelings, what she might have pend.[8]

His Octavia is intelligent and spirited and her feelings about her own situation lead her to contemplate the injustice of men's behaviour towards women in general, and to lament the attractiveness of vice and the weakness of human nature. The whole poem and the possibilities of reflection on far-reaching themes may have interested Greville. Daniel was tutor to the Countess's daughter, Lady Ann Clifford, and so knew the Countess and her circumstances at first hand. Greville may not have known Lady Cumberland personally but his *Letter to an Honourable Lady* is a companion piece to Daniel's. It is typical of the difference in temperament between the two men that whereas the situation is seen in Daniel's poem as an eminently personal one and he tries very sensitively to recreate Octavia's feelings, Greville's *Letter* deals with large abstract concepts of virtue and honour, power and obedience, and puts human motivation, as Greville commonly does, into the two main categories of hope and fear. When Daniel returned to the situation a few years later and wrote the verse epistle to the Countess of Cumberland he adopted something of Greville's lofty tone to describe the inviolability of the man (or woman) who:

> of such a height hath built his minde,
> And rear'd the dwelling of his thoughts so strong,
> As neither feare nor hope can shake the frame
> Of his resolved powres, nor al the winde
> Of Vanitie or Malice, pierce to wrong
> His setled peace, or to disturbe the same;
> What a faire seate hath he, from whence hee may
> The boundlesse wastes and weildes of man survey.

But what his poem celebrates is a refined stoicism: he never reaches the religious exaltation of Greville.

The common interest shown by Daniel and Greville in the theme of the ill-treated wife and the patience of Octavia suggests that Greville's *Letter to an Honourable Lady*, and also his lost play dealing with the Antony and Cleopatra story, were written just about the turn of the century. The particular interest of Greville's *Letter* is that it appears to show an early stage in the evolution of a Greville play, and in doing so to reveal the intellectual and creative processes at work. He begins with a theme and then proceeds to develop it on three levels, moral, political, and religious, and to gather illustrations for it. In the course of this, one of the illustrations opens out and presents itself to him as capable of carrying, through the images it provides, the whole weight of meaning which he finds in the original theme. He then abandons straight didactic discourse for the 'spreading ocean of images' and a form of dramatic writing which will make his points more succinctly and give sharper definition to what he has to say.

Daniel's *Letter from Octavia* appears to have another point of contact with a Greville play. Stanza 41 reads:

> Wretched Mankinde, wherfore hath nature made
> The lawful undelightfull, th' unjust shame?
> As if our pleasure onely were forbade,
> But to give fire to lust, t' adde greater flame;
> Or else, but as ordained more to lade
> Our heart with passions to confound the same.

This is Daniel writing well below his best, and it is a weak treatment of the theme of the Chorus Sacerdotum of *Mustapha*:

> Oh wearisome Condition of Humanity!
> Borne under one Law, to another bound:
> Vainely begot, and yet forbidden vanity,
> Created sicke, commanded to be sound:
> What meaneth Nature by these diverse Lawes?
> Passion and Reason, selfe-division cause:
> Is it the marke, or Majesty of Power
> To make offences that it may forgive?
> Nature herselfe, doth her owne selfe defloure,

To hate those errors she her selfe doth give.
For how should man thinke that, he may not doe
If Nature did not faile, and punish too?
Tyrant to others, to her selfe unjust,
Onely commands things difficult and hard.
Forbids us all things, which it knowes is lust,
Makes easie paines, unpossible reward.
If Nature did not take delight in blood,
She would have made more easie waies to good.

Which version came first, Greville's or Daniel's, we do not know, but
a comparison of the two demonstrates how much Greville gets out
of the dramatic context of his writing. The sentiments expressed
by Daniel have scarcely any force, whereas in *Mustapha* all the
power of the debate between God and the world which has gone
before is included in them and words like Passion, Reason, Nature,
carry a high charge because of the attention previously given
to them. The role of the priesthood in the play and the fact
that it is priests who speak the chorus gives a special edge to the
comments.

The choruses of *Alaham* illuminate the action of the play. The significances of *Mustapha* are worked out in dialogue and action, and the
choruses do not have the same effect. They raise, in fact, a number of
problems. When he rewrote the CQ version of the play, Greville rearranged the order of the scenes so that the act divisions in the earlier
and later versions do not come at the same points. CQ has no chorus
for act II although there is a heading for one in Q. Act IV ends in the
early versions with a chorus on death which is not included in WF.
Act V has no chorus. Early and late versions have in common the
Chorus Sacerdotus, but this comes at the end of act I in CQ, does not
appear in W, and is printed in F right at the end of the play and
separated from the rest of the text by a deep ornament.[9] The Chorus
Tartarorum also occurs both early and late, though not in C. It
is differently placed, occurring in Q at the end of act III, and in
WF at the end of act V. W and F have to themselves a Chorus of
Bashas and Caddies (act I), a Chorus of Priests (act II), a Chorus of
Time and Eternitie (act III), and a Chorus of Converts to Mahometism
(act IV).

The choruses of CQ are short and quite closely linked with the preceding act. The Chorus Sacerdotum, for example, in its original placing at the end of act I, takes up the point made by Soliman's vision of creation, that man is a compound of reason and passion, and the priests speak of the 'selfe-division' which this mixed nature causes. The Chorus Tartarorum comes effectively after the interview between Mustapha and Heli and comments on what has taken place much in the manner of the Beglerbie's speech which in WF introduces the scene. Instead of the line which stands in the WF text:

Vast *Superstition*! Glorious stile of Weakness!

Q reads:

Religion, thou vaine and glorious stile for weaknesse

and throughout the chorus exalts 'Nature' at the expense of faith and jeers at the religion for which Mustapha embraces suffering and death:

Courage, and Worth abjure thy painted heavens.
Sicknesse, thy blessings are; Miserie, thy triall;
Nothing, thy way unto eternall being;
Death, to salvation; and the Grave to Heaven.
So Blest be they, so Angel'd, so Eterniz'd
That tie their senses to thy senselesse glories,
And die, to cloy the after-age with stories.

The chorus comments directly on Mustapha's situation. Nature is the only law and if a man transgresses nature by threatening to kill, then:

Nature doth, for defence, allow offences.
*She neither taught the Father to destroy:*
*Nor promis'd any man, by dying, joy.*

When Greville decided to enlarge the Beglerbie's part and prefaced the Mustapha–Heli scene with a new speech of his, he built the sceptical, anti-religious point of view more thoroughly into the structure of the play. He seems to have wanted, in all versions, to make sure that it was closely associated with the Mustapha scene so that the reader's attention would be sharply focused on the contrast between the two attitudes of mind.

The choruses which occur in WF and not in CQ are more difficult to account for. The first is a long analysis of the uses and abuses of power, having only a slight connection with the particular situation in the play. The second is a comparison between the relation of church and ruler in Christian and Mohammedan countries and a discussion of the relative condition of the people. In the third, Time and Eternity make their rival claims, and in the fourth are described the various stages by which the bonds which tie together the estates of a kingdom are loosened. What Greville says in the *Life of Sidney* about the original choruses which he afterwards cut out and made into the treatises seems to apply very well to the WF choruses which we have: 'not borne out of the present matter acted, yet . . . the largest subjects I could then think upon, and no such strangers to the scope of the Tragedies, but that a favourable Reader might easily find some consanguinitie between them . . . my apprehensive youth, for lack of a well touched compasse, did easily wander beyond proportion.'

The style of these choruses is also surprising. In contrast with the taut, lapidary style of the rest of the play, they are discursive and employ elaborate and extended images. The second chorus changes half way through from six-lined stanzas to rhymed couplets as if two poems, or parts of poems, had been brought together. It contains the splendid lines:

> *Hee whom God chooseth out of doubt doth well:*
> *What they that choose their God do, who can tell?*

The Time-Eternity chorus, though Eternity has some fine stanzas, lacks much of the thrust and bite with which Greville usually invigorates such oppositions. Only the fourth chorus speaks in Greville's full tones, and here he uses poulter's measure, as he did in *Alaham*, with force and authority. The fact is that when Greville revised his play and packed so much into it, he left no function for the choruses to perform. He may have been puzzled to find material for them and have made use of verses that went back to the earliest drafting of the play. He retained the Chorus Tartarorum from CQ, but put it back to the end of the last act. It is less immediately appropriate there than it was in its original position at the end of act I, but provides a striking final ironic comment on the gulf which separates those whose souls are given to the world from the elect of God. It was probably not his own intention to preserve the Chorus Sacerdotum as well, but whoever was responsible for printing it after the Chorus Tartarorum had a happy inspiration. Though the points it makes have been made elsewhere in the play, this chorus gives cogent expression to the dilemma of the man *moyen spirituel*, like Heli, who would, if he could, be faithful to his creed but who finds the fears and desires of the flesh too much for him. It is in keeping with Greville's attitude as it appears elsewhere that the last word in the play should be with those who are tormented by the pull between God and the world. He loved to recognize a high and noble soul who could rise above the trammels of the world, but he never counted himself as one of these. His own place was rather with Achmat and he would not have denied that the 'wearisome condition of humanity' weighed upon him as it did upon the priests of the last chorus.[10]

It is, though, rather ironic that these should be perhaps Greville's most famous lines. Archbishop Tillotson composed one of his sermons to refute, as he says,

> those celebrated Verses of a noble *Poet* of our own, which are so
> frequently in the mouths of many, who are thought to have
> no good will to Religion –
> Oh wearisome Condition of Humanity!
> Borne under one Law, to another bound:
> Vainely begot, and yet forbidden vanity,
> Created sicke, commanded to be sound.[11]

Greville claimed no exemption for his own work from the 'common Fortune of Bookes', which depends on the 'grace, and capacity of the Reader': with his experience of men, he might have been less astonished than many others to find his works misapplied even to the service of those who 'have no good will to Religion'.

# 8 Humanist and Calvinist

To call a man of the sixteenth or seventeenth century a Calvinist is to indicate an attitude of mind rather than adherence to a formal set of doctrines. The particular shape and colour of the individual's Calvinism will be determined by experience and temperament and this is well illustrated by Greville. The relation of Greville's political interests to his theological attitudes and the stance he adopted in various other activities of his life have already been described; but in so far as the main interest of this study is in Greville as a writer, one major point has so far not been raised: how did Greville relate his engagement with literature to his view of the corruption of all worldly matters? What function did he allow to poetry? To what extent, if at all, did he have an artist's care for the medium he worked in? His *Treatie of Humane Learning* provides some of the answers to these questions, but it will be useful, before discussing the poem, to put it in a context of contemporary thinking about the issues it raises.

> When we read Demosthenes or Cicero, Plato or Aristotle or some others of their kind, I confess indeed that they wonderfully attract, delight and move us, even ravish our minds. But if from them we turn to the reading of the Holy Scriptures, whether we will or no they so pierce us to the heart and fix themselves within us that all the power of the rhetoricians and philosophers, compared with them, seems no more than smoke.

So wrote Calvin.[1] So also wrote Milton in a famous passage in *Paradise Regained* which has disturbed some of his readers ever since.

There is no need to argue for Milton's literary sensitivity, and as for Calvin, François Wendel writes: 'His conversion no doubt lowered the ancient authors in the hierarchy of values he admired, to the advantage of the Scripture; but it did not cause him to condemn them without reservation. In his commentaries and dogmatic treatises he continued to quote them abundantly, and with a mastery that betokens long familiarity.' Wendel quotes another scholar to the effect that: 'The Hellenic spirit faded little by little before the Christian spirit; nevertheless, Calvin preserved to the end the reputation of an excellent humanist.'[2] The same words might apply to Milton. Their austere religious creeds confronted their respect for learning and their delight in classical literature and created an intellectual situation which they had to resolve. The same situation impinged on Greville for he shared their theocentric view and their insistence on the Fall of Man as the dominant fact of human history, and he shared as well their humanism. The placing of human learning and the pursuit of literature in the scale of activities open to fallen man was a matter of importance to all three of them.

Calvin makes rather surprising allowances for what he distinguishes as man's earthly interests. Corrupt though man's intellect is, it may operate effectively in some spheres: 'When the human understanding applies itself to some study, it does not so labour in vain as not to profit at all.' The earthly interests to which human intellect may apply itself not altogether vainly are defined by Calvin as follows: 'I call those things earthly', he writes in the *Institutes of the Christian Religion*, 'which do not touch at all upon God and his kingdom nor upon the true righteousness and immortality of the future life, but belong to the present life and are as though enclosed within the limits of it. . . . In [this] first class are included political doctrine, the right way of managing one's house, the mechanical arts, philosophy and all the disciplines that are called liberal.' Through the operation of divine grace, 'there is some universal apprehension of reason imprinted naturally in all men', and 'if we recognize the Spirit of God as the unique fountain of truth, we shall never despise the truth wherever it may appear, unless we wish to do dishonour to the Spirit of God; for the gifts of the Spirit cannot be disparaged without scorn and opprobrium to himself.'[3] Milton in 1644 has a clear place for learning in his scheme of things: 'The end then of learning is to repair the ruins of our first parents by regaining to know God aright, and out of that knowledge to love him, to imitate him, to be like him, as we may the nearest by possessing our soule of true virtue, which being united to the heavenly grace of faith, makes up the highest perfection.'[4] Sidney had a similar view though he claimed rather less for the results which knowledge could achieve:

> This purifying of wit, this enritching of memory, enabling of judgement, and enlarging of conceyt, which commonly we call learning, under what name so ever it come forth, or to what immediate end so ever it be directed, the final end is to lead and draw us to as high a perfection as our degenerate soules, made worse by theyr clayey lodgings, can be capable of.'[5]

His claims for the efficacy and the status of poetry are very special. The poet outgoes the work of nature:

> Neither let this be jestingly conceived, because the works of the one be essentiall, the other, in imitation or fiction; for any understanding knoweth the skill of the Artificer standeth in that *Idea* or fore-conceite of the work, and not in the work it selfe. And that the Poet hath that *Idea* is manifest, by delivering them forth in such excellencie as hee hath imagined them. Which delivering forth also is not wholie imaginative, as we are wont to say by them that build Castles in the ayre: but so farre substantially it worketh; not onely to make a *Cyrus*, which had been but a particular excellencie, as *Nature* might have done, but to bestow a *Cyrus* upon the worlde, to make many *Cyrus's*, if they will learne aright why and how that Maker made him. Neyther let it be deemed too sawcie a comparison to ballance the highest poynt of mans wit with the efficacie of nature: but rather give right honor to the heavenly Maker of that maker, who having made man to his owne likeness, set him beyond and over all the workes of that second nature, which in nothing hee showeth so much as in Poetrie, when with the force of a divine breath he bringeth things forth far surpassing her dooings, with no small argument to the incredulous of that first accursed fall of *Adam*, sith our erected wit maketh us know what perfection is, and yet our infected will keepeth us from reaching unto it.[6]

This is Sidney's wording of Coleridge's description of the processes of the poetic imagination as 'a repetition in the finite mind of the eternal act of creation in the infinite I am.' Like Sidney, Bacon also justifies the 'feigned history' of poetry but for different reasons. The use of poetry, he declares, is

> to give some shadow of satisfaction to the mind of man in those points wherein the nature of things doth deny it; the world being in proportion inferior to the soul; by reason whereof there is agreeable to the spirit of man a more ample greatness, a more exact goodness, and a more absolute variety, than can be found in the nature of things. . . . So as it appeareth that poesy serveth and conferreth to magnanimity, morality, and to delectation. And therefore it was ever thought to have some participation of divineness, because it doth raise and erect the mind, by submitting the shews of things to the desires of the mind, whereas reason doth buckle and bow the mind unto the nature of things.[7]

In the passage which D. G. James quotes, poetry is described as 'a dream of learning' merely, not a reality; 'a thing sweet and varied, and that would be thought to have in it something divine; a character which dreams likewise affect'.[8]

For Bacon the reality of learning lay in the operation of reason upon the phenomena of the natural world and the right end of the pursuit of learning was 'to give a true account of their [men's] gift of reason, to the benefit and use of men.' Knowledge and learning are 'a rich storehouse, for the glory of the Creator and the relief of man's estate.' He goes on:

> as both heaven and earth do conspire and contribute to the use and benefit of man, so the end ought to be, from both philosophies to separate and reject vain speculations and whatever is empty and void, and to preserve and augment whatsoever is solid and fruitful; that knowledge may not be as a courtesan, for pleasure and vanity only, or as a bondwoman to acquire and gain to her master's use; but as a spouse, for generation, fruit and comfort.[9]

A recent study of Bacon's intellectual background gives prominence to his Calvinist inheritance. 'Bacon betrayed the practical bent of the

Calvinistic Protestantism that he absorbed as a boy, not least from his
mother, who was a Calvinist of strong piety . . . the effect of Calvinist
views may reasonably be found at the centre of Bacon's thought.'[10]
The essence of Bacon's method, it is said, 'is to supply the senses with
such helps and so to govern the reason that elaborate methodology
will atone for the worthlessness of man's senses and understanding.'[11]
The wording here may be open to some cavil but the point in essence
will stand: 'Numberless are the ways, and sometimes imperceptible,
in which the affections colour and infect the understanding',[12] and 'the
course I propose for the discovery of sciences is such as leaves but little
to the acuteness and strength of wits, but places all wits and under-
standings nearly on a level.'[13] It is not the methodology but the
imaginative vision it was designed to serve, the prospect of enabling
man to resume dominion over nature, which has survived the centuries and exerted a powerful influence, and this vision has no place in
Fulke Greville's assessment of man; but the handful of quotations
offered in these pages may serve to illustrate how from the same root
of awareness of man's degenerate nature may spring divers fruit. How
far can man improve himself? How far can the 'gifts of the spirit' be
discerned in the ways of man? What, in particular, can poetry contribute, if it can contribute at all, to 'the relief of man's estate'?

Sonnet LXVI of the *Caelica* sequence gives cogent expression to some
of the fundamental issues, as Greville sees them, which are involved in
questions concerning the place of literature and learning in a sinful
universe:

> *Caelica*, you (whose requests commandments be)
> Advise me to delight my minde with books,
> The Glasse where Art doth to posterity,
> Show nature naked unto him that looks,
> Enriching us, shortning the ways of wit,
> Which with experience else deare buyeth it.
>
> *Caelica*, if I obey not, but dispute,
> Thinke it is darknesse, which seeks out a light,
> And to presumption do not it impute,
> If I forsake this way of Infinite;
> *Books be of men, men but in clouds doe see,*
> *Of whose embracements Centaures gotten be.*

The first lines of the next stanza may seem to strike a note of pastoral innocence but they do not really do so. Their relation is to an intellectual background of which Calvin's paraphrase of *Coeli enarrant gloriam Dei* in his preface to the Bible of Olivétan forms part. As he expresses it more briefly in the *Institutes*: 'God has so manifested himself [to men] in such a beautiful and exquisite edifice of heaven and earth, showing and presenting himself there every day, that they cannot open their eyes without being obliged to perceive him.'[14] Greville's version is:

> I have for books, about my head the Skyes,
> Under me, Earth; about me Ayre and Sea:
> The Truth for light, and Reason for mine eyes,
> Honour for guide, and nature for my way.
> With change of times, lawes, humors, manners, right;
> Each in their diverse workings infinite.
>
> Which powers from that we feele, conceive, or doe,
> Raise in our senses thorough joy, or smarts,
> All formes, the good or ill can bring us to,
> More lively farre, than can dead Books or Arts;
> Which at the second hand deliver forth,
> Of few mens heads, strange rules for all mens worth.

Then out of the same train of thought roll the powerful denunciations. Books become now:

> False antidotes for vitious ignorance,
> Whose causes are within, and so their cure,
> Errour corrupting Nature, not Mischance,
> For how can that be wise which is not pure?
> So that Man being but mere hypocrisie,
> What can his arts but beames of follie be?

Where the inward man is corrupt, books and learning can only serve corruption. Where the heart and mind are pure, on the other hand, the truths of revelation are the only learning worthy of contemplation. The conclusion is inevitable:

> What then need halfe-fast helps of erring wit,
> Methods, or books of vaine humanity?

> Which dazell truth, by representing it,
> And so entayle clouds to posterity.
> Since outward wisdome springs from truth within,
> Which all men feele, or heare, before they sinne.

This is the absolutist position but practice calls for a closer working out of its application to persons and situations. This is provided in the *Treatie of Humane Learning*.

The first fifty-nine stanzas of this poem are an expansion of the severe dismissal of books in the *Caelica* sonnet: 'False antidotes for vitious ignorance'. Greville directs his attention here to the sources of human learning and finds them all ineradicably tainted. Man's first perceptions are through the senses, but human senses are inferior to those of the animals and how inaccurate they are as registers we may see by noticing how sense impressions vary from person to person. When we move from our physical equipment to our mental the situation does not improve. Imagination, the mental image of our sense impressions, does not even reproduce faithfully the imperfect information provided by the senses but 'our desires, feares, hopes, love, hate, and sorrow' create visions, phantasms, and dreams, and instead of knowledge present us only with 'apparitions'. Memory 'corrupted with disguis'd intelligence' cannot help us, and as for our understanding:

> though it containe
> Some ruinous notions, which our Nature showes,
> Of generall truths, yet have they such a staine
> From our corruption, as all light they lose;
> Save to convince of ignorance, and sinne
> Which where they raigne let no perfection in. (Stanza 15.)

When he has cut the ground entirely from under confidence in our natural gifts, Greville turns to the possibility that with skill and learning we might yet improve our situation, 'as if restore our fall'. This is the hope on which Milton's *Of Education* is founded, but in Greville's eyes it is mere delusion. Men erect structures of words and substitute them for the realities of which they remain totally ignorant. Who, since time began, ever discovered 'one true forme' (probably Platonic, metaphysical forms are what he has in mind, not Baconian, physical forms)? With all our pride in our intellectual structures:

Yet all our Arts cannot prevaile so farre,
As to confirme our eyes, resolve our hearts,
Whether the heavens doe stand still or move,
Were fram'd by Chance, Antipathie, or Love?   (Stanza 28.)

His scepticism about all contemporary theories of cosmogony appears
more advanced here than Bacon's rejection of 'an assumption which
cannot be allowed, viz. that the earth moves'[15] but it is unlikely that
Bruno was deceived when they met. The attitude of mind is not
forward-looking, but coolly sardonic.

In stanza 29, Greville sums up all the fruitless learning he has sur-
veyed so far:

Then what is our high-prais'd *Philosophie*,
But bookes of Poesie, in Prose compil'd?
Farre more delightful than they fruitfull be,
Witty apparance, Guile that is beguil'd;
Corrupting minds much rather than directing,
The allay of Duty, and our Prides erecting.

The doom of man is to go on in his vanity while the world, 'in lapse
to God', struggles to erect its 'fleshly idols' 'upon the false foundation
of his Guilt'. Is it then better to be ignorant and reject learning? The
questions of stanza 60 introduce the second part of the treatise in which
Greville, after all the belittling descriptions of the earlier stanzas, goes
on to concede relative value to learning. That he does so indicates a
double view of life and human activity but not a divided one, for like
Calvin he believes that man must labour in the world and like Calvin
he believes that within the limits of his corrupted reason he may
achieve some things. What he must not do is to overestimate these
achievements and to presume in his pride that they have any claims to
comprehend the truths which are in the keeping of God alone.

Man must not therefore rashly Science scorne,
But choose, and read with care; since *Learning* is
A bunch of grapes sprung up among the thornes,
Where, but by caution, none the harme can misse;
Nor Arts true riches read to understand,
But shall, to please his taste, offend his hand.   (Stanza 62.)

The first exercise of a sound learning is to pare away useless knowledge: use must stand higher than delight and the end of learning must be to inform men's practice in the affairs of the world. 'The outward Churches' are a major instrument of government and are therefore to be numbered among the affairs of the world and they, like laws, the second arm of authority, should concentrate on maintaining decent restraints and observances in society.

What follows especially concerns the use of words:

> Now for these instrumentall following *Arts*,
> Which, in the trafficke of Humanity,
> Afford not matter, but limme out the parts,
> And formes of speaking with authority:
> I say who too long in their cobwebs lurks,
> Doth like him that buyes tooles, but never works.
>
> For whosoever markes the good, or evill,
> As they stand fixed in the heart of Man:
> The one of God, the other of the devill,
> Feele, out of things, Men words still fashion can:
> So that from life since lively words proceed,
> What other *Grammar* doe our natures need?   (Stanzas 102–3.)

The relation between words and things is at the heart of much of Greville's thinking and is crucial to his conception of the style and material of poetry. He has scorned intellectual speculation, however refined and however ingenious, which fails to produce substantial knowledge, and he rejects also the branches of learning which deal in verbal niceties, erecting mental structures without foundation in truth and experience. Logic is learning of this kind, ripe for reform. Modes of argument which depend only on verbal subtleties must be got rid of, and only such precepts be admitted:

> As without words may be conceiv'd in minde.

Rhetoric similarly hides the truth which it pretends to serve 'with the painted skinne of many words':

> Whereas those words in every tongue are best,
> Which doe most properly expresse the thought;

For as of pictures, which should manifest
The life, we say not that is fineliest wrought,
Which fairest simply showes, but faire and like:
*So words must sparkes be of those fires they strike.*

For the true Art of *Eloquence* indeed
Is not this craft of words, but formes of speech,
Such as from living wisdomes doe proceed;
Whose ends are not to flatter, or beseech,
Insinuate, or perswade, but to declare
What things in Nature good, or evill are.   (Stanzas 109–10.)

After rhetoric comes poetry, and with it music, 'arts of recreation' both, as Greville describes them, 'esteem'd as idle mens profession' because their effective power is strictly limited. They can move men by pleasing but they cannot make any real change in their natures:

This makes the solid Judgements give them place,
Onely as pleasing sauce to dainty food;
Fine foyles for jewels, or enammels grace,
Cast upon things which in themselves are good;
Since *if the matter be in Nature vile,*
*How can it be made pretious by a stile?*   (Stanza 112.)

Greville is following his usual method here. As with the whole subject of human learning, he begins with a slighting account of the human activity, dismissing it as a worthless thing relative to the wisdom of God or the purity of mind necessary for salvation; but having established the true scale of values he is willing to grant a modified usefulness to human arts in the sphere of this life. So of poetry and music he grants that 'in this Life, both these play noble parts.' Music is justified by its power to rouse appropriate emotions in worship, and also in war. The juxtaposition of these two 'noble' uses may strike a modern reader as cynicism but it would be unhistoric to ascribe this point of view to Greville. The combination of ideas here illustrates a characteristic situation, for when he turned his mind to the things of this world he firmly held that a clear-eyed pragmatism was not only appropriate but also fully consistent with his theology.

He does not, all the same, count its capacity to move a warlike spirit among the virtues of poetry, though Sidney had done so. He gives it instead an exclusively moral function of a high order:

> The other twinne [i.e. poetry], if to describe, or praise
> Goodnesse, or God she her *Ideas* frame,
> And like a Maker, her creations raise
> On lines of truth, it beautifies the same;
> And while it seemeth onely but to please,
> Teacheth us order under pleasures name;
> Which in a glasse, shows Nature how to fashion,
> Her selfe againe, by ballancing of passion.   (Stanza 114.)

Both music and poetry are, consequently, legitimate activities 'not pretious in their proper kind' and a 'disease of mind' if studied for their own sakes, but capable of exerting useful influences. Poetry cannot raise a man to virtue but it can propose ideal images for his contemplation and it can teach. Both poetry and music are:

> *ornaments to life, and other Arts,*
> *Whiles they doe serve, and not possesse our hearts.*

Arithmetic, Geometry, and Astronomy are considered next, and Greville is again concerned to discredit theoretic speculation and to insist on practical application. This attitude is constant throughout the varying contexts of the treatise and is summed up with a generality that includes all particular applications, including especially, of course, the duty of man to God, in the concluding stanzas of the poem where Greville pulls together all the threads of his discussion:

> For onely that man understands indeed,
> And well remembers, which he well can doe;
> The *Laws live, onely where the Law doth breed,*
> *Obedience to the workes it bindes us to:*
> And as the life of Wisedome hath exprest,
> If this you know, then doe it, and be blest.   (Stanza 140.)

To seek knowledge 'merely but to know' is idle curiosity; to use it for the benefit of others is charity; but the first duty of the individual is to 'build' himself on 'that *sure rocke of truth*; *Gods Word, or Penne*.'

So finally, Greville admits learning, hedged against irreverent enquiry into the secrets of the deity on the one hand and impractical theoretical speculation on the other, and founded on a knowledge of the weakness of 'this fraile fall'n humane kinde'. The pursuit of knowledge must never seduce us into love of the world:

> we must not to the world erect
> Theaters, nor plant our Paradise in dust,
> Nor build up *Babels* for the Divels elect;
> Make temples of our hearts to God we must;
> And then, as *Godlesse wisdomes follies be*,
> So are his lights our true Philosophie.   (Stanza 147.)

The whole poem is a very striking working out of the situation which developed from the impact of Calvinism and Humanism upon each other. The experience it reflects and the problems arising from it were not at all uncommon even before Bacon and the new philosophy called all in doubt, but the new learning and Bacon's glowing vision of modern progress naturally sharpened the issues involved. Professor Bullough sees Greville's *Treatie of Humane Learning* as being in part an answer to Bacon's *Advancement of Learning* and there are many points of contact between the two works. Greville's insistence on the practical application of learning is Baconian and the description of the four classes of idols in *Novum Organum* comes close to Greville's estimate of the impediments to knowledge. The differences between Bacon and Greville are at the same time perfectly evident. Bacon acknowledges 'that general map of the world, that *all things are vanity and vexation of spirit*',[16] and he is well aware that the mind of man is, as he puts it, 'like an enchanted glass, full of superstition and imposture, if it be not delivered and reduced',[17] but his emphasis falls differently from Greville's, on to the note of confidence, enthusiasm and excitement: 'This it is then which I have in hand, and am labouring with mighty effort to accomplish – namely to make the mind of man by help of art a match for the nature of things, – to discover an art of Indication and Direction whereby all other arts with their axioms and works may be detected and brought to light.'[18] 'Arts', in Bacon's use of the word, are associated with hope. They denote the skills man may acquire which will relieve his estate and lead him into a land bright with promise. 'The enlarging of the bonds of human empire, to the

14—F.G.

effecting of all things possible'[19] is a prospect of immense dimension which man has scarcely begun to explore.

When Greville writes of 'arts', the word rings very differently:

> *What then are all these humane Arts, and lights,*
> *But Seas of errors? In whose depths who sound,*
> *Of Truth finde onely shadowes, and no ground.*
>
> (*Humane Learning*, stanza 34.)

Arts work on nature, but not, in Greville's eyes, to improve it – rather to flatter and deceive. They are 'Formes of Opinion, Wit, and Vanity', '*strange Chimeras*', testimonies of nothing but man's sin. In the *Treatise of Religion* the language is the same. Some abuse religion by making it:

> nothing else but Art
> To master others of their owne degree,
> Enthrall the simple well-believing hart.   (Stanza 30.)

Sin and error wander in 'arts and pompes'. The holy disciplines of faith and obedience are unacceptable to arts:

> those riddles of the sinne
> Which error first creates, and then inherits;
> This light consumes those mists they florishe in,
> At once deprives their glorie, and their merits:
> Those mortall formes, moulded in humane error,
> Dissolve themselves by looking in this mirror.   (Stanza 107.)

Of course, arts must in the end be admitted for worldly use, but chastened and cleansed, and severely subordinated to practical utility. Sciences should be drawn from nature, arts should be drawn from practice, never out of books: the ideas sound congenial to Bacon, but the spirit which informs them is not. Greville sees no wide horizons opening through 'arts' and his use of the word is tinged always with distrust if not contempt.

If the *Treatie of Humane Learning* was written as a counterstatement to the *Advancement of Learning*, it would probably have been composed not long after the appearance of Bacon's book in 1605. Professor G. A. Wilkes argues,[20] on other grounds, that it comes very late in Greville's career and he minimizes the connection with Bacon. The chronology of Greville's works as a whole is bedevilled with uncertainties, and external evidence is lacking here as elsewhere. It is true that Bacon and Greville cover much common ground and that their works can be read as thesis and anti-thesis, but this is not enough to establish a deliberately close relationship between them. As has been pointed out already in this chapter, the extent to which man could redeem himself from original sin by knowledge was a question with which men of the sixteenth and seventeenth centuries were concerned both before and after Bacon and the same arguments, with varying emphasis according to the cast of mind of the writer, are likely to occur whenever the subject is handled. Greville's acquaintance with Bacon may very probably have given a special impetus to his own thoughts on the subject and he may even have drafted a version of his treatise on this impulse, but whether it took final shape then or whether he worked on it again at any other time in his long life, the Baconian influence alone will not decide.

Greville's attitude to learning in general has an important bearing on his attitude to literature, but the remarks on poetry in the treatise which have been quoted are of special interest. The insistence throughout that words should have reference to experience and not be employed to create self-contained structures devised merely for the sake of their ingenuity or prettiness seems to imply a diction of resolute plainness and a style limited only to declaration, with insinuation or persuasion rejected as illegitimate. But Greville allows for beauty and he allows also a subtler effectiveness to poetry than at first seems likely. If poetry raises her creations 'on lines of truth', they gain in beauty and, furthermore, while poetry seems only to minister to our delight it also 'teacheth us order under pleasures name'. There is something more than straightforward didacticism involved here. Harmony and proportion and decorum are all contributors to 'order', and Greville has gone some way towards admitting aesthetic pleasure as an instrument of moral good. An earlier stanza on the subject of rhetoric adds another touch. 'Scarcity of words', Greville writes, 'forced' rhetoric at first to use 'Metaphorike wings' because, he goes on:

> no language in the earth affords
> Sufficient Characters to expresse all things.

Rhetoric has since abused the power of metaphor, 'playes the wanton with this need', but metaphor is not to be eschewed on this account. The stanza which follows, insisting that:

>        those words in every tongue are best,
>    Which doe most properly expresse the thought

goes on to compare language to painting and to claim that it is not beauty alone which is admirable in a picture but its faithfulness to the object represented. Greville drives home his point with a metaphor:

> *So words must sparkes be of those fires they strike.*    (Stanza 109.)

Metaphor, a picture in words, is thus admitted as a means of effective statement and most certainly Greville himself uses it. 'Vain wombs' and 'false moulds' occur elsewhere in Greville's poetry to denote the tainted sources of human knowledge and the perverse forms of human institutions but they are the common coin of the vocabulary of the *Treatie of Humane Learning*. The language is in fact highly metaphoric throughout, whether in a stanza composed of a tissue of images like number 38, or in a passing reference as in stanza 36, lines 1 and 2. Once there is an extended image of some beauty, in stanza 72:

> Besides, Where *Learning*, like a *Caspian Sea*,
> Hath hitherto receiv'd all little brookes,
> Devour'd their sweetnesse, borne their names away,
> And in her greenesse hid their chrystall lookes;
> Let her turne *Ocean* now, and give backe more
> To those cleare Springs, than she receiv'd before.

Quite often Greville makes use of the allusive power of metaphor, as in stanza 4:

> No marvell then, if proud desires reflexion,
> By gazing on this Sunne, doe make us blinde,
> Nor if our Lust, Our *Centaure*-like Affection,
> Instead of Nature, fadome clouds and winde,
> So adding to originall defection,
> As no man knowes his owne unknowing minde:
> And our *Aegyptian* darkness growes so grosse,
> As we may easily in it, feele our losse.

Classical fable and a biblical plague combine to illustrate Calvinist theology here, and throughout Greville's work the 'lively images'[21] of the poets' fables are drawn on for their telling statement of truths of human conduct. Poets, Greville writes in *A Treatise of Monarchy*, are:

> In *Ideas* farr more free,
> Then any other arts of mortall brest.    (Stanza 476.)

His attitude seems to be the same as Sidney's when he spoke of the poet's liberty of 'freely ranging onely within the Zodiack of his own wit'. That is to say, the poet's inventions, because they are limited only by his imaginative capacity and not by anything external, are in peculiarly sympathetic accord with the moral experience of humanity and because of this they compel recognition and assent. Greville's use of the illustrative power of fables is, consequently, distinguished from heavy-handed allegorizing by virtue of the fact that he recognizes and exploits the imaginative vitality of the 'speaking picture' which the poets' fables provide.

All in all, *A Treatie of Humane Learning* tells us a great deal about Greville's intellectual attitudes in general and his practice of poetry in particular. The juxtaposition in his mind of belief in the absolute worthlessness of human achievements, and the relative worth of some of them, has been described. As for poetry, when he considers it absolutely, he sees it as an idle thing:

> Then what is our high-prais'd *Philosophie*,
> But bookes of Poesie, in Prose compil'd?
> Farre more delightfull than they fruitfull be,

but when he considers it relatively, though he insists that all the arts of language must be subordinate to the soundness of the subject-matter, yet he finds room for beauty, 'order', and imagery. Sometimes, he knows, meaning can only be communicated by metaphor, and this kind of language comes naturally to him. He uses it for effects of divers kinds whenever he writes, for it was in part a natural consequence of his translating of moral and theological doctrines into the terms of their practical application that he should think largely in images. This feature of his style, indeed, while it adds vividness, also contributes considerably to the difficulty of reading him, for what his language often provides is, so to speak, the second term of the equation from which we have to work back to construct the whole thought. The result can make for a very tough texture of discourse, requiring unremitting intellectual exertion on the part of the reader.

The combination in the *Treatie of Humane Learning* of a rigorous relativism, by which poetry and all the arts of men are rejected as dross in comparison with the works of the spirit, and at the same time a recognition and care for the properties of language and the image-making faculty, might in another man have led to an uneasy dualism in his approach to his own work. But Greville was essentially a strong-minded and a consistent thinker. Having begun on the pursuit of poetry and found its power and its attractiveness for him personally, he sought then to use and develop its skills for the sake of the higher truth by the side of which no purely artistic pleasure could be worth a moment's concern, but in the service of which, nevertheless, art might so refine itself as to attain a qualified merit. The history of Greville's endeavour to make poetry capable of truth is the history of his career as a poet. The essential features which characterize this emerge particularly clearly in Greville's relation with his younger disciple, Samuel Daniel, and the tracing of this association will help to bring into focus what has emerged so far, from the study of separate works, about the nature and degree of Greville's achievement as a poet.

# 9 · Poetry and truth

The political and intellectual associations of Greville's lifetime were many and various. His poetical associations were with two men preeminently, Sidney and Daniel. It was from Sidney that Greville received the first impulse to write, at first when he and Sidney and Dyer were all young together and writing was one of the expressions of their companionship, and later when, frustrated in his attempts to see service overseas, he settled down to follow Sidney's example and put into verse what he could not put into action. As he writes of this decision in the *Life of Sidney*, he makes it sound as though literature were an alternative form of public service, another way of putting one's gifts and education at the service of the State and one's fellow men. It is not play, or self-expression, or the pursuit of beauty, but rather an extension of action or a substitute for it.

He refers to Sidney as his example in all this but, to modern eyes at least, he misinterprets his master; for Sidney's perception of the values of the imagination in itself seems to be lost on him and he is uneasy even with the fictions of *Arcadia*. 'For my own part,' he writes, 'I found my creeping Genius more fixed upon the Images of Life, than the Images of Wit.' It is true that when Greville writes the *Life of Sidney* he is a much older man than Sidney was when he died, but it is not age alone which makes the tone of the parts of the *Life* which deal with his own and Sidney's writings very different from that of the *Apologie for Poetry*. Greville's whole approach to the business of poetry was fundamentally different from that of his friend, though it seems likely that the real nature of his own attitude only became clear to him after Sidney's death and he may never have seen how far it was from

Sidney's. To juxtapose a comment of Chapman's and a line from the third chorus of Greville's play *Alaham* is to bring out sharply the essential quality of Greville's distinctive attitude to poetry. The subject-matter of poetry, Chapman wrote, 'is not truth, but things like truth'. In the third chorus of *Alaham* the good spirits confront the evil spirits and part of the general condemnation of them which they make is that: 'Not truth, but truth-like grounds is that you worke upon.'

We are presented here as distinctly as possible with the central fact concerning Greville's poetry: that he wants to find a way to project truth as he sees it, not incidentally or by oblique methods, but so that the images and the statements will have a direct impact upon the reader and etch themselves upon his mind. His endeavour is to burn away adventitious ornament and to make his verse capable of intellectual argument and moral discrimination of the most rigorous kind.

In the 1590s he found a disciple, Samuel Daniel. Daniel was some eight years younger than Greville and he may already have been a dependent in the household of Sidney's sister, the Countess of Pembroke, when Greville first met him. Some of his sonnets from the *Delia* sequence were published in a pirated edition of *Astrophil and Stella* in 1591 and this would certainly have been enough to draw Greville's attention to him as it did the Countess of Pembroke's. Daniel was scholarly and retiring and, having no means of his own, dependent upon patronage for his livelihood. Greville was independent and wealthy and his active, worldly-wise career puts him to all appearances at the opposite pole from Daniel. But their common acquaintance with the Countess of Pembroke brought them together and they were drawn to one another by affinity of mind. Circumstances obliged Daniel to accommodate himself to the tastes of others and temperament made him particularly susceptible to influence. The impact of Greville's strong mind and firm ideas about the potentialities of poetry made a great impression upon him. Wilton, the Pembroke seat, was a place where poetry was taken very seriously, and Daniel had already been urged by one of the circle, Spenser, to 'rouze his feathers'[1] and take a higher flight than that represented by his love poetry. Lady Pembroke herself had enlisted him to fight for culture and learning by composing a Senecan drama, *Cleopatra*, in defiance of 'this tyrant of the North: Grosse Barbarisme'.[2] Greville extended yet further his conception of the range and power of poetry and Daniel's comments enable us to see fairly clearly the lines on which their discussions proceeded.

Daniel's *Musophilus* (1599) was designed as a 'generall defence of all learning', a large undertaking about which Daniel is characteristically nervous, but he is confident that Greville will support the enterprise:

And if herein the curious sort shall deeme
My will was carried far beyond my force,
And that it is a thing doth ill beseeme
The function of a *Poem* to discourse:
Thy learned judgement which I most esteeme
(Worthy *Fulke Grevil*) must defend this course.   (lines 995–1000)

It was with Greville that Daniel tried over his arguments for *A Defence of Ryme*. As Daniel says, Campion's *Observations in the Art of English Poesie* of 1602 prompted him to write 'a private letter, as a defence of mine owne undertakings in that kinde [i.e. rhyme] to a learned Gentleman a great friend of mine, then in Court,' and the *Biographia Britannica* of 1750 amplifies this with the statement that Daniel and Greville exchanged a number of letters

> upon some improvements or reformation that had been proposed
> to be made, in the masques, interludes, or other dramatical enter-
> tainments at Court. . . . Their sentiments they also exchanged in
> writing upon the topic of our English versification, about the
> time that Daniel had his controversy with Dr. Campion there-
> upon, and Sir Fulke's judgement is often applauded, with his
> munificence to several practitioners therein.

These letters, unfortunately, can no longer be found. What Greville thought about attempts to introduce quantitative scansion in English can probably be deduced from the pages of Sidney's *Apologie for Poetry* and Daniel's *Defence of Ryme* and from the fact that only one exper- iment in classical scansion is known to be his (*Caelica* VI). It would be interesting to have his comments on masques, those fragile and ephemeral productions of which his friend Francis Bacon said 'these things are but toys'. To guess at Greville's views from Daniel's prac- tice, it seems likely that Greville may have been at least partly re- sponsible for the ambiguities in Daniel's attitude to the two masques that he himself wrote, *The Vision of the Twelve Goddesses* (1604) and *Tethys Festival* (1610). The basis of *The Vision of the Twelve Goddesses* is a serious allegory of State, a 'hieroglyphic of empire and dominion', and Daniel justifies his approach in his dedication of the printed version to the Countess of Bedford: 'these ornaments and delights of peace are in their season, as fit to entertaine the world, and deserve to be made memorable as well as the graver actions – both of them concurring to the decking and furnishing of glory and Majesty, as the necessary complements requisit for State and Greatnesse'; but at the same time, both here and in his preface to *Tethys Festival*, he speaks slightingly of the form itself as being unworthy of serious attention. 'Dreames and shewes' he calls the masque, and those who provide them are merely 'the poore Inginers for shadowes and frame onely images of no result'. He goes on in the preface to *Tethys Festival* to combine typical Grevillean themes with some more distinctively his own in a splendidly-worded retort to the critics who have disparaged him:

> Seeing there is nothing done or written, but incounters with detraction and opposition; which is an excellent argument of all our imbecilities and might allay our presumption, when we shall see our greatest knowledges not to be fixt, but rowle according to the uncertaine motion of opinion, and controwleable by any surly shrew of reason; which we do find is double edged and strikes every way alike. And therefore I do not see why any man should rate his owne at that valew, and set so low prises upon other mens abilities. L'homme vaut l'homme, a man is worth a man, and none hath gotten so high a station of understanding, but he shall find others that are built on an equall floore with him, and have as far a prospect as he; which when al is done, is but in a region subject to al passions and imperfections.

In 1593–4 Daniel left the Pembroke household and soon after came under the protection of Charles Blount, Lord Mountjoy, Essex's friend, and of Greville himself. In April 1595 Greville wrote to Cecil on his behalf asking him to grant the reversion of some property rights in the Isle of Wight as 'a good deed to help the poor man'.[3] Everything suggests that Greville and Daniel remained in close contact for a number of years, working and talking together and discussing a programme for poetry. Under Greville's tuition, Daniel became a 'discourser' in verse, a handler of large subjects and, what was to prove a discomforting development, a theorist about the relations between style and subject. Yet Daniel was not quite the malleable material hoped for by Greville, and by Lady Pembroke too when she induced him to write *Cleopatra*. Suggestible, easily deflected, and easily abashed as to some extent he was, Daniel had in the last analysis a character of his own and his imagination was warmer, more humane, and more sympathetic than Greville's. *Cleopatra*, for all its frigid, neo-classical structure, breathes with the life of an intensely realized study of Cleopatra herself, and *Musophilus*, 'a generall defence of all learning', is very different in tone and character from Greville's *Treatie of Humane Learning*.

The Greville–Pembroke influence may well have damaged Daniel. Greville, in particular, disquieted him and caused him deeply to distrust his own gifts. In *Musophilus* he held enthusiastically the humanist belief in eloquence:

> Powre above powres, O heavenly *Eloquence*,
> That with the strong reine of commanding words,
> Dost manage, guide, and master th'eminence
> Of mens affections, more than all their swords:
> Shall we not offer to thy excellence
> The richest treasure that our wit affoords?
> Thou that canst do much more with one poor pen
> Then all the powres of princes can effect:
> And draw, divert, dispose, and fashion men
> Better then force or rigour can direct:
> Should we this ornament of glorie then
> As th'unmateriall fruits of shades, neglect?   (Lines 939–50.)

As for poetry, he goes on:

> That breeds, brings forth, and nourishes this might,
> Teaching it in a loose, yet measured course,
> With comely motions how to go upright:
> And fostring it with bountifull discourse
> Adorns it thus in fashions of delight,
> What should I say? since it is well approv'd
> The speech of heaven, with whom they have commerce
> That only seeme out of themselves remov'd,
> And do with more then humane skils converse:

Those numbers wherewith heaven and earth are mov'd,
Shew, weakenes speaks in prose, but powre in verse.

(Lines 970–80.)

Four years later, in the *Defence of Ryme*, he is beset by doubts. Eloquence is dismissed as merely 'the garnish of a nice time', and 'the outside of words' is now as nothing compared with the substance to be
conveyed which may appear 'in what habite it will', since 'all these
pretended proportions of words, howsoever placed, can be but words,
and peradventure serve but to embroyle our understanding, whilst
seeking to please our eare, we inthrall our judgement.'

Perhaps the most Grevillean line that Daniel ever wrote occurs near
the beginning of his long historical poem, the *Civill Warres*:

I versify the truth, not poetize.

This was written in the early years of their acquaintance and it reflects
Greville's often scornful use of 'poetry' to denote the fanciful and un-
founded, and his insistence on truth as against 'things like truth'.
Greville himself sustained his endeavour to carve out a poetry of truth,
but Daniel was a poet of a different stamp and Greville's unremitting
analysis of the relation between literary art and the substance of the
poem in the end depressed him. In his dedication of the last instalment
of the *Civill Warres* in 1609 he confesses that he is ready to abandon
poetry:

For mine owne part, I am not so far in love with this form of
Writing (nor have I sworne Fealtie onely to Ryme) but that I
may serve in any other state of Invention, with what weapon of
utterance I will: and so it may make good my minde, I care not.
For, I see, Judgement and Discretion (with whatsoever is worthy)
carry their owne Ornaments, and are grac't with their owne
beauties; be they apparayled in what fashion they will. And
because I finde the common tongue of the world is Prose; I
purpose in that kinde to write the Historie of England.

When Daniel writes his late poetry, it is not Grevillean at all:

Love is a sicknesse full of woes,
    All remedies refusing:

A plant that with most cutting growes,
   Most barren with best using.
            Why so?
More we enjoy it, more it dyes,
If not enjoy'd, it sighing cries,
            Hey ho.

Love is a torment of the minde,
   A tempest everlasting;
And Jove hath made it of a kinde,
   Not well, nor full nor fasting,
            Why so?
More we enjoy it, more it dyes
If not enjoy'd, it sighing cries,
            Hey ho.

The cutting edge of sharp commentary on experience is never so rounded off by Greville for the sake of sheer lyric pleasure, even in his earliest lyrics.

Daniel was intelligent and sensitive, too much aware of too many sides of a question for his own comfort. Greville, by contrast, had a vein of iron in his character. It showed when he screwed the last drop of profit out of his investments and when he preserved through years of exclusion the will and the vigour to come into high public office at the age of sixty. It showed when he retained through a long and active career the memory of the friend of his youth, dead long ago, whose spirit he invoked to measure later contemporaries by and find them wanting; and it shows in his poetry. It is there in the lightest of his lyrics and it stiffens him to persevere in the task which Daniel gave up, the making of poetry out of 'truth' as he conceived it, that is, the unsanctified nature of man and the demands of religion. These are the 'images of Life' which he deals in, and these truths are not to be adorned or adulterated by 'images of Wit'. The 'poetic', that is to say the fictional, is to be eschewed. The garnish of 'sweete hony-dropping' rhetoric is also to be avoided unless it can be justified by its function: words are to be joined to things as they were in Adam's naming of the creation. Daniel followed him for a time, excited by the prospect of establishing a new status for poetry, grander than anything which had so far been allowed it in English:

To see if we our wronged lines could raise
Above the reach of lightnesse and contempt.[4]

But Daniel cared for literature itself, as part of the artistic culture of a civilized society, and he cherished it as an activity whose refinement gave pleasure and was also a way of knowledge. He could never quite give up the aesthetic pleasure of literature. Greville, more rigorous, held always the stance which he ascribed to Sidney: 'his end was not writing, even while he wrote; nor his knowledge moulded for tables, or schooles; but both his wit, and understanding bent upon his heart, to make himself and others, not in words or opinion, but in life, and action good and great.'

Greville never abandoned poetry for prose as Daniel did. His most important prose work, the *Life of Sidney*, is intended as a dedication merely and the *Letter to an Honourable Lady* is unfinished. When he chose poetry as his 'weapon of utterance' in preference to prose, 'the common tongue of the world', he meant to use the heightening power and the discipline of verse to give point and effect to what he had to say. He described poetry as a 'spreading Ocean of images' and images came plentifully to him both in verse and prose. He had at least some parts of the traditional poetic equipment in a very high degree: he handled a variety of verse forms with ease and subtlety and he had a prolific image-making power. There is, in fact, some paradox in the paragraph in which, disclaiming the images of wit, he uses the proverb of the black ox and unrolls one of the sea images which occur so frequently in his works, often with great imaginative effect. The result, finally, is that in Greville we have, not as has often been assumed, a writer of minimal poetic talent working relentlessly to pound his thought into verse form, but a man of natural gifts who worked to discipline them and evolve a new form of poetic language which would bring poetry out of the pupilage of fiction into the 'real' world of 'truth'.

# Appendix

## Further notes on dating

Professor G. A. Wilkes in an article some years ago (*Studies in Philology*, lvi (1959), pages 489–503) argued that the passages in the *Life of Sidney* concerning Greville's treatises (*Life*, pages 152–5, quoted above, pages 120–1) help us to some important facts about the sequence of Greville's writing. He points out that the title which Greville gives to the treatise whose composition he describes in particular detail is *The Declination of Monarchy*, and that when he goes on to speak of 'the rest', the subjects he names are Church, Laws, Nobility, War, and Peace. All these are names given to sections of the treatise we now have called *Of Monarchy*. 'Declination of Monarchy to Violence' is the title of section 2, 'Of Church' is section 6, 'Of Lawes' is section 7, 'Of Nobility' is section 8, 'Of Peace' is section 11, and 'Of Warr' is section 12. Professor Wilkes concludes that it is to these sections that Greville is referring in the *Life* and that the other treatises, *Of Warres*, *Of Religion*, *Upon Fame and Honour* and *Of Humane Learning* had not yet been written. At the time of composing the references in the *Life* Greville was still, apparently, thinking of what later became parts of a single poem as separate treatises. Professor Wilkes deduces that *Of Monarchy* is, at least for the greater part and in its origins, the earliest of the treatises and the others are to be dated after the composition of the *Life*; that is, after 1610–14.

This interpretation of the passage in the *Life* seems, on the face of it, to be very reasonable. If the title *The Declination of Monarchy* which Greville uses were held to cover the first five sections of *Of Monarchy* as we now have it, the section 'Of Church' would immediately follow it and this would accord with Greville's statement that the church is the subject of the first of the treatises which follow *The Declination of Monarchy*. The first five sections, which are at present entitled 'Of the Beginning of Monarchy', 'Declination of Monarchy to Violence', 'Of Weak Minded Tyrants', 'Cautions against these Weake Extremities', and 'Strong Tyrants' could well have been subsumed under the one generic title and could be divided quite appropriately into three parts. In the 1670 text there is a page title over stanzas 185–91 of section 5 reading 'Cautions against Weak Extremities' which although it is plainly wrong as it stands since it repeats, inappropriately, the heading of section 4, may all the same be a useful indication that a parallel section – 'Against Strong Extremities'? – was at some time intended, and if so this would make a neat tripartite arrangement for the material of the present first five sections.

Further study of *Of Monarchy*, unfortunately, casts doubt on Professor Wilkes's neat programme. The language of the *Life* is, as it happens, echoed most closely in the section 'Of Lawes', which is section 7 of *Of Monarchy* and therefore not covered by the title 'The Declination of Monarchy' whether this is held to apply to section 2 alone or to the first five sections of the poem as we have it. The sentence about 'indigested crudities, equally applied to Kings, or Tyrants' has a close parallel in stanzas 320–1 of 'Of Lawes', and in stanza 276 there are references to the 'harsh severity of the *Lacedemonian* Government' and to Athenian learning which might be among those which Greville said he 'forced in' to give the treatise more weight. Stanzas 304–6 provide examples of 'the Roman gravity, and greatnesse' but Roman polity, naturally enough, serves to illustrate many points throughout the poem. As for the reference in the *Life* to a treatise on the church, it could be held to point either to the treatise *Of Religion*, which a note in Greville's hand in the Warwick manuscript directs to be placed before the treatises of Humane Learning, Fame and Honour, and Warre, or to the section 'Of Church' in *Of Monarchy* as Professor Wilkes supposes: but the work which most closely fits the description in the *Life* occurs in section 12, entitled 'Of Warr', and runs from stanza 543 to stanza 566. The passage in the *Life* reads as follows:

> The first limme of those Treatises (I mean that Fabrick of a superstitious Church) having by her masterfull ambition over Emperours, Kings, Princes, free States, and Councels, and her

Conclave deceits, strengths, and unthankfulnesse, spred so far beyond my *Horizon*, as I at once gave over her, and all her derivatives to *Gamaliels* infallible censure; Leaving Lawes, Nobility, War, Peace, and the rest, (as glorious Trophies of our old Pope, the sin) to change, reforme, or become deformed, according as vanity, that limitlesse mother of these Idolatries, should either winne of the truth, or the truth of them. (*Life*, page 155.)

In the section 'Of Warr' Greville first describes war as an inevitable consequence of man's sin, and then goes on to define the causes of 'right and defence' which may be grounds of warfare. He speaks also of the wisdom of maintaining a state of preparedness and of the desir-ability of alliances to safeguard the balance of power. Stanza 543 turns to apply this doctrine to the contemporary situation, and Greville insists that it is of the first importance 'as the tymes now stand' to keep open the cleavage between Catholic and Protestant countries. No vision of wealth or power to be bought by a Catholic alliance is to be toler-ated, for any sacrifice is worthwhile to preserve 'everlastinge health' and this depends on absolute refusal to compromise with the Pope. Tolerance at home or failure to support the enemies of the Catholics abroad are alike disastrous, for:

> This flesh borne Church supremacie,
> Whether form'd in monarchall governemente,
> Or state *Aristocraticall* it be,
> With less then all, can never be content;
> But by the sophistries of witt and will,
> Stryve ever to be head of good and ill. (Stanza 551.)

Kings must learn from her tactics how to counter them: if she makes use of inquisitions, Kings should freely invoke the power of the law and:

> When by confession she seekes to maintaine
> That mapp of secretts, which she doth abuse;
> Then must Kinges by all tryalls gage her neast,
> So as her byrds may neither hatch, nor rest. (Stanza 554.)

If the Catholics plead freedom of conscience, so ought we, and we should be especially on guard to parry the church's attempts to increase her influence abroad. Stanzas 559–61 are strongly denunciatory:

> Trust not their Church with her scope infinite,
> As King-shipps in this worlde, more in the other;
> Heere to seeme greater then refined righte,
> There both of grace and innocence a mother;
> For God, a Pope; for Angells, Cardinalls;
> A Church more overbuilt then Babells walls.

> An outward Church, that must stand as it grew,
> By force, crafte, rapine, and hypocrycie,
> An earthlie faith, even every day made new,
> Builte on the base of ones supremacie;
> A pride borne of that Angells pride that fell,
> Prisinge for Peeters pence, heav'ne, purgatorie, hell.

> Trust not this myter, which forgiveth none,
> But damns all sowles, that be not of her creedes;
> Makes all Saints Idolls, to adorne her throne,
> And reapes vaste wealth from superstitious seeds;
> For must she not with wett, or burnt wings fall,
> Which soares above him, that created all?

This whole sequence of stanzas ends with a statement about the duties of the clergy. They should be:

> greate within, religious true,
> As heralds sent by God to worcke progression
> From synne to grace, and make the old man new.

They should not:

> fall into those common moldes
> Of fraile humanitie, which skandall give

but they should keep decorum in their lives:

> For messingers of heav'ne must still appeare
> As if that heav'ne, not earth, were to them deere.

Finally Greville returns to the point he makes in the *Life*, that in giving his advice he is not distinguishing between kings and tyrants, but he adds:

Yet beames and bodies beinge divers thinges,
Fynelie in shadows may resembled be:
Whence in the outward varienge forme of thinges,
Tyrants may well use rules set downe for Kinges.

All this, with its strongly anti-Catholic bent and its vehement warnings against the temporal ambitions of the Church, seems to correspond much more closely to the tone of the description given in the *Life* than does either the meditative *Of Religion* or the section 'Of Church' in the treatise *Of Monarchy* which treats of church government as a branch of state-craft. 'Of Church' includes an attack on the Roman Catholic church, it is true, but this is comparatively short (stanzas 211–16) and subsidiary to the main material of the section. The anti-Catholic stanzas of section 12 are noticeable, on the other hand, not only because of their vigour but also because they are so tenuously attached to the main line of discussion. The whole passage could in fact be taken out and the treatise would read perfectly well without what at present appears to be an extensive digression.

There is one other feature of the anti-Catholic stanzas of section 12 which relates them to the passage in the *Life* and that is the references to the Pope. The phrase in the *Life* 'glorious Trophies of our old Pope, the sin' is baffling as it stands, but less so if stanzas 546–50 of *Of Monarchy* are used as a commentary on it. The emphasis in these stanzas is on the ambition of the Pope who strives for temporal power and seeks to absorb all rivals. Pride, Greville warns:

had never such an elevation,
As when aspiringe superstition ranged

and pride is an ingrained characteristic of the outward church:

Wherbie she still unform'd lives, till a head
Supreame she findes, or to her self makes many;
A bodie such as must be governed
Within it selfe, not subject unto any;
And in each minute of her nature swells,
Even with that pride, wherwith the whole excells.

There seems to be a common association of ideas in these stanzas and the passage in the *Life* between the Roman church and its supreme head, the Pope, and the sin of pride which dominates the outward church and which infects all the activities of human society, laws, nobility, war, peace, 'and the rest'.

Greville's words in the *Life*, then, do not give us strong grounds on which to construct the probable sequence of his work since we cannot by any means be sure that, supposing the list of themes, Laws, Nobility, etc., does in fact represent titles of treatises (and it is not certain that it does), the works denoted are the sections of *Of Monarchy* which carry similar titles now. It follows that the evidence is not clear enough to support Professor Wilkes's argument that the treatises of *Religion*, *Fame and Honour*, and *Warres* must all be dated after the composition of the *Life of Sidney*. Since we cannot be certain which poems Greville was referring to in the *Life*, we cannot be sure that they did not include versions of these treatises. We cannot be sure either that the *Life of Sidney* was composed in one piece, and there is some evidence that it was not. Between the time of the Shrewsbury manuscript text and those collated by Nowell Smith, Greville rearranged and added to the material of the chapters concerning Sidney's speculations about European policy. The passage about Essex and the three chapters about Queen Elizabeth interrupt Greville's account of his plays and seem likely to be interpolations in an original which did not contain them. The Essex–Elizabeth pages seem almost certain to have been composed in or near 1611 when Greville was angry at Cecil's frustration of his plans to write a history of the preceding reign. If they are additions to an already existing manuscript, there can be no assurance that the situation described in the surrounding material represents the situation in 1611: that is to say, supposing that when Greville wrote about the treatises in the *Life* there existed only a version of *Of Monarchy*, it does not necessarily follow that when he added chapters XV, XVI, and XVII in 1611 or thereabouts he had not written other treatises.

Professor Wilkes's conclusion from his chronological argument is that Greville redefined his attitude to experience at a late stage of his career – i.e. post-1614 – and wrote new poems to expound a new vision. This would surely have to be dismissed even if the chronological evidence he adduces were acceptable. Greville's work and thought do not lend themselves to linear description of such a kind, as this whole book demonstrates.

# Notes

Notes to Chapter 1
1 *Life of Sir Philip Sidney*, ed. Nowell Smith, Clarendon Press, 1907, pp. 73–6.
2 R. Naunton, *Fragmenta Regalia*, Arber's English Reprints, 1869, p. 50.
3 There is a letter from Greville to John Coke at Melbourne Hall in Derbyshire (pkt 15) in which Greville thanks Coke for his 'gatherings' and refers to 'the daintiness of the council chest'. The letter is dated March 1611 and the year may be either old or new style. The reference appears to be to the episode described in the *Life*.
4 *Life of Sidney*, ed. Nowell Smith, pp. 217–20.
5 J. Spedding, *Letters and Life of Francis Bacon*, 1868, iv, p. 219.
6 The sentence occurs in a letter of Greville's (it is printed in *Reports of the Historical Manuscripts Commission*, xii, Appx pt i, p. 77) and in its context it is a piece of self-congratulation for having seen through an untrustworthy servant. There is no hint of any kind of tension as the words appear in the passage.

Notes to Chapter 2
1 The principal sources of the biographical material in this chapter are: (i) *The Dictionary of National Biography*; (ii) *The Victoria County History – Warwickshire*; (iii) J. Edmondson, *An Historical and Genealogical Account of the Noble Family of Greville*, 1766; (iv) F. L. Colville, *The Worthies of Warwickshire*, 1870. Sources other than these are noted below.
2 B. M. Egerton MS. 2988.
3 There is a reference to Greville's claim on the Marquis of Winchester's estates in *Reports of the Historical Manuscripts Commission*, Hatfield 11, p. 584.
4 Elizabeth Willoughby was *de jure* Baroness Willoughby de Broke and when in 1621 Fulke Greville was created Lord Brooke he also requested a barony by right of descent from Robert Willoughby. The claim was disallowed at the time but allowed in 1696 when Sir Richard Verney, grandson of Fulke Greville's sister, Margaret, made the same claim.
5 MS. life of Robert, Lord Brooke, quoted by Edmondson.

6 Ibid.

7 *Calendar of State Papers*, Dom., 1605, Addenda pp. 468–9 The manuscript life of Robert, Lord Brooke, has a fuller account of Sir Fulke's anti-papist energy: 'His zeale and soundnesse in Relligion, made Henry Garnet (that notorious Powder-traytor) provinciall over the Jesuites here in England, take small delight to stay at Coughton a mile off him. Fryars of lesse note must abide the hazard of his search and justice. He had a quick apprehension, and a cleare and prompt judgment. No sooner did he heare of the taking of the great horses, upon the Wednesday morning, from the Castle Stable at Warwicke, by Graunt and Winter, but knowing them to be violent Papists, and calling to minde the insolencie and boldnesse of some other papists, before him in his course of justice; he presentlie concluded, from those premises, that the papists had some dangerous Treason a foot, and therefore made speedie preparation, to crush the horride Serpent at the first breaking out of the shell. . . .'

8 *Calendar of State Papers*, Dom., 1605, p. 271.

9 Somerset House 99, Huddlestone.

10 *Reports of the Historical Manuscripts Commission*, Hatfield 18, p. 348.

11 *Reports of the Historical Manuscripts Commission*, xii, Appx pt i, pp. 27–8. The letter dates from about 1600.

12 E. I. Fripp, *Master Richard Quyny*, O.U.P., 1924, p. 83.

13 *Reports of the Historical Manuscripts Commission*, Hatfield 11, p. 433. There is a quaint account in the manuscript life of Robert, Lord Brooke. Before Fulke Greville acquired the castle, the writer (Thomas Spencer) says, it 'for a time became a neglected desert; only Caesars Tower was an uncouth prison of felonious persons clogd with fetters and bolts of yron. But the rest was an habitation of night-monsters, a court of satyres, an house of hagges, a dwelling of the scritch-owle, and the flying mouse. . . .' Greville, he adds, when it came into his possession, 'built a faire wall of stone about the Orchards and Gardens which he had there planted, restored it to its former strength, beautie, and magnificence. . . .'

14 Warwick Castle MS. 2829.

15 Ibid. 2556.

16 W. Dugdale, *The Antiquities of Warwickshire*, editions of 1765 and 1786.

17 Warwick Castle MS. 6767.

18 'Iter Boreale', in Chalmers's English Poets, v, 1810.

19 J. Nicolls, *Progresses of James I*, 1828, iii, p. 431.

20 *Reports of the Historical Manuscripts Commission*, xii, Appx pt i, p. 88.

21 Ibid., p. 110.

22 J. E. Neale, *The Elizabethan House of Commons*, Penguin Books, 1949, pp. 48–9.

23 *Acts of the Privy Council*, 1601–1604, pp. 247–8.

24 *Reports of the Historical Manuscripts Commission*, xii, Appx pt i, pp. 39, 69–71, 86. See also Greville's will.

25 Ibid., pp. 64–7.

26 Warwick Castle MS. 2701. I am making use of a transcript kindly given to me by Mr Philip Styles, Reader in History at the University of Birmingham.

27 *Calendar of State Papers* Dom., 1595–7, p. 444; *Reports of the Historical Manuscripts Commission*, xii, Appx pt i, pp. 50–1.
28 The City Archivist of Coventry has kindly supplied me with copies of three letters in his care, dated 1592.
29 Staffordshire County Record Office, Anglesey Collection D/1734/2/10.
30 Staffordshire County Record Office Xerox copies of early Paget correspondence, vol. ix, f. 91.
31 Folger Library MS. L.a. 482.
32 Ibid., L.a. 483.
33 Ibid., L.a. 679 and L.a. 939.
34 Ibid., L.a. 1048 and 1050.
35 Ibid., L.a. 339, and *Reports of the Historical Manuscripts Commission*, Hatfield 6, p. 96.
36 Folger MS. L.a. 926.
37 *Reports of the Historical Manuscripts Commission*, xii, Appx pt i, pp. 27–8.
38 Staffordshire County Record Office, early Paget correspondence, vol. xi, f. 78.
39 *Reports of the Historical Manuscripts Commission*, Hatfield 6, p. 37.
40 *Reports of the Historical Manuscripts Commission*, xii, Appx pt i, p. 365.
41 A scurrilous poem of the time which accuses Greville of being parsimonious is printed in *Inedited Poetical Miscellanies 1584–1700* edited by W. C. Hazlitt, 1870, and by A. B. Grosart in volume i of his edition of Greville's *Works*, pp. xcix–c. The tone and substance of these verses are such that it seems very unlikely they were based on real information and they cannot be taken seriously as a comment on Greville's character.
42 *Reports of the Historical Manuscripts Commission*, xii, Appx pt 4, p. 487.
43 Edmondson writes (p. 86) that he 'was buried with great solemnity; sir William Segar, Knight, garter; sir Henry St George, Knight, Richmond herald; and Henry Chitting, esquire, Somerset herald, directing the funeral.'
44 Extracts from Greville's letter and Coke's reply are printed in *Reports of the Historical Manuscripts Commission*, xii, Appx pt i, pp. 89–91. The Report unfortunately omits all the detailed comments which Coke made on the drafts submitted to him by Greville and these are particularly interesting since Coke quotes a number of lines from Greville's verses in the course of his comments. These lines exist nowhere else and the full text of the letters affords an interesting glimpse of a Greville poem in the making as well as, in Coke's comments, a piece of seventeenth century 'practical criticism'. I have printed the relevant extracts in an article, 'Greville's Epitaph on Sir Philip Sidney' in *Review of English Studies*, New Series xix (1968), pages 47–51. A very recent article by N. K. Farmer Jnr, 'Fulke Greville and Sir John Coke: An Exchange of Letters on a History Lecture and Certain Latin Verses on Sir Philip Sidney', discusses the letters from an historian's point of view and adds some new information. (*Huntington Library Quarterly* xxxii (May 1970), pp. 217–36.)
45 Bullough's edition, i, p. 275.
46 Quoted in W. Benham, *Old St Paul's Cathedral*, 1902, p. 21.
47 Its size invites the speculation that Greville transferred his designs, or some version of them, for the tomb in St Paul's to Warwick, but this does not appear to be so. Dr Pevsner describes the tomb in St Mary's as a six-poster

with two tiers of black columns, the lower carrying arches, the upper standing against the blank attic storey. There are top pediments and corner obelisks. The sarcophagus is black with big Roman lettering and no effigy. It is the work of Thomas Ashby. (*Warwickshire*, pp. 447–8.) Greville describes the projected monument in St Paul's to Coke in quite different terms. See pp. 22–4.

### Notes to Chapter 3

1 Greville prepared a report for the Queen on trading conditions in the East Indies as early as 1600. He was concerned with the company again many years later. *Annals of the Honourable East India Company*, ed. J. Bruce (1810), i, pp. 121–6; *Calendar of State Papers*, E. Indies, 1622–4, pp. 158, 409.

2 The manuscript life of Robert, Lord Brooke, says of Greville's choice of his heir that he [Greville] had 'a great desire to continue and support his owne name in the Countie of Warwick. And so much the rather because he did foresee the ruine and decay of Milcote house which did come to pass in his dayes. . . . Wherefore he did cast a fatherlie affection, upon Robert Grevill, the next braunch of the line male of his owne house, being his Uncle Roberts grandchild, tooke him at the age of foure yeeres, and carefullie provided for his education and breeding, that he might be fit, for that estate and dignitie, which he did purpose one day to conferre upon him.'

3 *Life of Sidney*, ed. Nowell Smith, pp. 146–8.

4 *Acts of the Privy Council*, 1588, p. 168. B.M. Harley MS. 286, f. 144.

5 *Calendar of State Papers*, Ireland, vol. lxxiv, nos. 28, 58: vol. lxxv, no. 37.

6 See especially *Reports of the Historical Manuscripts Commission*, Hatfield 7, p. 370, where Greville writes enthusiastically of the *Triumph*, which he was later to command.

7 *Calendar of State Papers*, Dom., 1598–1601, *passim* for references to Greville's activities in this office.

8 Ibid., p. 282; W. L. Clowes, *The Royal Navy*, 1897, i, p. 529.

9 *Reports of the Historical Manuscripts Commission*, Hatfield 8, pp. 347–8.

10 Ibid., Hatfield 9, p. 336.

11 J. Nichols, *Progresses of Queen Elizabeth*, 1823, iii, p. 60 f.; G. Peele, *Polyhymnia*.

12 *Reports of the Historical Manuscripts Commission*, Hatfield 9, pp. 4, 162.

13 *Reports of the Historical Manuscripts Commission*, xii, Appx pt i, pp. 27–8.

14 Ibid., De L'Isle and Dudley, ii, p. 448.

15 *Sidney Papers*, ed. Collins, ii, p. 147.

16 *Calendar of State Papers*, Dom., 1603–10, p. 182.

17 See for example *Sidney Papers*, ii, pp. 65, 8, and *Reports of the Historical Manuscripts Commission*, Hatfield 8, p. 168.

18 J. Harington, *Nugae Antiquae*, 1779, ii, p. 265.

19 *Calendar of State Papers*, Dom., 1603–10, p. 24.

20 *Reports of the Historical Manuscripts Commission*, xii, Appx pt i, pp. 50–5.

21 Lansdowne 88, ff. 123 and 125, quoted by Grosart in the Memorial Introduction of his edition of Greville's *Works*.

22 *Calendar of State Papers*, Dom., 1603–10, p. 98.

23 G. Bullough, *Modern Language Review*, xxviii (1933), pp. 1–20.

24 *Calendar of State Papers*, Dom., 1603–10, pp. 110 and 192; *Reports of the Historical Manuscripts Commission*, Hatfield 16, p. 357.

25 *Reports of the Historical Manuscripts Commission*, Hatfield 17, p. 597.

26 Ibid., Hatfield 16, pp. 196–7.

27 Ibid., Hatfield 17, pp. 364–5.

28 Lansdowne 89, f. 140, quoted Grosart, Memorial Introduction.

29 *Reports of the Historical Manuscripts Commission*, Hatfield 18, p. 348.

30 Ibid., Hatfield 19, pp. 96–7.

31 Penry Williams, *The Council in the Marches of Wales under Elizabeth I*, 1958.

32 *Calendar of State Papers*, Dom., 1603–10, p. 364.

33 *Reports of the Historical Manuscripts Commission*, Hatfield 19, pp. 256, 324.

34 *Calendar of State Papers* Dom., 1603–10, p. 373.

35 *Reports of the Historical Manuscripts Commission*, Portland Manuscripts, vol. ix, pp. 142–3.

36 P. M. Handover, *Arbella Stuart*, 1957.

37 *Reports of the Historical Manuscripts Commission*, Portland MS., vol. ix, p. 39.

38 Ibid., xii, Appx pt i, p. 77.

39 *Calendar of State Papers*, Dom., 1611–18, pp. 256, 257.

40 *Lives and Letters of the Devereux, Earls of Essex*, ed. W. B. Devereux, 1853, ii, p. 265.

41 J. Nichols, *Progresses of James I*, 1828, iii, p. 172.

42 See *Calendar of State Papers*, Col. E. Indies for 1617–21, p. 239; 1622–4, pp. 409–12; and *Calendar of State Papers*, Dom., 1625–6, p. 19.

43 *Calendar of State Papers*, Dom., 1623–5, p. 214; 1625–6, pp. 7, 328; S. R. Gardiner, *History of England, 1603–42*, 1883, v, pp. 223, 323.

44 *Calendar of State Papers*, Venetian, 1625–6, p. 21. Professor Bullough, in *Modern Language Review*, xxviii (1933), p. 16, states that at the beginning of 1627 Greville obtained a new sinecure, as Deputy Vice-Admiral for the Isle of Wight, and Grosart (vol. iv) gives references to this appointment and to affairs connected with it (it was clearly not a sinecure) in *Calendar of State Papers*, Dom., 1627–8, 1628–9, and even 1629–31. Apart from the fact, which Grosart notes with an exclamation mark, that Greville died in 1628, the appointee is always referred to as Sir Fulke Greville and the sort of thing said of him and the kind of duties required of him clearly relate to a younger and less well-known man than the senior statesman who had been Lord Brooke since 1621 and who in 1627 was seventy-three years of age.

45 Quoted in J. Spedding, *Letters and Life of Lord Bacon*, 1868, v, pp. 200–1.

46 *Calendar of State Papers*, Dom., 1625–6, p. 9.

47 *Reports of the Historical Manuscripts Commission*, xii, Appx pt i, p. 232.

48 *Calendar of State Papers*, Dom., 1625–6, p. 133.

49 *Reports of the Historical Manuscripts Commission*, xii, Appx pt i, p. 217.

50 The consistency with which Greville read domestic and foreign affairs in terms of Catholic–Protestant antagonism is seen again in his welcome of the news that Bishop Williams was to be replaced as Lord Keeper by Coventry (*Reports of the Historical Manuscripts Commission*, xii, Appx pt i, pp. 230–1). Gardiner's comment on the new appointment also indicates a strong reason for Greville's support of Buckingham: 'His [Coventry's] accession to office . . .

was one more announcement of the Protestant tendencies of Buckingham' (*History of England*, vi, p. 32).

51 These letters are Harleian MS. 1581 f. 270; and Tanner MS. vol. lxxiii, f. 382. They are quoted in Grosart's Memorial Introduction.

52 *Reports of the Historical Manuscripts Commission*, xii, Appx pt i, pp. 89–90. This was not the first time Greville had concerned himself with the furthering of learning by an academic appointment. In 1604 he recommended a scholar for a lectureship at Gresham College and solicited Cecil's support for his candidate. The joint advocacy of Cecil and Greville was successful and it is worth noting, since Greville at his death was charged with meanness, that he adds in his letter to Cecil: 'I have satisfied the competitor to the full [i.e. given financial compensation to an unsuccessful rival for the post], lest the honour you did me should anyways prove envious to you' (*Reports of the Historical Manuscripts Commission*, Hatfield 16, p. 176). Of course this might have been politic generosity.

53 *Calendar of State Papers*, Dom., 1623–5, p. 446.

54 *Calendar of State Papers*, Dom., 1627–8, p. 470.

55 Christopher Hill, *Intellectual Origins of the English Revolution*, 1965, adds to his account of Dorislaus's Cambridge experiences: 'Dorislaus's one lecture, and his silencing, seem to have made a strong impression on at least one young Cambridge man – John Milton', and he refers to the 5th and 7th Prolusions (p. 176). Some details of this affair are included in R. Parr, *The Life of Ussher*, London, 1686, pp. 393–4, and J. B. Mullinger, *The University of Cambridge*, iii, pp. 83–9, C.V.P., 1911.

56 *Reports of the Historical Manuscripts Commission*, xii, Appx pt i, pp. 370, 427, 449.

57 A. à Wood, *Athenae Oxonienses*, 1815, ii, p. 342.

58 W. Camden, *Britain*, 1610, under 'Warwickshire', pp. 565–6.

59 J. Speed, *Prospects of the most famous parts of the World*, Book i, f. 49–50. Quoted from *John Speed's England*, Phoenix House, 1954. Also *Calendar of State Papers*, Dom., 1598–1601, p. 62.

60 *Reports of the Historical Manuscripts Commission*, Hatfield 11, pp. 236, 246.

61 Wood, *Athenae Oxonienses*.

62 *Reports of the Historical Manuscripts Commission*, Hatfield 5, p. 166. See also my book *Samuel Daniel*, Liverpool University Press, 1964, pp. 62–7.

63 In *Statesmen and Favourites of England since the Reformation*, 1670, p. 728.

64 E. K. Chambers, *William Shakespeare*, Oxford University Press, 1930, ii, p. 250.

65 Davenant was Shakespeare's godson and some said his natural son. Davenant did not discourage the rumour.

66 They are printed in *Letters and Life of Bacon*, ed. J. Spedding, i, pp. 298, 302, 359; and also in Grosart, i, pp. lxiv–lxviii.

67 *Letters and Life of Bacon*, v, p. 135. Spedding quotes a letter (ii, pp. 21–6) which he dates 1595–6, signed by Essex but probably composed, Spedding believes, by Bacon. It is in reply to a request from Greville for advice about the best way of making use of amanuenses. He is going to Cambridge and wishes to employ 'gatherers', i.e. men who will read and make notes for him. It is a

splendid letter, Baconian whoever wrote it, but why Greville should address himself to Essex for such advice is puzzling. V. F. Snow in an article, 'Francis Bacon's Advice to Fulke Greville on Research Techniques' (*Huntington Library Quarterly* xxiii (1959–60), pp. 369–78), discusses this letter but his answer to the questions it raises is not entirely convincing.

68 J. Spedding, *Letters and Life of Bacon*, vii, pp. 325–6.

*Notes to Chapter 4*

1 Jean Robertson, 'Sidney and Bandello', *The Library*, xxi (1966), pp. 326–8.

2 Public Record Office, SP 12/195/33, quoted by W. A. Ringler in his edition of *The Poems of Sir Philip Sidney*, Oxford University Press, 1962, p. 530.

3 I have made some suggestions about interpretation and related matters in an article, 'Fulke Greville and the Revisions of *Arcadia*,' *Review of English Studies*, New Series, xvii (1966), pp. 54–7. Miss Jean Robertson, who is preparing an edition of *Arcadia*, tells me that she agrees with my main argument.

4 *Ricerche Anglo-Italiane*, Rome, 1944, p. 68.

5 A modern scholar has made a striking claim for the substance of the revised *Arcadia*: 'a treatment of political commonplaces emerges which is more complicated, more realistic, more conducive to ironies than that represented by any Elizabethan world-picture of a musically simple order and degree.' E. W. Talbert, *The Problem of Order*, University of North Carolina Press, 1962, p. 117.

6 I take it that the reference to the dashes of Sidney's pen beautifying the margins of his works does not refer, as Nowell Smith suggests, to drawings in the margins of Sidney's manuscript of *Arcadia*, but that Greville is intending to describe *Arcadia* as standing in relation to Sidney's more serious activities as an embellishment in the margin does to a manuscript.

7 Miss Frances Yates in *John Florio* (Cambridge University Press, 1934) suggests that Greville's co-editor was Florio, but Dr Ringler presents the evidence for identifying him with Gwynne on page 532 of his edition of Sidney's *Poems*. On the same page are listed the contemporary references to Greville's responsibility for the 1590 edition.

8 *The Complete Works of Sir Philip Sidney*, ed. A. Feuillerat, Cambridge University Press, 1922, i, p. 4.

9 This is a political poem and Greville makes use of Languet's story for his own purposes in *A Treatise of Monarchy*, stanzas 121–4. In l. 40 of Sidney's poem 'worthy Coredens' is referred to as a friend to whose care Languet entrusted Sidney when 'forste to parte' from him on the banks of the Danube. The name (co-redens) may signify one returning with Sidney from Vienna and it is probably meant to designate Greville. In 1577 Languet was sending his 'dutiful respects to the excellent Master Greville' with a reference to the journey which Greville and Sidney had taken together to the Emperor Rudolph II (*The Correspondence of Sidney and Languet*, ed. S. A. Pears, 1845, p. 108).

10 A clear table of the arrangement of the eclogues in the old *Arcadia* and the editions of 1590 and 1593 is printed by Dr Ringler on pages 381–2 of his edition of Sidney's *Poems*.

11 For details of the Philisides poems, see Ringler, pages 417–18 and 492.

12 *The Complete Works of Sir Philip Sidney*, ed. A. Feuillerat, i, p. 524.

13 I take the 'direction sett down undre his [Sidney's] own hand' mentioned in Greville's letter to Walsingham to refer to the old *Arcadia*, not, as Dr Ringler understands it, to the revised text. See my article in the *Review of English Studies* cited above.

14 Dedication of the old *Arcadia* to the Countess of Pembroke (Feuillerat, i, p. 3).

15 Dr Nowell Smith collated the manuscript of the *Life* in the Library of Trinity College, Cambridge, with the printed text of 1652 and records variants in his edition of 1907. He concludes that the two versions represent different recensions of the text made, in all probability, by the author himself. He was unable to decide which had the greater authority. Since Nowell Smith's day a new manuscript of the text has come to light in Shrewsbury Public Library. This is a scribal copy, though not in any of the hands of the Warwick MSS. It has been described by S. Blaine Ewing in 'A New Manuscript of Greville's *Life of Sidney*', *Modern Language Review*, xlix (1954), pp. 424–7.

16 Marshall was the servant who tended Sidney as a boy. His account book, itemizing expenditure on behalf of the young Philip, is printed in the *Life of Sir Philip Sidney*, by M. W. Wallace, 1915.

17 As a political work the *Life of Sidney* had a burst of popularity in the 1660s. On 1 January 1667–8 Samuel Pepys recorded that 'my Lord Crew did turn to a place in the Life of Sir Philip Sidney wrote by Sir Fulke Greville, which do foretell the present condition of this nation, in relation to the Dutch, to the very degree of a prophecy; and is so remarkable that I am resolved to buy one of them, it being quite throughout, a good discourse.' Next day he found a copy only with difficulty: 'the book-seller told me that he had sold four, within this week or two, which is more than he sold in his life of them: and he could not imagine what should be the reason of it: but I suppose it is from the same reason of people's observing this part therein, touching his prophesying our present condition here in England in relation to the Dutch, which is very remarkable.'

18 Villiers did not appear at Court till 1614 when there was a struggle for power between him and Somerset. If Greville is referring to this in particular, his comments would give a late date for the *Life*, but he probably has in mind the general quarrelsomeness among the Scots at Court.

19 An interesting passage which occurs in the Shrewsbury manuscript and not in Nowell Smith relates to Sidney's death: 'Immediately after God had given Sir Phillip this opportunity to expresse a modell of his worth to the world, Even then to manifest that the same God is all he hath created and infinite besides, to take away this same patterne, perchance least we should make Idolls of our selves, and so give his honour unto men; And yet (like the Almighty) not intending to destroy the way of worth in one Creature, he presently stirs up that excellent Princesse Queene Elizabeth to step againe into the same path, which herselfe had formerly troden out to the world, for she had no sooner perfected her virgin Tryumph over that sanctified, and invincible Navy. . . .' The text then joins that of Nowell Smith on page 206 and treats of Elizabeth's actions against Spain. Blaine Ewing

builds a theory concerning the history of Greville's revision of the text on this passage but his argument is based on a misinterpretation. He takes the 'he' in 'he presently stirs up' to refer to Sidney, whereas it must certainly refer to God Who is demonstrating His almighty providence in partially repairing the loss of Sidney by leading the Queen to enact some of his policies. For further comments on the dating of the *Life of Sidney* see the Appendix.

*Notes to Chapter 5*

1 Sidney's *Two Pastoralls* commemorate the time of:
   Striving with my Mates in Song,
   Mixing mirth Our Songs among.
   (*The Poems of Sir Philip Sidney*, ed. W. A. Ringler, Oxford University Press, 1962, pp. 260–4.)

2 There is a certain amount of external evidence relating to the sonnets though it does not take us very far. Number I was set to music by M. Cavendish in 1598, v and LII by Dowland in 1597 and XXIX, by Dowland again, in 1600. In 1586 Puttenham was counting Greville among those 'who have written excellently well as it would appeare if their doings could be found out and made publicke with the rest' (*The Arte of English Poesie*). Probably he is basing his judgement on some of the *Caelica* poems. The Oxford *Exequiae* on Sidney (1587) contain a reference to Mirafilus which seems to point to *Caelica* LXXIII and this must consequently have been written by 1587. Another poem in the collection contains the same pun on Greville's name which he himself uses in *Caelica* LXXXIII. This poem, according to a note in the Warwick manuscript, should in fact have been copied as Number LXXVI. If the order of the Warwick manuscript is meant to be chronological we should therefore be able to put the first seventy-six poems at least before the *Exequiae*. Internal evidence relating to dates concerns the influence of Sidney on certain poems and whether or not dates can be arrived at by the study of features of style and mood. Professor Bullough goes into these questions in his section on dating in volume i of his edition of the *Poems and Dramas of Fulke Greville*, taking account of the evidence and the conclusions embodied in M. W. Croll's *The Works of Fulke Greville* (Philadelphia, 1903). G. A. Wilkes's contribution to discussion of the chronology of Greville's works appears in his article, 'The Sequence of the Writings of Fulke Greville, Lord Brooke' in *Studies in Philology*, lvi (1959), pp. 489–503. I have myself suggested that sonnets LXXXI and LXXXII belong to 1615 or nearabouts, when Greville was endeavouring to compose an epitaph for the double tomb he planned for Sidney and himself (*Review of English Studies*, New Series, xix (1968), pp. 47–51).

3 R. Naunton, *Fragmenta Regalia*, p. 50.

4 Thomas Fowler to Archibald Douglas, *Reports of the Historical Manuscripts Commission*, Hatfield 3, p. 375.

5 *Works of Francis Bacon*, ed. Spedding, Ellis and Heath, 1870, vi, p. 883.

6 Ringler, *Poems of Sidney*, pp. 66–7.

7 Ibid., pp. 462–3.

8 Ward's *English Poets*, quoted by Bullough, i, p. 252.
9 R. M. Sargent, in *At the Court of Queen Elizabeth*, Oxford University Press, 1935, makes a study of the life and lyrics of Sir Edward Dyer and prints the poems which he believes to be his. My quotations from Dyer are from this book.
10 See my article on this poem in *Review of English Studies*, New Series, xix (1968), pp. 47–51.
11 Bullough, i, p. 45 and Ringler, pp. xxx and 446–7 n. 5.
12 *Times Literary Supplement*, 1937, p. 576, and 'The Emblematic Conceit in Giordano Bruno's *De Gli Eroici Furori* and in the Elizabethan Sonnet Sequences', *Journal of the Warburg Institute*, vi–vii (1943–4), pp. 101–21.
13 It is sometimes suggested that some of the Cynthia poems are addressed to Queen Elizabeth; but the only poem which must certainly refer to her is number LXXXI and no name at all is used in that.
14 The textual history of this poem suggests that it may have been completed in two parts (see Bullough, i, p. 266) and this may account for the change of name. On the other hand, the name Cynthia also appears in the poem and though it may denote here, as Professor Bullough declares it does, the goddess of chastity, the presence of all three of the names used for the mistress may indicate that in Greville's opinion the behaviour described in this group of poems is not that just of *a* woman, but of Woman.
15 Professor Bullough glosses Greville's lines: 'for I could not lose more by being melancholy' but the more natural sense seems to be 'my only regret is that I had no more to give' which is also the meaning of Sidney's lines.
16 I am relying very largely for comments on Calvin on François Wendel's book, *Calvin*, Fontana Library, 1965. See especially the section on Predestination. The influence of Calvin on Greville's work is discussed by H. W. Utz, *Die Anschauungen über Wissenschaft und Religion im Werke Fulke Grevilles*, Bern 1948.
17 An appreciative account of *Caelica* is offered by F. Inglis in his article, 'Metaphysical Poetry and the Greatness of Fulke Greville' (*The Critical Review*, Melbourne, Sidney, 8, 1965, pp. 101–9). There is also a study by William Frost, *Fulke Greville's 'Caelica': an Evaluation*, (Pleasantville, New York, 1942).

*Notes to Chapter 6*

1 It slightly strengthens this suggestion that there is a letter from Sir Ralph Winwood in Venice to Fulke Greville, dated 1606, in which he discusses Garnet's case at length and inveighs against equivocation. Incidentally, he prefaces his review of some outstanding concerns of the moment with the remark that so long as Salisbury lives he and Greville must be 'but standers by in the state'. (Sloane MS. 3106.)
2 See also stanzas 575–9. The reference to Queen Elizabeth in stanza 578 does not indicate whether she is alive or dead.
3 Philip Styles, 'Politics and Historical Research in the Early Seventeenth Century' in *English Historical Scholarship in the Sixteenth and Seventeenth Centuries*, ed. Levi Fox, Oxford University Press, 1956.
4 *Caelica* LXXVII condenses Greville's indictment of the abuse of the law by

'Our moderne Tyrants' into five six-lined dynamic stanzas. Of course, Greville is not concerned in the lyric with argument and exposition but is free to make a forceful personal statement.

5 Some of the background of Greville's political thought is described by Hugh N. Maclean in two articles: 'Fulke Greville: Kingship and Sovereignty', *Huntington Library Quarterly*, xvi (1952-3), pp. 237-71, and 'Fulke Greville on War', *H.L.Q.*, xxi (1957-8), pp. 95-109. There is a study of political aspects of *Of Monarchy* in M. Kupffer, *Fulke Grevilles 'Poems of Monarchy' als Spiegel seiner politischen Ansichten*, Riga, 1929. For a fuller description of contemporary thought on the nature and power of monarchy, see J. W. Allen, *A History of Political Thought in the Seventeenth Century*, London, 1928, especially Part 2, chapter X. See also 'George Buchanan and the Sidney Circle' by J. E. Phillips in *H.L.Q.*, xii (1948-9), pp. 23-55.

6 For a discussion of other material in Section 12, see the Appendix.

7 It is possible, nevertheless, as I suggest in my discussion of *Mustapha*, that the poem or poems which later composed the second chorus had been written in some form early, although they are not included in any extant version of *Mustapha*.

8 The Harvard College Library possesses a manuscript (MS. Eng 36) with the title *Monarchie in its Excellence compared with Aristocratie and Democratie severally, and with both Joyntly. Written by the honble. and learned Sr. Foulke Grevill Lord Brooke and left in Manuscript.*

It consists of the first two stanzas of Section I of *A Treatise of Monarchy* followed by Section XIII (The Excellencie of Monarchy compared with Aristocratie), Section XIV (The Excellencie of Monarchie compared with Democratie) and Section XV (The Excellencie of Monarchie compared with Aristocratie and Democratie Joyntlie). These parts of the *Treatise* are arranged as a self-contained poem in three sections and the stanzas are numbered from 1 to 91. (There is a misnumbering: stanza 73 is followed by 78.) There is a dedicatory letter signed Richard Graves and addressed to Doctor Sainte Barbe. The writer says that the manuscript was left to his brother, then Fulke Greville's chaplain, by Greville at his death, and then bequeathed by the brother to himself: 'A Legacy unto mee for my better supportance.'' The letter continues: 'But the Press not admitting of it, to let it lye sullied in the dust of this cankering age, or be raked in oblivion (being A Gemme of inestimable vallue, and so necessary to be weren in thiese times) I ho[ld] it A Sinne unpardonable. . . .'

There are no significant variants from the printed text in the MS. Some readings which might be attempts to improve the text are probably to be accounted for by a rather careless copyist (there are a number of slips and erasures) substituting a more familiar form for an unusual one. The manuscript does not appear to throw any light on the textual history of the *Treatise*. The sections of which it consists seem to have been copied from a complete manuscript but why, and in what circumstances Richard Graves came to possess it, is not clear. The only chaplain referred to in Greville's will is named William Burton. It seems likely that Richard Graves may have been connected with the family of Colonel Richard Graves of Kings Norton, Worcestershire. This family had dealings with John St Barbe of Hampshire in 1663. (See

*Graves Memoirs of the Civil War compiled from Seventeenth Century Records* by
F. A. Bates, Edinburgh and London, 1927, pp. 124 and 134.)

I have been allowed to see and quote from this manuscript by courtesy of
the Harvard College Library.

*Notes to Chapter 7*

1  In *Review of English Studies*, New Series, i–ii (1950–1), pp. 308–23.

2  Nowell Smith notes that: 'The black ox treading on a person's foot is given
as a proverb for adversity first by J. Heywood (1562).' He adds that he does
not know if the proverb is of English origin or not. It survived in Scotland
at least for a long time. In *The Antiquary* Edie Ochiltree greets Elspeth after
the death of Steenie Mucklebackit with the words: 'I'm fain to see ye looking
sae well, cummer; the mair, that the black ox has tramped on ye since I was
aneath your roof-tree.' Yeats's use of it, particularly appropriate to Greville,
is quoted on the title-page of this study. There is an interesting account of this
proverb in 'The Proverb "The black ox has not trod on his foot" in Renaissance Literature' (*Philological Quarterly* xx (1941), pp. 266–78) by Archer
Taylor. Greville's use is cited under meaning 2: 'He is inexperienced, he has
not known sorrow or care.'

3  For an analysis of the verse-patterns, which incorporates material supplied by
Croll, see Bullough, ii, pp. 50–7.

4  Professor Bullough offers some possibilities on page 44 of volume ii of his
edition. See also R. M. Cushman's 'Concerning Fulke Greville's Tragedies
*Alaham* and *Mustapha*', *Modern Language Notes*, xxiv (1909), pp. 180–1.

5  There is also a manuscript of the early version in the Folger Library. I have
left this out of account in my general discussion of the revisions because it is
not significantly different from C and Q and as these are the texts collated by
Bullough the reader will find it simpler to follow my comments with his
edition if I confine my references to the texts used by him. There is an interesting point relating to the choruses in the Folger manuscript and this is
noted later on.

6  Grosart, iv, pp. 281–2.

7  There is a second letter included in the 1633 edition of Greville's works. It is
addressed to his sister's son, Greville Verney, while he was in France. Greville
sends the young man £30 and advice about how to make good use of his
time abroad. In the first place he is not to be seduced by Roman Catholicism
and in the second he should inform himself about the geography of the
country and about the social, political, and commercial habits of the people.
The letter has one outstandingly Grevillean passage:

'Now for the world, I know it too well to persuade you to dive into the
practices thereof: rather stand upon your guard against all that tempt you
thereunto, or may practise upon you in your conscience, your reputation,
or your purse. Resolve that no man is wise or safe, but he that is honest.
And let this perswasion turne your studies and observations from the
complement and impostures of this debauched age to more reall grounds
of wisdome, gathered out of the stories of Time past, and out of the government of the present State.' (Grosart, iv, p. 303.)

This is evidently a genuine letter, actually posted, and dated 'From Hackney this 20 of November, 1609'. How 'genuine' the *Letter to an Honourable Lady* is, is problematical. When the 1633 volume was being prepared, John Verney, Greville Verney's brother, wrote an angry letter to John Coke denying that his brother had been the recipient of the advice on travel and the £30, but he seems not to have persuaded Coke. (*Reports of the Historical Manuscripts Commission*, xii, Appx pt i, pp. 483–4.)

In a recent article in *Renaissance Quarterly* ('Fulke Greville's Letter to a cousin in France and the Problems of Authorship in Cases of Formula Writing,' *R.Q.*, xxii (1969), pp. 140–7), N. K. Farmer Jr. describes MS. versions of this letter which are ascribed to different authors and different recipients. He suggests that the letter was regarded as a model treatment of the subject of travel, to be made use of by anyone on a suitable occasion; the original authorship is probably unascertainable. The passage quoted above, with its characteristic sentiments and vocabulary makes, nevertheless, a strong case for Greville's authorship.

8  *A Letter from Octavia to Marcus Antonius* is printed by Grosart in *The Complete Works in Verse and Prose of Samuel Daniel*, 1885, i, pp. 117–38.

9  In an article on 'Réligion et raison d'état dans l'œuvre de Fulke Greville' in *Etudes Anglaises*, v (1952), pp. 211–22, M. Jean Jacquot refers to a copy of the 1633 volume of Greville's works in the Bibliothèque Nationale which contains manuscript annotations in the margin of *Mustapha*. The words 'vast superstition' in the Chorus Quintus Tartarorum are underlined and in the margin is written: 'In the originall, it is *Blind Religion* thou glorious, etc. But this seemed too Atheisticall to be licensed att the presse.' 'Religion' is the reading of Q. At line 10 'Superstitious' is underlined and in the margin is 'Religious'. Q has 'this dreame, Religion'. In the margin of the Chorus Sacerdotum ('Oh wearisome Condition of Humanity!') is written: 'This chorus is misplaced; but rather then lose it, I caused it to be inserted here to fill up this page.' M. Jacquot was unable to identify the hand in which all the notes are made and I have not so far had any success in tracing the history of the volume.

10  The manuscript in the Folger Library, which preserves a text very closely related to CQ, has an interesting variation of the chorus arrangement. Like CQ it has the Chorus Sacerdotum at the end of act I and, like Q, the Chorus Tartarorum at the end of act III, but at the end of act II, where CQ has nothing, it has the second part of the chorus on death which occurs in the C manuscript of act IV (Q has only a truncated version of this chorus). This is the section beginning 'Man dreame no more, examine what life is' to the end (pages 269–70 in Professor Bullough's text). Act IV of the Folger manuscript ends with the first part of this death chorus, 'When will this lives sparke putt in our spiritte' down to 'As I ende joyes, I ende all imperfection'; and act V, where CQ has no chorus, repeats 'Man dreame no more, examine what life is', already used at the end of act II. This is beautifully written out at the end of the play. Incidentally, in both occurrences of these verses the Folger manuscript supplies the word missing from the C text (Professor Bullough's line 113) and the line reads: 'Since Life in Liveinge hetherwards maks haste.'

16—F.G.

Presumably it was not Greville's final intention to use the same chorus twice, but the 'Man dreame no more' lines make a very appropriate ending to the play, and the splitting of the verses which act IV of C puts together draws attention to a fact about the play: that it is very much about death, and attitudes to death are used to reveal sharply the orientation of the characters towards this world or the next.

11 *Works of Dr John Tillotson,* 4th ed., London, 1704, p. 329.

*Notes to Chapter 8*

1 *Institutes of the Christian Religion,* Book 1, chapter 8, paragraph 1. I am again indebted in this chapter to François Wendel's book on Calvin, from which this passage is quoted.

2 Wendel, p. 34.

3 *Institutes of the Christian Religion,* Book II, chapter 2, paragraphs 13 and 15. Quoted by Wendel.

4 Milton, *On Education.*

5 Sidney, *Apologie for Poetry,* ed. Churton Collins, pp. 12–13.

6 Ibid., pp. 8–9.

7 'The Advancement of Learning,' in *The Philosophical Works of Francis Bacon,* ed. J. M. Robertson, 1905, p. 88.

8 *De Augmentis,* Robertson, p. 453.

9 *The Advancement of Learning,* Robertson, p. 60.

10 Virgil K. Whitaker, *Francis Bacon's Intellectual Milieu,* University of California, 1962, p. 22.

11 Ibid., p. 23.

12 *Novum Organum,* i, axiom xlix.

13 Ibid., i, lxi.

14 *Institutes of the Christian Religion,* Book I, chapter 5, paragraph 1. See Wendel, p. 161 and n. 36.

15 *Novum Organum,* ii, axiom xlvi.

16 *The Advancement of Learning,* Robertson, p. 164.

17 Ibid., p. 118.

18 Ibid., p. 115, n. 142.

19 *New Atlantis,* Robertson, p. 727.

20 'The Sequence of the Writings of Fulke Greville,' *Studies in Philology,* lvi (1959), pp. 489–503.

21 *Of Monarchy,* stanza 653.

*Notes to Chapter 9*

1 In *Colin Clouts Come Home Again.*

2 Daniel's dedication of the 1594 edition of *Cleopatra* to the Countess of Pembroke.

3 *Reports of the Historical Manuscripts Commission,* Hatfield 5, p. 166.

4 *Musophilus,* lines 1011–12.

# Select bibliography of printed material

# Select bibliography of printed material

(Only works referred to in this book are listed here.)

a *Texts of Greville's Works*

Bullough, G., *Poems and Dramas of Fulke Greville*, 2 vols., Edinburgh and London, 1939

Butter, N., *Mustapha*, 1609

*Certaine Learned and Elegant Workes of the Right Honorable Fulke Lord Brooke written in his Youth, and familiar Exercise, with Sir Philip Sidney . . .*, London, 1633

Ellis-Fermor, U., *Caelica*, The Gregynog Press, 1936

Grosart, A. B., *The Works of Fulke Greville*, 1870

*Life of Sir Philip Sidney*, London, 1652

Smith, Nowell, *Life of Sir Philip Sidney*, Clarendon Press, 1907

*The Remains of Sir Fulke Grevill, Lord Brooke: being poems of Monarchy and Religion*, London, 1670

Wilkes, G. A., *The Remains being poems of Monarchy and Religion*, Oxford University Press, 1965


b *Critical, biographical, and background works*

*Acts of the Privy Council*

Alexander, William, *The Poetical Works*, ed. Kastner and Charlton, Manchester, 1921–9

Allen, J. W., *A History of Political Thought in the Sixteenth Century*, London, 1928

Bacon, F., *Philosophical Works*, ed J. M. Robertson, London, 1905

Bates, F. A., *Graves Memoirs of the Civil War compiled from Seventeenth Century Records*, Edinburgh and London, 1927

Baxter, Richard, *Poetical Fragments*, London, 1681

Benham, W., *Old St Paul's Cathedral*, London, 1902

*Biographia Britannica*, 1750

Bruce, J., *Annals of the Honourable East India Company*, 1810

Bruno, Giordano, *La Cena de le Ceneri*, 1584, ed. G. Aquilecchia, 1955
  *Spaccio de la Bestia trionfante*, 1584 (the dedication is translated in
  F. B. Newman, 'Sir Fulke Greville and Giordano Bruno: a possible
  echo,' *Philological Quarterly*, XXIX, 1950, pp. 367–74)
  *De Gli Eroici Furori*, 1585. Trans. P. E. Memmo, *Studies in the Romance
  Languages and Literature*, University of North Carolina, pp. 48–52,
  1964–5
Bullough, G., 'Fulke Greville, First Lord Brooke', *Modern Language Review*,
  XXVIII, 1933, pp. 1–20
*Calendars of State Papers*, Domestic and Foreign
Camden, W., *Britain*, London, 1610
Chambers, E. K., *Shakespeare. A Study of Facts and Problems*, Oxford, 1930
Clowes, W. L., *The Royal Navy*, London, 1897
Collins, A., *Letters and Memorials of State* . . . , London, 1746 (sometimes
  known as *The Sidney Papers*)
Colville, F. L., *The Worthies of Warwickshire*, Warwick, 1869
Corbet, Richard, *Poems and Life*, in *Chalmers' English Poets*, v, 1810
Croll, M. W., *The Works of Fulke Greville*, Philadelphia, 1903
Cushman, R. M., 'Concerning Fulke Greville's Tragedies *Alaham* and
  *Mustapha*', *Modern Language Notes*, XXIV, 1909, pp. 180–1
Daniel, Samuel, *Works*, ed. A. B. Grosart, 1885–96
  *Poems and a Defence of Ryme*, ed. A. C. Sprague, Harvard University
  Press, 1930
Devereux, W. B., *Lives and Letters of the Devereux, Earls of Essex*, London,
  1853.
*Dictionary of National Biography*
Donne, John, *The Divine Poems*, 1633, ed. H. Gardner, Oxford, 1952
  *The Elegies and the Songs and Sonnets*, 1633, ed. H. Gardner, Oxford,
  1965
Dugdale, William, *The Antiquities of Warwickshire*, Coventry, 1765;
  Warwick, 1786
Edmondson, J., *A Historical and Genealogical Account of the Noble Family of
  Greville*, London, 1766
Ellis-Fermor, U., *The Jacobean Drama*, London, 1936
Ewing, S. Blaine, 'A New Manuscript of Greville's *Life of Sidney*',
  *Modern Language Review*, XLIX, 1954, pp. 424–7
Farmer, N. K., 'Fulke Greville's Letter to a Cousin in France and the
  Problems of Authorship in Cases of Formula Writing,' *Renaissance
  Quarterly*, XXII, 1969, pp. 140–7
  'Fulke Greville and Sir John Coke: An Exchange of Letters on a History
  Lecture and Certain Latin Verses on Sir Philip Sidney', *Huntington Library
  Quarterly* xxxii (May 1970), pp. 217–36
Feuillerat, A., *The Complete Works of Sir Philip Sidney*, C.U.P., 1922
Florio, John, *The Essayes of Montaigne*, London, 1603
Fripp, E. I., *Master Richard Quyny*, O.U.P., 1924
Frost, William, *Fulke Greville's 'Caelica': an Evaluation*, New York, 1942
Gardiner, S. R., *History of England*, London, 1883–4

Garnier, R. *Œuvres complètes*, ed. Pinvert, Paris, 1923

Harington, J., *Nugae Antiquae*, London, 1779

Hazlitt, W., 'Of Persons one would wish to have seen,' *Essays*

Hazlitt, W. C., *Inedited Poetical Miscellanies 1584–1700*, London, 1870

Hill, Christopher, *Intellectual Origins of the English Revolution*, Oxford, 1965

Inglis, F., 'Metaphysical Poetry and the Greatness of Fulke Greville,' *The Critical Review*, Melbourne, Sidney, no. 8, 1965, pp. 101–9

Jacquot, J., 'Réligion et raison d'état dans l'œuvre de Fulke Greville', *Etudes Anglaises*, August, 1952, pp. 211–22

Kelliher, W. H., Letter in *Times Literary Supplement*, 29 May 1969

Kupffer, M., *Fulke Grevilles 'Poems of Monarchy' als Spiegel seiner politischen Ansichten*, Riga, 1929.

Kyd, T., *Works*, ed. Boas, Oxford, 1901

Lloyd, D., *Statesmen and Favourites of England since the Reformation*, London, 1670

Maclean, H. N., 'Fulke Greville: Kingship and Sovereignty', *Huntington Library Quarterly*, XVI, May 1953, pp. 237–71

'Fulke Greville on War,' *Huntington Library Quarterly*, XXI, 1957–8, p. 95–109

Milton, John, *Tractate of Education*, 1644

Moore, Thomas, *Letters and Journals of Lord Byron*, London, 1875

Mullinger, J. B., *The University of Cambridge*, iii, C.U.P., 1911

Naunton, R., *Fragmenta Regalia*, Arber's English Reprints, London, 1869

Neale, J. E., *The Elizabethan House of Commons*, Penguin Books, 1963

Nicolls, J., *Progresses of Queen Elizabeth*, London, 1823

*Progresses of James I*, London, 1828

Orsini, Napoleone, *Fulke Greville tra il Mondo e Dio*, Milan, 1941

Parr, R., *The Life of Ussher*, London, 1686

Pears, S. A., *Correspondence of Sidney and Languet*, London, 1845

Peele, G., *Works*, ed. A. H. Bullen, London, 1888

Peerson, Martin, *Mottects or Grave Chamber Musique*, 1630

Pembroke, Mary, Countess of, *Antonie*, ed. Luce, Weimar, 1897

Peterson, D. L., *The English Lyric from Wyatt to Donne*, Princeton University Press and O.U.P., 1967

Pepys, Samuel, *Diary*

Pevsner, N., *The Buildings of England: Warwickshire*, Penguin Books, 1966

Praz, M., *Ricerche Anglo-Italiane*, Rome, 1944

Puttenham, G., *The Arte of English Poesie*, 1586 (in *Elizabethan Critical Essays*, ed. Gregory Smith, Oxford, 1904)

Rees, Joan, *Samuel Daniel*, Liverpool University Press, 1964

'Fulke Greville and the Revisions of *Arcadia*,' *Review of English Studies*, n.s. xvii, 1966, pp. 54–7

'Greville's Epitaph on Sir Philip Sidney', *Review of English Studies*, n.s. xix, 1968, pp. 47–51

Letter in *Times Literary Supplement*, 5 May 1969

*Reports of the Historical Manuscript Commission*

Ringler, W. A., *The Poems of Sir Philip Sidney*, Oxford, 1962

Robertson, Jean, 'Sidney and Bandello,' *The Library*, XXI, 1966, pp. 326–8

Sargent, R. M., *At the Court of Queen Elizabeth*, O.U.P., 1935

Seneca, L. A., *Works*, trans. T. Lodge, London, 1614

Sidney, P., *The Poems*, ed. W. A. Ringler
  *Arcadia*, ed. A. Feuillerat
  *Apologie for Poetry*, ed. Collins, Oxford, 1907

Snow, V. F., 'Francis Bacon's Advice to Fulke Greville on Research
  Techniques,' *Huntington Library Quarterly*, XXIII, 1959–60, pp. 369–78

Spedding, James, *Letters and Life of Francis Bacon*, London, 1868

Speed, John, *John Speed's England*, Phoenix House, 1954

Spenser, Edmund, *Poetical Works*, ed. Smith and de Selincourt, London, 1929

Styles, Philip, 'Politics and Historical Research in the early Seventeenth
  Century,' in *English Historical Scholarship in the Sixteenth and Seventeenth
  Centuries*, ed. Levi Fox, O.U.P., 1956

Talbert, E. W., *The Problem of Order*, University of North Carolina Press, 1962

Taylor, Archer, 'The Proverb "The black ox has not trod on his foot" in
  Renaissance Literature,' *Philological Quarterly* xx (1941), pp. 266–78

Tillotson, John, *Works*, 4th ed., London, 1704

Ure, Peter, 'Fulke Greville's Dramatic Characters', *Review of English Studies*,
  1950–1, n.s., 1–2, pp. 308–23

Utz, H. W., *Die Anschauungen über Wissenschaft und Religion im Werke
  Fulke Grevilles*, Bern, 1948

*Victoria History of the Counties of England: A History of Warwickshire*

Wallace, M. W., *Life of Sir Philip Sidney*, Cambridge, 1915

Wendel, F., *Calvin*, The Fontana Library, 1965

Whitaker, V. K., *Francis Bacon's Intellectual Milieu*, University of California, 1962

Wilkes, G. A., 'The Sequence of the Writings of Fulke Greville, Lord
  Brooke', *Studies in Philology*, LVI, 1959, pp. 489–503

Williams, Penry, *The Council in the Marches of Wales under Elizabeth I*,
  Cardiff, 1958

Winters, Yvor, 'The Sixteenth Century Lyric in England', *Poetry: a Magazine
  of Verse*, Chicago, vols 53 and 54, February, March, April, 1939.

Wood, A. à, *Athenae Oxonienses*, ii, London, 1815

Yates, Frances A., *John Florio*, C.U.P., 1934
  Letter in *Times Literary Supplement*, 1937, p. 576
  'The emblematic Conceit in Giordano Bruno's *De Gli Eroici Furori* and in
  the Elizabethan Sonnet Sequences', *Journal of the Warburg Institute*, 6–7,
  1943–4, pp. 101–21

## Sources of manuscript material referred to in this study

Bodleian Library, Oxford
British Museum
City Record Office, Coventry
Folger Shakespeare Library,
  Washington
Harvard College Library

Melbourne Hall, Derbyshire
Shrewsbury Public Library
Somerset House
Staffordshire Country Record Office
Trinity College, Cambridge
Warwick Castle

# Index

# Index